17.29

DM 3/01

New Subediting

Titles in the series

Series editor: F. W. Hodgson

Broadcast Journalism   Andrew Boyd
Computerized Newspaper, The   Paul Williams
Creative Newspaper Design   Vic Giles and F. W. Hodgson
Freelance Journalist, The   Christopher Dobson
Law and the Media   Tom Crone
Journalist's Guide to Sources   David Spark
Magazine Journalism Today   Anthony Davies
Modern Newspaper Practice   F. W. Hodgson
Newspaper Language   Nicholas Bagnall
Picture Editing: An Introduction   Tom Ang
Practical Newspaper Reporting   Geoffrey Harris and David Spark
Practical Photojournalism   Martin Keene
Printing: A Guide to Systems and Their Uses   W. R. Durrant
New Subediting: Apple-Mac, QuarkXpress and After   F. W. Hodgson
Writing Feature Articles   Brendan Hennessy

New Subediting
Apple-Mac, QuarkXpress and After

Third Edition

F. W. Hodgson

Oxford   Boston   Johannesburg   New Delhi   Singapore   Sydney

Butterworth-Heinemann
Linacre House, Jordan Hill, Oxford OX2 8DP
225 Wildwood Avenue, Woburn, MA 01801-2041
A division of Reed Educational and Professional Publishing Ltd

ℛ A member of the Reed Elsevier plc group

First published as Subediting: A Handbook of Modern Newspaper Production 1987
Reprinted 1987, 1992
Second edition 1993
Reprinted 1995, 1996
Third edition 1998

British Library Cataloguing in Publication Data
Hodgson, F. W.
  New Subediting: Apple-Mac, QuarkXpress and
  After – 3rd (Media manual) ed
  1 Newspaper layout and typography
  2 Journalism
  I Title
  070.4′1′0285

ISBN 0 240 51534 X

Composition by Genesis Typesetting, Rochester, Kent
Printed and bound in Great Britain

CONTENTS

List of illustrations   vii

Preface   viii

Acknowledgements   xv

Introduction: The Quark revolution   **1**
The arrival of Quark – 'Subs with Quark experience'
– Sub or page editor? – Technology and the sub

Chapter 1   **What is editorial production?**   **12**
Creating the news – The newsroom – The copytaster –
Measuring the news – News patterns – Production
start-up

Chapter 2   **A sub's guide to design and typography**   **26**
Format – Balance of contents – Who does what –
Designing the pages – Typography – Using type –
Design workshop

Chapter 3   **Dealing with pictures**   **48**
Role of pictures – Picture sources – The photo
briefing – Choosing pictures – Editing pictures – The
design function – Uses of pictures – Graphics

Chapter 4   **Handling text**   **69**
The subs' table – The editing function – Getting it
right – Check sources – Making it fit – Editing for the
page – Order and shape – The intro – The delayed
drop – Story sequence – Using quotes – Geography –
Time – Background

Chapter 5   **Fault-finder's guide to English**   **87**
The sentence – Paragraphs – Punctuation

Chapter 6   **Word traps**   **107**
The right word – Clichés – Vogue words – Misused words – House style – Journalese

Chapter 7   **Writing headlines**   **125**
The words – Symbols – Word accuracy – Headline punctuation – Headline abbreviations – Content – Composing a headline – Headline thoughts – Things to avoid

Chapter 8   **Headline typography**   **140**
Shape – Arrangement – Type style – Character counts – Spacing – The creative moment – Alternative words

Chapter 9   **Further techniques in subbing**   **159**
Subeditors and the law – Legal traps – Privilege – When to rewrite – Revising and editionizing – Caption writing – Writing contents bills

Chapter 10   **Handling a running story**   **176**
Dealing with the text

Chapter 11   **Features: Planning and design**   **189**
Copy sources – Planning – Features production – Page design – Guiding the reader – Features workshop

Chapter 12   **Features: Editing and projection**   **205**
Accuracy – Language – Ghost writing – Reader participation – Features and the law – Projection – Features headlines

Appendix   ***Press Complaints Commission Code of Practice***   *217*

Glossary   *223*

Index   *243*

ILLUSTRATIONS

Figure 1 The leap into full-screen composition: Apple-Mac page-making terminals in use at the *News of the World* before the introduction of their Windows-based Unisys Hermes system. Make-up here is using the QuarkXpress program, but with separate subbing and page-building screens.   2

Figure 2 A page on screen (with zoom section), using the Unisys Hermes pagination module. It provides for WYSIWYG composition, continuous object and status monitoring and image cropping on page. Multi-user access allows several people to work on the same page.   5

Figure 3 The command desk system of editorial production: it aims at centralizing edition inputs and decision-making, with direct back bench control of make-up through designated page editors working with specialist and rewrite subs.   6

Figure 4(a) Pages take shape on Apple-Mac screens at the *Nottingham Evening Post*, which utilizes the Quark Publishing System (QPS). Subeditors are using the zoom facility to work on sections of pages. The latest version of this system extends QPS applications also to the Windows market for use with PCs equipped with Windows 95 and Windows NT   7

Figure 4(b) Tracking the material – an information header for a news story or feature is created on the Quark database server and filled in by users as the feature moves through the editorial and production processes   7

Figure 5 Picture editing on screen with Unisys Hermes. Their NewsCrop tool allows cropping, mirroring, zooming, and adjusting tonal curves in mono and colour, enabling quick last minutes changes to be made. The system permits the integration of applications such as Adobe PhotoShop if additional image handling is needed.   9

Figure 6 Halfway house: the cut-and-paste method of page composition. A compositor attached cut-up text and picture bromides to a page grid. The page was photographed to create the negative from which the printing plate was derived. Note the stick-on tape rules that had to be used. This method has now mostly given way to screen make-up.   10

Figure 7 A cleaner environment: smooth polymer plates are used on this modern web-offset press at the News Centre, Portsmouth, where once all was hot metal. The pages are printed by being offset via a 'blanket' which picks up the ink by chemical means and transfers it to the paper.   11

Figure 8   The electronic newsroom shown as the fulcrum of copy flow on a typical national daily. Stories are keyed into the system by the writers, checked by the news editor, sorted by the copytaster, planned and placed by the back bench or chief sub, and called up on screen for subbing and building into the page.   16

Figure 9   Serving the community – this well filled broadsheet front page from the weekly *Cumberland News* uses a stylish lower case type dress and well planned highlights to present ten newsy stories, all from the circulation area. For good measure it runs an edition blurb with page cross-references.   19

Figure 10   How the tabloid evenings do it – an inside news page from the *Birmingham Evening Mail* and a smart front page from Bristol's *Evening Post*. Effective placing of pictures and polished use of the tabloid style characterize these sans type layouts.   22

Figure 11   With its full-width masthead, use of blurbs and front page colour (though sometimes oddly printing on pink), the *Financial Times* has come a long way in the last few years. This page one, with its Times Roman lower case format and studied elegance of design, shows that a paper with a mostly business readership does not have to look dull.   23

Figure 12   A Sunday paper in parts: how the logo identifies the *Sunday Times* sections.   27

Figure 13(a) How a layout becomes a page: this example from *The Sun* in the run-up to full screen make-up still carried written headline, intro and picture instructions for the subeditor.

Figure 13(b) *The Sun* news page as it appeared when printed.   32

Figure 14   How a leading provincial morning paper covers its territory: place names flag the stories in this busy *Western Mail* news page.   33

Figure 15   All-serif lower case type, standard column measure throughout, and thick-and-thin-cut-off rules, produce elegance and readability in the *Sunday Times's* news pages. Note, in this one, the use of a cut-out, which are easier to achieve in screen make-up programs.   34

Figure 16   Examples of different weights in a well used stock type. Caslon in four of its variants (top to bottom): light, regular italic, extra bold, black.   37

Figure 17   Two variants from the Times New Roman range: extra bold and bold italic.   37

Figure 18   Helvetica (sometimes bit-mapped as Geneva) in three of its guises. Top to bottom: light, medium and bold.   38

Figure 19   Taking variants to an extreme: the slab-seriffed Rockwell light and its partner, Rockwell extra bold.   38

Figure 20   A line of Bembo lower case showing the x-height of the characters in relation to the ascenders and descenders – in this type their length results in a type 'small on its body'.   39

Figure 21   A space problem with these *Times* crossword clues has forced the subeditor to squeeze four of the lines to keep them within the measure.   40

Figure 22   Giving emphasis to lists: black blobs and squares are used to separate as well as emphasize these connected items. Bold caps in a roman context have a similar function in the horoscope setting, bottom right.   43

Figure 23   Six-line drop letters give style to the *Daily Mail* feature, left, as well as acting as eye-breakers in place of crossheads in a long text. Drop letters are used as guides for the reader in the *Western Mail's* question-and-answer medical column, above.   44

Figure 24   Another device used in place of crossheads to break up a long text: poignant quotes have been taken from this news feature and used between thick-and-thin rules as breakers. They are located in mid-paragraph to avoid halting the eye above the rule.   44

Figure 25   Run-on sideheads in 14pt italic are used under a stock logo to tabulate the items in this column of news brief from the *Liverpool Echo*. Note the text setting – set left, ragged right.   45

Figure 26   The use of white space and bold setting for times and titles is important in giving the reader easy-to-follow TV programme details.   46

Figure 27   A *News of the World* page on-screen awaiting two pictures.   48

Figure 28   A photograph that made news: the famous Reuters picture of the frigate *HMS Antelope* exploding into a fireball after being hit by an Excocet missile in San Carlos Bay in the Falklands War.   50

Figure 29   How the pictures flow: the part played by the electronic picture desk in routing pictures from their source to the page.   51

Figure 30   Even a mood picture needs a caption, especially where a model has been used in setting it up. The caption on this *Birmingham Evening Mail* picture of a girl plagued by a stalker makes it clear that the person shown is a lookalike.   53

Figure 31   Choosing for the page: what makes a good picture.
★ The *Aberdeen Press and Journal* photographer went for mood in the shot, opposite, of an American sailor and his Scottish wife at the lowering of the Stars and Stripes at a Scottish base.
★ The shot a sports photographer hopes for. The theme is action in the *Western Mail's* Allsport picture of Juventus scoring a goal against Manchester United in the European Champions' League.
★ Expression is the theme of this well-caught picture in London's *Evening Standard* of Prince Charles and his son Prince Harry about to fly off on a Royal tour.   59

Figure 32   As taken at the ringside: *News of the World* cameraman Brian Thomas captures the moment of triumph in a big boxing match.   60

Figure 33 The picture as it was cropped and used to show the two fighters in close-up. 60

Figure 34 Eight diverse fashion shots are imaged together into a montage in this women's page presentation in London's *Evening Standard*. 64

Figure 35 Cut-out pictures and bastard setting are easily achieved in modern page make-up programs. In this *Evening Standard* example the setting spills round the bent cane in a typical Charlie Chaplin look-back picture. 65

Figure 36 Successful blurbs, especially those at the top of the front page, are best achieved by a composite of boldly presented pictures, headline type and cross-references printed in colour. In this example from *The Express*, attractive girlie cut-outs, one extending into the masthead area, take the eye. Headings and cross references are here reversed on to red and blue. 66

Figure 37 Cropping and sizing a picture on the back of the print by the diagonal method before shooting it for the page. Nowadays, under full-page composition, photographs are cropped in the scanner at the outset. The crop and size can be further adjusted on screen, if need be, by the page editor. 66

Figure 38 Jobs that graphics can do:
Top left: in this working graphic, a *Daily Mail* artist shows the method by which a man survived in the sea by turning his waders into a lifejacket. Also included is the time scale and geography of the man's rescue.
The Guardian's map pinpoints deep coal mines threatened with closure in an accompanying story about problems in the power industry.
Right: Symbol graphics – an example from the *Western Mail's* horoscopes column. 67

Figure 39 Subbing at an editing screen: the text rearranges itself and gives a line count in response to cuts and adjustments made by the cursor. 70

Figure 40 Sports production: the copy flow from reporters and writers is filtered through the sports desk to the chief subeditor, specialist subs and page editors in a replica of the news and features operation. On most papers sports writing and production is independent of the rest of the paper. 71

Figure 41 Column width setting by the inch: a useful guide in text editing for new subeditors. 76

Figure 42 Style and pace in writing: an example from the world of golf (courtesy *The Times*) 98

Figure 43 Punctuation that a headline can do without: one that appeared. 131

Figure 44 First inkling of a disaster story – layout 1 178

Figure 45   The story develops – layout 2   180

Figure 46   It takes more of the page – layout 3   182

Figure 47   and still more – layout 4   186

Figure 48   The features department: copy flow from writers to features editor and thence to page make-up.   190

Figure 49   The agony aunts – mainstay at the popular end of the market in the national tabloids and in many provincial papers. These examples are from the *Birmingham Evening Mail* and *The Sun*.   192

Figure 50   The furniture of the features pages: a selection of columnist by-lines and logos for a variety of service columns and special features.   196

Figure 51   How a big evening paper handles a double-page features spread: a *Birmingham Evening Mail* special report on women plagued by stalkers.   198

Figure 52   Features display *Guardian* style: daring white spaces and the eye-grabbing big picture.   201

Figure 53   The elegance of a *Daily Mail* books page: stand-up drop letters, neat picture balance and clean uncluttered setting are the ideal foil against uncluttered advertising.   202

Figure 54   A leader page for all tastes: a strongly pictured main feature, a perceptive leading article and a light-hearted columnist go together well in this *Liverpool Echo* design.   203

Figure 55   Reader participation: letters are rated highly in all manner of newspapers, but there can be traps in running a Letters to the Editor column. These busy, well-filled examples are from the *Nottingham Evening Post* and the *Hull Daily Mail*.   210

Figure 56   The front page blurb – and sometimes the back page – is the shop window for the day's big feature offering.   212

PREFACE

So embedded is the computer in today's newspaper practice that it is hard to imagine how life was without it. Writers and production journalists alike have learnt to love their screens and keyboards. Above all, it has revolutionized the editing process. For the subeditor the computer is the ultimate tool that gives visual control of the product in a way that was impossible under old-time printing

What it does not do, of course, is to replace the creative skills it takes to edit the modern newspaper to the standard that its readers – and owners – have come to expect. In *New Subediting* I have taken advantage of a timely new edition of my much used textbook on the subject to reassess these skills in the light of the very latest advances in computerized editorial systems, and to examine what the systems builders have to offer.

The chapters that follow spell out in detail what today's young sub needs to know across the varied spectrum of computer-led editorial production. They examine and draw lessons from work in contemporary newspapers in text and presentation. They consider multi-skilling, and define the varied techniques of copy-tasting, the handling of news and features material, headline writing, and the use of typography and pictures to build attractive pages on screen.

Nor is language neglected. *New Subediting* takes account of the development of English as a vehicle of mass communication in an important section on word usage, polishing and fault-spotting.

Finally, it makes the point that previous editions of this book have made – that technology, however, advanced, exists to serve the purposes of editors and journalists and that, in whatever language or country, a newspaper is only as good as the creative skills of those who write, edit and put it togehter.

F.W. Hodgson
Ninefield, Sussex
September 1998

ACKNOWLEDGEMENTS

I found the following works useful in my chapters dealing with the knotty problems of text editing that confront subeditors: Robert Burchfield's 1997 revision of *Fowler's English Usage* (Oxford University Press); Sir Ernest Gower's *The Complete Plain Words* (Penguin Books, 1987); Eric Partridge, *Usage and Abusage* (Penguin Books, 1882), and G. V. Carey, *Mind the Stop* (Penguin Books, 1976 – and still the best). I would be failing in my duty if I did not acknowledge the example of my old colleague Harold Evans, whose five-volume work, *Editing and Design* (Heinemann), produced in the early 1970s, remains a repository of wisdom and expertise on the craft on newspaper journalism as it stood at the onset of 'new technology'.

For permission to reprint material and whole pages as examples, I am indebted to the editors of *The Guardian*, the *Sunday Times, The Times, Daily Mail, Financial Times, The Sun,* the *Bristol Evening Post, Birmingham Evening Mail, Western Mail, Liverpool Echo, Cumberland News, Hull Daily Mail* and the London *Evening Standard*. I am glad to have permission from the editor of the *Nottingham Evening Post* to use the picture of the editorial room at his newspaper on page 7, and from the editor of the *News of the World* and News Group Newspapers Ltd for the use of pictures on pages 48 and 60.

Quark Inc, of 1800 Grant Street, Denver, USA and Unisys Italian Spa, of Via Benigno Crespi 57, Milan, Italy, have helped with information on their products and permission to reproduce technical illustrations. For special help and facilities I am grateful to the Newspaper Society and to Richard Beamish and Alan Shanks, and to Portsmouth and Sunderland Newspapers Ltd, and News Group Newspapers.

INTRODUCTION: THE QUARK REVOLUTION

A sociologist writing about the press divided newspaper staffs into gatherers and processors. The gatherers: reporters of all types, photographers, feature writers and, of course, news and picture agencies. The processors: editors of all types including departmental heads, layout artists, subeditors and not forgetting the office lawyer by whatever title.

The writer in question noted that the processors marginally exceeded the gatherers in numbers. This was to be expected since, unlike books, newspapers are complicated things requiring a good deal of planning, decision taking, sorting and choosing of material and targeting on particular readerships, whence stem techniques in text editing, headline writing, illustrating and typographical display. These, of course, can vary considerably from paper to paper. Newspapers require editing at its most varied and complex.

At the heart of the process are the subeditors. The editor of a newspaper – that is *the* editor – cannot carry out, and never has carried out, all the editing functions, although he (or she) remains responsible, legally and practically, for what appears when the paper is printed. It is the subeditors, varying in numbers depending on the size of the paper, and multi-skilled to a greater degree since the demise of old printing, who produce the paper to the editor's broad policy and plan.

Editorial production, for that is what this complicated process is called, calls for a great variety of skills from subeditors. Knowledge of type and page design and the use of pictures are needed to produce balanced and eye-catching layouts in the style of the paper. Knowledge of page make-up is needed to see that everything fits correctly without clash and problems and that the finished page is finely honed – these days on screen – ready for the plate-maker. There is no old-fashioned print overseer to see to this aspect.

Editing the text is a fundamental skill in all newspapers, and in all parts of a newspaper. It requires a sound knowledge of language so as to spot faults, an unswerving dedication to accuracy, taste and legal fitness, an ability to collate from various sources a story of required length and style, to rewrite copy swiftly as and when required, to provide a readable and meaningful headline that fits, and to do all these things coolly in the face of deadline pressure.

The fact that, on some papers, making up pages on screen and even designing them, may fall to the same sub who edits the text is a measure of the technological change that has come over editorial production.

The arrival of Quark

The use of the computer in newspaper production which started in America in the early 1960s and spread across Europe had, by the mid-1980s, freed Britain forever from the centuries-old dominance of hot-metal printing. For the first time, journalists could generate their own type effortlessly as they sat at their keyboards writing and editing the text that went into the newspaper. In fact, it was the writers, as they keyboarded their stories into the office computer for editing, who effectively set the newspaper in type.

The computer, in this new production mode, allowed pages to be made up photographically, hence the term photoset type. Text and headlines were typeset and output on bromides; these were cut up by *photo-compositors* with scalpels (Figure 6) and attached to a page card in accordance with a *page layout* supplied by the editorial. Pictures were laser-printed on to bromides and likewise put into the page and trimmed by scalpel as required. The adverts arrived in the composing room as page-ready bromides and were pasted into position. When

Figure 1 The leap into full-screen composition. Apple-Mac page-making terminals in use at the *New of the World* before the introduction of their Windows-based Unisys Hermes system. Make-up here is using the QuarkXpress program, but with separate subbing and page-building screens

complete, and after being copied for inspection by the editor and advertising manager, each page was photographed and the negative sent to the platemakers to be made into a printing plate. It should be said that this system of page production is still in use in some newspaper offices.

Since type could be set and corrected hundreds of times faster than on hot-metal Linotype machines, and the pages put together much quicker than by the old method with its heavy metal type, the new photoset type and cut-and-paste make-up gave newspapers instant benefits in speed, safety and cost saving. Moreover, through interfacing easily with web-offset presses through the use of transfer-image polymer plates instead of direct-impression metal ones, the photo-produced pages enabled colour to be used for the first time in run of press.

The change, through the loss of traditional printing jobs, also brought to an end the years of confrontation and bad labour relations that had existed between managements and the old print unions, and resulted in the move of long-established newspapers from city centres to purpose-built premises in suburban locations with rooms full of keyboards and monitors and a press hall with banks of new web-offset presses.

But a revolution in newspaper production as big, or bigger, was round the corner. Hot metal and traditional typesetting had gone; the old rotary presses, with their heavy direct-impression metal plates had gone; the computer reigned supreme – but there was still a composing room, still camera operators and a dark room used in page production.

In the early 1990s a number of national papers, both daily and Sunday, began experimenting with page composition on screen. They used Apple-Macintosh desktop computers via a page make-up program called QuarkXpress which could be linked with the office mainframe computer, in which text was stored, by means of an interface. It was not trouble-free but it did enable pages to be put together on special make-up screens. Subs were selected to take charge of this new function, while text editing continued as before on the older editing screens.

It was then found that Apple-Macs used in clusters and driven by powerful file servers had the speed and memory required to handle complex layouts on screen without reliance on a mainframe database. Moreover, the new method accepted text and graphics inputs on page more easily and allowed the subeditor in charge of making up the page, using the Quark program and mouse controls, the flexibility needed to build to any nominated style. Full electronic pagination had arrived.

Primitive page-making systems offering formula pages had been around for years in some provincial papers, but they lacked the speed and memory, and also the flexibility, to produce pages of a variety and standard acceptable to the bigger national papers. There was a continuing problem with graphics generation in the computer. The harnessing of QuarkXpress and Apple-Mac desktop computers, plus developments in servers, picture scanning and imaging, especially in colour, solved these problems.

By 1995 all the national dailies and Sundays had adopted the Apple Mac-QuarkXpress solution, through a variety of configurations, and had moved into full screen composition. The composing room was no more. The dark room still played a role in the creating of high resolution page negatives required as an interface between screen and plate, but the arrival of direct-to-plate programs began to phase out even this. By 1998, a number of national newspapers made up on screen were delivering pages straight to the platemaker at the stroke of a key.

The incentive towards page-to-plate production in the nationals stemmed from the move, for distribution purposes, into decentralized printing at provincial sites since it simplified and speeded up the transmission of pages straight to the press. At Canary Wharf, in East London, where seven national papers owned by Mirror Group Newspapers and the *Daily Telegraph*, were published there were no presses at all. The papers were printed in a variety of centres including some abroad.

Meanwhile, in the provinces the move was towards concentration of printing on fewer sites as companies and papers replanted and merged their interests, which included contract printing for the nationals. On the editorial production side, provincial papers were less advanced. While the bigger ones had introduced the latest screen make-up systems, more than a quarter of titles were still using cut-and-paste in the middle of 1998.

'Subs with Quark experience'

Screen page make-up is still new and novel enough for its effect on editorial production to be over-stated by those in awe of it. Advertisements for subs request 'experience of using QuarkXpress.' In fact, senior subs, wearing their production hats, have always been responsible for page make-up, whether the work entailed guiding the inky hand of an old-time stone hand or the scalpel of some newly trained paste-up compositor. The advantage of screen make-up is that the subeditor – and not an intermediary – now does the moving about of ingredients and the polishing of space. The journalist is in charge of the product.

It is not an arduous job. The page plan, originating as ever as a 'rough' drawn on a sheet of paper by the executive concerned, is blocked out on the screen in the type style of the paper, with the contents indicated. Stories are called up ready subbed to fit their space. Pictures and graphics are imaged into their boxes from the scanners and adjusted on screen for a fine fit. Adverts are likewise called into their boxes and given a tweak. Mouse and key controls are instantaneous. The work of putting the page together is easy compared to what it used to be.

(a)

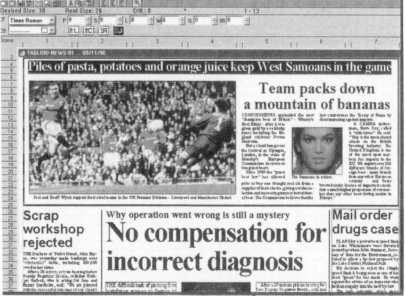

(b)

Figure 2 A page on screen (with zoom section), using the Unisys Hermes pagination module. It provides for WYSIWYG composition, continuous object and status monitoring and image cropping on page. Multi-user access allows several people to work on the same page

Sub or page editor?

What is the effect of this new situation? The speed of technological change has produced some weird ideas. Should subs be left to design their own pages (as they have always done on many weekly papers) as well as edit and typeset the material? Have subs, as a result of technological change, mysteriously less subbing to do than they used to have?

Should the subs' table be redesigned as what someone has called the 'command desk system', with the editor in the middle and executives, page builders and the rest of the subs in declining order of importance ranged around in concentric circles (Figure 3), with a 'rolling conference' going on all the time – a daunting intrusion into the peace needed for editing?

Should there be 'page editors' who each take a page on to their screen and sub every item, be it a feature or a news item, be it political or be it some sexy scandal, be it a crusty columnist or a clutch of readers' letters? Alternatively, should newspaper editors – as *The Independent* tried briefly to do in 1987 – let writers edit and project their own material and get rid of subs altogether?

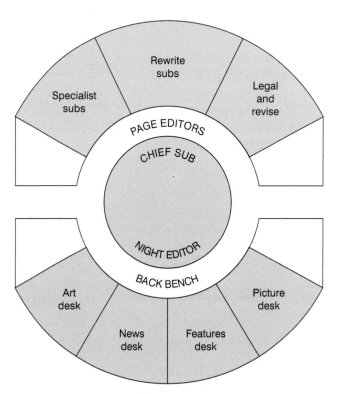

Figure 3 The command desk system of editorial production: it aims at centralizing edition inputs and decision-making, with direct back bench control of make-up through designated page editors working with specialist and rewrite subs

(a)

(b)

Figure 4(a) Pages take shape on Apple-Mac screens at the *Nottingham Evening Post*, which utilizes the Quark Publishing System (QPS). Subeditors are using the zoom facility to work on sections of pages. The latest version of this system extends QPS applications also to the Windows market for use with PCs equipped with Windows 95 and Windows NT. **(b)** Tracking the material – an information header for a news story or feature is created on the Quark database server and filled in by users as the feature moves through the editorial and production processes

Technology and the sub

Developments in technology are pointing the way to the future. The early Apple Mac-QuarkXpress solutions – which can still widely be found – were hybrids in which problems of interfacing with ageing editing systems and databases meant that page building and text editing had to be done on different screens.

Improved applications which entailed the use of clusters of Apple-Macs driven by powerful servers, which did not have to rely on the mainframe, speeded up both editing and make-up and allowed subs to edit on-page. Later, integrated Apple Mac-QuarkXpress systems, such as QPS and, more recently, the Microsoft Windows-based Unisys Hermes system, brought with them improved on-screen graphics handling and vastly upgraded and faster database management. These systems integrated make-up and text editing on every workstation in the editorial department if it were so required.

Hermes, the first fully-fledged solution not using Apple Mac computers and QuarkXpress, offered papers, and groups of papers, a powerful constantly updated text storage and retrieval system delivering through new-type servers. It had a multimedia archive which claimed 'virtually no limits on the type of data that can be stored and manipulated' which was aimed at companies moving towards electronic publishing via the Internet.

It also worked on any standard PC running Microsoft Windows 95 by means of text handling, design and make-up, and image handling modules, and could be customized to any size of operation, including multi-format papers on the same site.

While facilities in the new systems introduced might make subbing on a 'whole page' basis through page editors seem logical, the reasons for doing this were less so. Specialisms for many papers, especially those selling strongly on text as opposed to display, relied on special skills and experience, on subs who were good at such things as captions or rewrites. With the new systems, multi-access, in fact, allowed any number of subs to work on the same page – which they could all have on-screen at the same time – so there was no problem. Specialist subs could fit in the bridge column or a technology report. Chunks of artwork such as blurbs could be taken out of the frame to be worked on by an artist and returned page-ready, while simultaneously a sub might be grappling with a long-running story as the lead.

The page deadline, however, required that one sub – or a production editor? – should be responsible for deciding when it was ready and, in this respect, nominated page subs or page editors made sense.

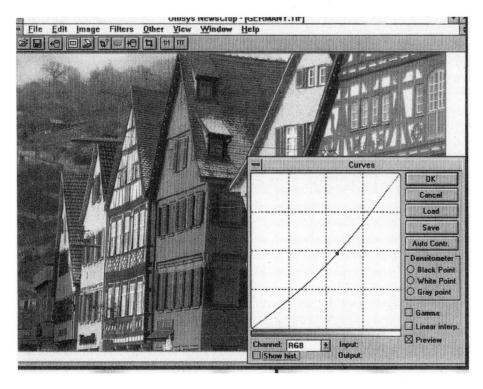

Figure 5 Picture editing on screen with Unisys Hermes. Their NewsCrop tool allows cropping, mirroring, zooming and adjusting tonal curves in mono and colour, enabling quick last minute changes to be made. The system permits the integration of applications such as Adobe PhotoShop if additional image handling is needed

Other changes blurred the old boundaries in editorial production. By 1998 some newspapers, despite their scorn of the early modular make-up systems, had begun setting up page 'modules' that could be called up and adapted on screen for fast routine pages, thus reducing the work of layout artists, whose graphics role had already been reduced by computer-generated graphics. More imaginative designs and 'spreads' still required an art desk, especially on the big national papers.

In another development some national and provincial papers announced contracts for agreed plate-ready pages of news from *PA News's* new page production team to supplement their copy input. The attraction for provincial papers – the *Liverpool Post* was one – was that they obtained coverage, set up in their own type format and fitting round the adverts, of national and international news that was outside their normal staff deployment. A number of national papers used the arrangement to input made-up pages of agreed regional content, including some sport, for edition areas where they were not well represented. While the agency contracts could be used by some papers for cost-cutting they led, in fact, to more jobs for subs at *PA News* who built up their editorial production staff as business grew.

All these developments were spin-offs of the all-dominant computer which had moved into the centre of editorial production. Which ideas you used and how you used them depended on the sort of newspaper you were, and what you were trying to do.

If the editing and presentation of text and pictures and their projection and targeting on the readers were important, as they surely are on most newspapers (and if you are not trying to run entirely on a shoestring), you needed specialists with skills in these areas. They are not, for instance, matters that can be left to reporters or features writers, whose skills and techniques are for different ends. The working time of those staff is best spent gathering and writing news and researching and composing features – things that chair-bound subeditors might not be very good at.

There is no doubt that involvement in page make-up, which is a very computer-organized and not intrinsically difficult task, has made life more interesting for subeditors. When, in response to your cursor and mouse control (if the task falls to you), you see a page taking shape on your screen in a way that it will appear to the readers, you feel far closer to your newspaper. Apart

Figure 6 Halfway house: the cut-and-paste method of page composition. A compositor attached cut-up text and picture bromides to a page grid. The page was photographed to create the negative from which the printing plate was derived. Note the stick-on tape rules that had to be used. This method has now mostly given way to screen make-up

Figure 7 A cleaner environment: smooth polymer plates are used on this modern web-offset press at the News Centre, Portsmouth, where once all was hot metal. The pages are printed by being offset via a 'blanket' which picks up the ink by chemical means and transfers it to the paper

from this, however, the techniques of editing and projecting the contents of your newspaper to the readers have not mysteriously changed. As subs, you have simply been given better tools with which to do the job. This should make for better newspapers and probably more of them if proprietors and editors get the formula right and are prepared to maintain standards.

It is to these techniques that this book now turns.

1

WHAT IS EDITORIAL PRODUCTION?

Editorial production on a daily paper, morning or evening, begins with the selection of the contents for the day's issue. This does not mean that the writing part has finished. News will continue to be gathered and written up to the last deadline of the last edition, background features will be prepared and photographs shot, but once decisions begin to be taken about the placing of stories in the pages, that is editorial production.

Central to this process is the paper's team of subeditors, by whom the various tasks of editing are carried out. A prime mover in this early stage of producing the paper is the senior subeditor who selects and shortlists from the mass of incoming material the stories most likely to be used. Since *copy* is the name for all the material keyboarded in by the writers, copytasting is the word used for the selecting of this material, and the person who initiates the process is the *copytaster*.

News creation is a round-the-clock operation into which a newspaper tunes during its hours of production. On an evening paper, where work begins about 8 a.m., the *newsroom* deals first with overnight stories and follow-ups from the previous day's news. Because of the time difference, foreign copy will be at first predominantly from America. This is why the early editions of evening papers often carry American-originated material which is later thrown out as the flow of home and European stories picks up with the start of the day's activity cycle.

As edition succeeds edition, from about midday there is a strengthening of the home news-of-the-day content with *running stories* being updated between editions into the late afternoon, peak time for the inflow of stories being around 2 to 3 p.m. Afternoon cricket scores replace morning and overnight ones; the lateness of racing results is a guide to the press time of the edition you have bought.

The morning paper cycle begins at about 11 a.m. or midday, with edition press times from about 7 p.m. depending on the distribution areas and where the printing presses are that serve them. National papers, printing in a variety of centres these days, publish earlier for more distant areas. Provincial morning papers with their closer distribution can afford to work until well into the evening before getting their first edition away.

Morning paper newsrooms first of all mop up the news of the day, looking for follow-ups where stories have had a good run in the evenings and on television, and giving more detailed versions of stories the evenings have only nibbled at. They have the benefit of evening events, speeches, meetings, functions and theatres and have more time for set-piece interviewing. Because of the time difference, morning papers are stronger on European news and are first with the day's events from Australia and the Far East. They also have time for polished detailed background features and situationers which give depth and perspective to their coverage.

By the time the last bit of updating has been done and the last edition (not normally later than 2 a.m.) has gone to press, the flow of home and European stories has subsided and the first stories are coming in from America. The news cycle is ready once more for an 8 a.m. start-up by the evenings.

Creating the news

News – features are dealt with later in this book – arrives in a newspaper office from a variety of sources. Common now to all reporters, feature writers and agencies is the practice of keyboarding copy straight into the office computer, from which stories are recalled on to screens for editing into their page slots.

Agency copy is entered likewise and is automatically routed to the desk whose job it is to read and deal with it. Local references are typecoded to help local paper subscribers and draw the news editor's attention. There are not many jobs these days being carried out by village correspondents where ballpen, typewriter and telephone are the means of origination.

Staff reporters

Staff reporters are the most useful and controllable source of news and the likeliest source of *exclusives*; all papers like to have something their rivals haven't got. Numbers vary from about ten to twenty on a small evening paper to forty or more on a national daily. They work from the newsroom or from branch offices and sometimes independently in districts, and they are controlled and briefed by the news editor (or the chief reporter on smaller papers).

Jobs can vary from a simple telephone inquiry, or personal call resulting from a letter or information received, to complicated jobs involving a team of reporters and sometimes several locations. Some stories might have both local and national, or even foreign 'ends' and last all day or several days.

If there is no time to get to the office to keyboard copy into the computer, reporters, using portable workstations, file direct into the system by telephone modems; otherwise their copy is taken over the telephone by *copytakers*, who keyboard it in for them. Where there are bigger staffs a newspaper might use a number of reporters as an investigative team on long-term news projects under a leader or project editor. This is usually planned into the paper in advance as a special news feature.

Freelances

Freelance reporters are used mainly on specialist assignments or for holiday relief work and are paid for the job or days or weeks worked. They are not tied to a paper except where they have a specific contract covering a job or sequence of shifts. Some specialize in investigative writing which they sell to the highest bidder.

Local correspondents

These are journalists working for a local paper, or as local freelances, who are accredited by *retainer* fee or some special arrangement to a bigger paper to cover stories in the area. They get *lineage* (a fee per line) for stories used or ordered. The arrangement usually precludes them working for a rival paper. They cover wanted stories where a staff reporter is not available.

News agencies

National and international news agencies work round the clock to provide a variety of services for newspapers all over the world, collecting material from bureaux and correspondents in cities and countries, checking and editing it and distributing it to subscribers.

Most countries have their own national agencies whose services are used by small and medium-sized papers to fill gaps in coverage, or even provide all but local coverage. Agency stories can be used as check sources and many agencies provide news pictures. The international ones such as Reuters, Associated Press, United Press International and Agence France Press are the prime sources of foreign news for papers who have few, or no, foreign corespondents, and also of newsfilm and sound reporting for television and radio. They feed into national news networks stories affecting a country's own interests and their nationals abroad. News agency correspondents are often the first to break important foreign stories.

Agencies operate in a similar way to newspapers through staff reporters in main centres with local correspondents, or *stringers*, filing in from the districts. The subediting, which includes headlining, checking and editionizing for the various services, is carried out at the main offices and serves morning, evening and Sunday papers. Most papers in Britain take the Press Association (national) and Reuters general services and some sport, financial, situationer and other services, depending on their contracts. A rent is paid for each.

Handouts

Handouts arrive in newspaper offices in great numbers from all sorts of organizations, including the Government, and sometimes from celebrities, via press officers, whose aim is to reach the public through the newspaper. They are usually given to reporters to read or to specialists whose field they cover in case they contain something of interest to the readers. Reading them can be a tedious and even boring job, but it can yield important stories over a wide field including, for example, housing statistics, immigration, race problems, technology breakthroughs, new cars and copy for consumer columns.

The newsroom

Though the newsroom is the heart of the gathering side of the business (see Figure 8) it is concerned with production, too, for it is here that decisions are taken that will shape the news content of the paper. And, of course, the keystrokes made by the writers are the keystrokes, subject to editing, that set the paper in type.

The news editor, who runs the newsroom, is one of the busiest executives on the paper. The assessment of a news situation depends at the outset on the news editor's judgement: what news is to be covered, in what depth, and who is to do the work. Reporters and correspondents are briefed so that copy is filed on time and important aspects of stories not missed. Stories are commissioned from freelances and outside specialists, agency input monitored, work checked to see it is done properly, handouts, correspondence, expenses, travel arrangements, interviewing for jobs and a hundred and one other things dealt with. In this work the news editor is helped by a deputy, usually a couple of assistants and a secretary.

The news editor keeps a check on where the staff are, listens to their calls in, decides when to extend coverage of a story, when to ask for more copy and when to call it a day where a story has 'fallen down'. The advent of the *electronic newsroom* helps. News editors now check reporters' files on screen, send back stories where coverage is not enough or has failed in some way, and route stories to the copy taster and chief sub as they become ready for the pages. There is sometimes a reverse traffic on screen of stories sent back by the chief sub who is not happy with them.

The use of portable workstations by reporters has improved newsroom organization. District offices can be controlled electronically through the newsroom's keyboards, with stories and messages being routed to and fro.

Village and country correspondents of provincial papers now often have their own portable terminals: Women's Institutes and flower show results have entered the computer age. Most offices have a number of such terminals in use among part-time contributors, while many with their own PCs link up to the office computer by telephone modem to file copy. It all makes for more effective control of coverage.

By the time the editing and making up of the pages begins, a good deal of the decision-making has already taken place. The material has passed through the newsroom system. Stories have been checked by the news editor and sent

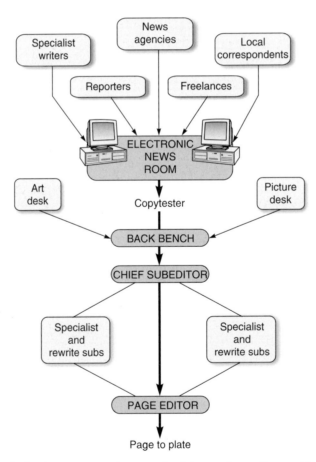

Figure 8 The electronic newsroom shown as the fulcrum of copy flow on a typical national daily. Stories are keyed into the system by the writers, checked by the news editor, sorted by the copytaster, planned and placed by the back bench or chief sub, and called up on screen for subbing and building into the page.

to the chief sub. Among them, depending on the facts of a story, the amount of space available and the volume of news about, are the candidates for the day's pages.

The copytaster

In theory, the editor reads everything that is likely to get into the paper. In practice this is seldom possible, although editors are usually given a copy of all reporters' stories, or can call them up on their personal screens.

The editor, through informal discussions with executives during the day and through the briefings and debate of the daily planning conference, is familiar with the more important stories that are being covered, and at an early stage has ideas about the thrust and balance of the paper. The likelihood of some big stories is known in advance and their place in the paper can be prepared. There are days, however, when because of other concerns, the editor has little time to focus on the whole news input and has to leave some decisions to his executives. The role of the copytaster who, come what may, reads everything that is written and submitted, is thus an important safeguard.

The copytaster is usually the first production journalist to arrive for duty in the editorial room. Here, at a desk close to the chief sub (Figure 8) and usually just in front of the back bench, the process of 'tasting' goes on until the last edition of the day has gone to press. The work is generally split into two shifts with a deputy taking over later in the day.

This is the journalist figure most maligned by the media sociologists. The copy taster is the 'gate-keeper', the one who lets in or shuts out stories according to the indoctrination practised by the proprietor/organization; who assesses news to a set of stereotypes deeply embedded in his professional soul; who bends circumstances to fit preconceived stereotypes and pigeon holes; the stopper when anything original or damning appears at the gate; the one who protects the readers, the people, the organization from truths that jar . . . and so on.

The job, in reality, is nowhere near as influential or as sinister. The copytaster is unfailingly a senior subeditor who understands the paper's market and readership, and his (or her) function is to sift through and sort all incoming stories and reject those that are unsuitable or unusable. The aim is to shortlist and reduce to manageable proportions what is sometimes a mountain of material so that the night editor, chief subeditor, or whoever is in charge of page planning, can set to work on the edition without their time being wasted.

The job is a 'hot seat'. The danger facing all copytasters is of 'spiking' a story that turns out be one the editor decides should have been carried. This is a special hazard on national papers when the rejected story can turn up in a rival paper. The safeguard against this happening is the copytaster's own finely tuned news sense and familiarity with the paper's style and content.

Measuring the news

A quick examination of newspapers on the same day will reveal that while some stories are common to many, there is a variety of opinion among them as to what news to carry. There is a difference in coverage in the daily press between newspapers that circulate nationally and regional and local ones. Within these bands are further differences in market and content.

Some papers exist to propagate the views of political parties or churches or minority groups or interests. Some national papers – in Britain, for instance, *The Times*, *The Guardian* and the *Daily Telegraph* – have an up-market readership interested in cultural things and world news, and in technology and education. Some are highly specialized, such as the *Financial Times* with its business news (and absence of sport). At the same time, many tabloid, or half-size, papers – which have a bolder display – such as *The Sun* and *The Mirror*, sell to a popular readership and are strong on pictures, human interest news and stories about TV personalities, showbusiness, sport and the Royal family.

Town evening papers reflect the life and activity in the circulation area and carry only the more important national stories and very little foreign news. Some county papers are full of news about the farming community, village activities, local wedding and social gossip of the area. News about dominant industries such as steel or textiles, in which many readers work, can feature strongly in regional papers. This is all quite natural. They are performing a service for their readers (see Figure 9).

There is also a difference in weight of coverage between daily and Sunday papers, and between provincial evening and weekly papers. The once-a-week publications devote more space to features giving depth and background to the news of the week, and to comment and opinion.

It will be seen from this brief survey that there can be no universals in news assessment. While a copytaster on a national 'serious' daily and one on a provincial evening follow the same routine, the yardstick by which they measure the copy input is not the same.

This does not mean there can be no definition of news. News remains, in any circumstances, the first tidings, or knowledge or disclosure of an event. By the same token, a secret or unknown event remains secret and unknown until, upon its disclosure, it becomes news. For example, the marriage in secret of a celebrity might take ten years to be revealed to the public. Then it becomes news. Thus we can say that, in terms of a newspaper's content, it is not the event itself that is news but its disclosure.

Figure 9 Serving the community – this well filled broadsheet front page from the weekly *Cumberland News* uses a stylish lower case type dress and well-planned highlights to present ten newsy stories, all from the circulation area. For good measure it runs an edition blurb with page cross-references

Once a news situation has been disclosed and made public it ceases to be news. A notable news story that appears in a paper one day will be referred to the following day only in the light of some new aspect that has cropped up. This is called a *follow-up*.

Yet it is not sufficient for an event to be news within this narrow definition for it to be worth printing. It must also be of likely interest to the readership which, as we have seen, varies from paper to paper. There is little point, for instance, in a country weekly on the Welsh border, filling its pages with news about Brazil or China, or the *Financial Times* concerning itself with the result of the three-legged race in a school sports in Cumbria. The journalists know their paper's market – they have to know it to do their job properly – and they select the sort of news that is right for it. Even so, copytasters will find that among the copy that flows into their electronic baskets each day is a percentage that does not fit the pattern. The first job is to weed this out.

Another consideration in news assessment is the sheer volume of the commodity available on the day. A newsroom or agency does not stop filing when it has reached a given number of stories; it goes on covering the news wherever it breaks. The gatherers accept that it is the job of the editor and the editorial staff to decide how much of it will be used and at what length. While the factors governing this measuring of news become instinctive in an experienced copytaster, it is worth noting down what they are. Also, it should be repeated that it is not the copytaster's job to select what goes into the paper but rather to exclude what, for various reasons, is unsuitable, shortlisting the remainder into a manageable amount.

A story is rejected if:

1 It is geographically outside the paper's market, unless it is of special importance (depending on whether it is a national, regional or local paper).
2 It is outside the readers' range of interests (whether quality, up-market, popular or specialist).
3 It does not extend any further material that already appeared in the papers.
4 It appears to be merely seeking publicity for someone and has otherwise little reader interest.
5 It is legally unsafe (unless it is worth making safe), in bad taste, racist, clearly inaccurate, silly, or based on rumour.
6 It is simply not good enough, or interesting enough, on a day when there is a great deal of news about.

The last point demonstrates why absolutes are not possible in measuring news value. Even if a story fulfils most of the normal criteria, the decision on whether it is used and, if used, how much space it will get, can depend on the number of good stories demanding to be used, the existence of other similar stories, and the space available on the day. It is not generally realized that the amount of space for editorial use in a newspaper rises and falls in response to the percentage flow of advertising and not to the volume of news available.

The consequence of this that a story that might justify being given a good space one day might warrant less on another. The best day for a good show to a story is when the copy flow is known to be slack – on the Sunday shift working for a Monday morning paper, for example.

The alternative on such days might seem to be to leave blank spaces in the pages, but this would look silly and also would not be liked by the reader. What happens is that certain exclusive stories are held back (or planned forward) for publication on slack days, a greater number of foreign stories used and more space given to features, or picture display. It has to be said that however uneven the flow of news, there are very few days in the year when the editor is at his (or her) wit's end what to put into the paper, but the phenomenon just described does account for the good and bad days that newspapers have, which are sometimes noticed by readers.

News patterns

The four pages reproduced in this chapter, three provincial and one national, demonstrate the working of the news selection patterns we have just described.

The *Cumberland News* page one (Figure 9) provides model coverage for a weekly serving communities in a far-flung area. The ten stories range from drug abuse in a hospital and a woman meeting her mother for the first time in 54 years, to a hunt supporters' demonstration, a competition for a new Millennium bridge at Carlisle, and a man of 88 found hanged. Even the fillers tell about a local lad who was the boyfriend of Louise Woodward, the au pair accused of killing a baby in the US, and about more local jobs expected following a Marks & Spencer's expansion. Inside there is hardly an area of activity from market and stock prices to Women's Institutes that does not get its space.

The two evenings from Birmingham and Bristol (Figure 10) cannot compete with this on scale but, in tabloid fashion, they provide a powerful display for stories of strong local interest in eye-catching layouts. Both are good-looking easy-to-read papers for busy city dwellers looking for a quick round-up of the day's news as it affects them.

The *Financial Times* (Figure 11) shows how a specialist broadsheet can pack in the news while still achieving quiet, readable elegance. The four main stories are given a good space. The air crash picture, by the standards of any daily, is an eye-catcher, and there are still to come a column of 17 briefs on companies and economies around the world, a currency chart, a contents list, and three colour blurbs about items in the inside pages.

Figure 10 How the tabloid evenings do it – an inside news page from the *Birmingham Evening Mail* and a smart front page from Bristol's *Evening Post*. Effective placing of pictures and polished use of the tabloid style characterize these sans type layouts

22

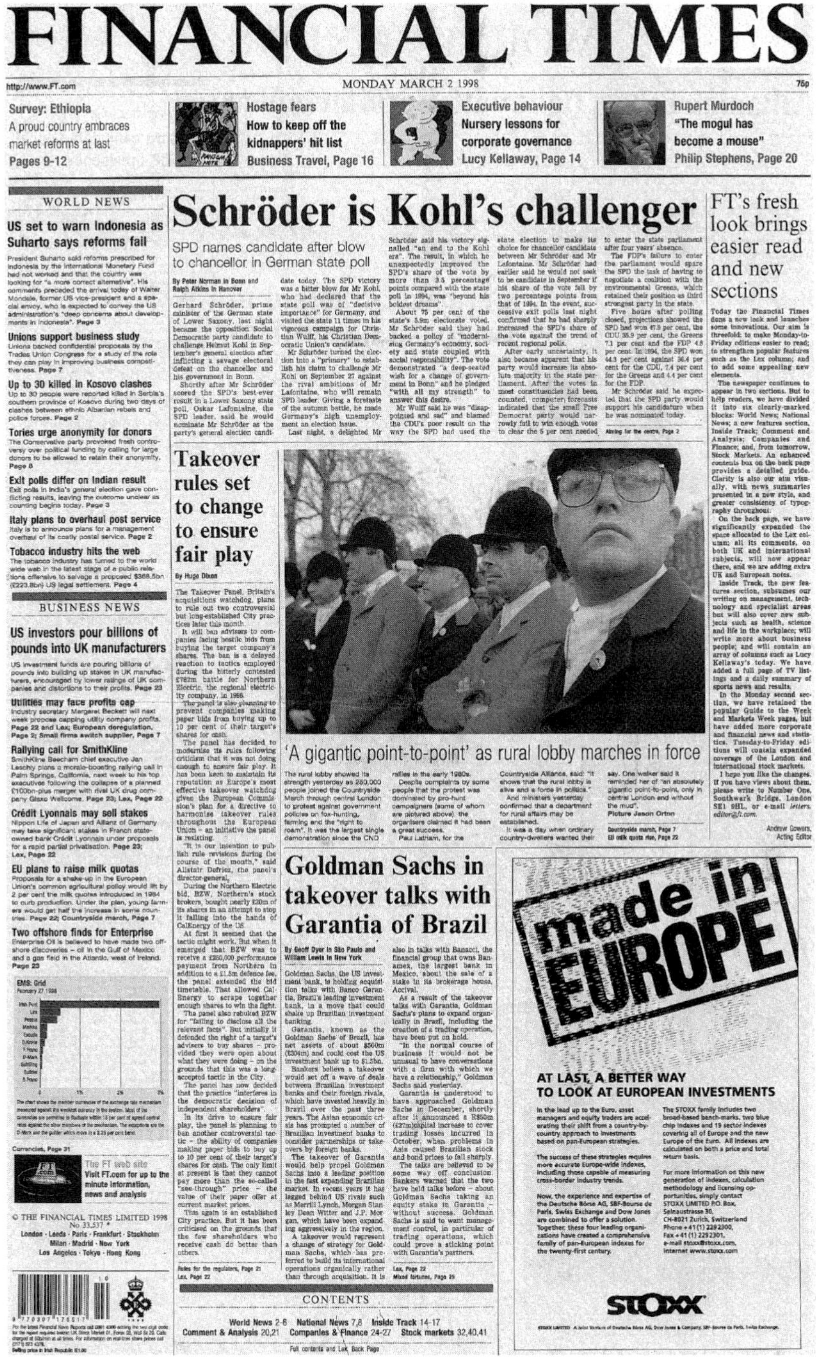

FINANCIAL TIMES

http://www.FT.com MONDAY MARCH 2 1998 75p

Survey: Ethiopia
A proud country embraces market reforms at last
Pages 9-12

Hostage fears
How to keep off the kidnappers' hit list
Business Travel, Page 16

Executive behaviour
Nursery lessons for corporate governance
Lucy Kellaway, Page 14

Rupert Murdoch
"The mogul has become a mouse"
Philip Stephens, Page 20

WORLD NEWS

US set to warn Indonesia as Suharto says reforms fail

Unions support business study

Up to 30 killed in Kosovo clashes

Tories urge anonymity for donors

Exit polls differ on Indian result

Italy plans to overhaul post service

Tobacco industry hits the web

BUSINESS NEWS

US investors pour billions of pounds into UK manufacturers

Utilities may face profits cap

Rallying call for SmithKline

Crédit Lyonnais may sell stakes

EU plans to raise milk quotas

Two offshore finds for Enterprise

EMS: Grid

The FT web site
Visit FT.com for up to the minute information, news and analysis

© THE FINANCIAL TIMES LIMITED 1998

London · Leeds · Paris · Frankfurt · Stockholm
Milan · Madrid · New York
Los Angeles · Tokyo · Hong Kong

Schröder is Kohl's challenger

SPD names candidate after blow to chancellor in German state poll

By Peter Norman in Bonn and Ralph Atkins in Hanover

FT's fresh look brings easier read and new sections

Andrew Gowers, Acting Editor

Takeover rules set to change to ensure fair play

By Hugo Dixon

'A gigantic point-to-point' as rural lobby marches in force

Picture Jason Orton

Goldman Sachs in takeover talks with Garantia of Brazil

made in EUROPE

AT LAST, A BETTER WAY TO LOOK AT EUROPEAN INVESTMENTS

STOXX

CONTENTS

World News 2-6 National News 7,8 Inside Track 14-17
Comment & Analysis 20,21 Companies & Finance 24-27 Stock markets 32,40,41

Figure 11 With its full-width masthead, use of blurbs and front page colour (though sometimes oddly printing on pink), the *Financial Times* has come a long way in the last few years. This page one, with its Times Roman lower case format and studied elegance of design, shows that a paper with a mostly business readership does not have to look dull

Production start-up

In today's computerized environment it is the tools rather than the principles that have changed but, if you can imagine an electronic pile of text, pictures and advertisements on the one hand and the printed paper coming off the press on the other, then editorial production is what happens in between. We will now look at how this process begins.

We will take, as our example, a small tabloid evening paper running a new page-to-plate make-up system based on Apple-Mac PCs and the latest version of QuarkXpress. It is operated by a small team of subs who, if you like, are page editors, each of whom sub the items for their page and make up the pages on screen, complete with pictures and advertisements, to plate-ready state. It is a system that suits a paper with modest staffing, few executives and no art desk.

The back bench, or control desk (in Figure 8), consists of the deputy editor (who would be the night editor on a national morning paper), and the chief subeditor and his deputy, who doubles as copytaster. The editor occasionally drops by and sits in when not tied to his (or her) office on other duties; it is a paper where the deputy editor has the role of production supremo.

Suppose you are the copytaster. Your 'in' queue of stories from the newsroom has already begun to mount by the time you report for duty and your first task is to check your directories or folders and 'read in'. You make a few notes on a pad (no office is entirely paperless!). The deputy editor and chief sub, who have called up particular stories on their screens, are roughing out early pages on half-size layout sheets which they will hand to the page subs who are beginning to arrive.

While you are reading in, the deputy editor and the chief sub confer with the editor about the general balance and expected main contents of the day's paper in the light of what is known. They tell you what important items are expected and any particular things to look out for.

Your job is now to read and draw the important stories – especially any unexpected ones – to the attention of the night editor or chief sub and put them into their queues; to put the clearly 'dead' ones into an electronic 'spike', and to put doubtful or possible stories into pending queues to be called up as needed. You look out for stories with edition area interest and bring them forward at the right time, and route to the picture desk any stories needing pictures in case this has not already been done.

You might feed a flow of useful shorter material into a special queue to the chief sub to be used as *fillers* at the bottoms of pages. The number of 'out' queues you operate depends on the amount of copy and the degree of pre-sorting needed to suit the number of pages.

Reading all copy before it is subbed is useful. It enables you to spot any errors or failings in stories and to send them back in good time to the newsroom for more work or inquiries. If you have a separate agency input it enables you to suggest to the newsroom ideas for local 'ends' to agency stories where these have not already been put in hand.

> Copytasting on screen makes life easier. You can call up the complete directory of stories held in a given queue (i.e. newsroom, agency, sport, etc.) and get the source, name, catchline and first few lines of any story, and also its length. Stories can be sorted into subject and priority queues within the computer so that the right material is drawn to the chief sub's attention at the right time. You can queue related stories together, including edition area copy.

Some national dailies refine the tasting process by filtering copy through a *rough* and *fine* taster, or through separate home and foreign tasters, where there is a heavy copy input and a lot of pages to fill. The aim is not only a fail-safe reading operation but also a continuously creative assessment of the copy flow throughout the editions.

CHAPTER TWO

A SUB'S GUIDE TO DESIGN AND TYPOGRAPHY

The plan of a newspaper – what it contains and the order in which it is presented – is decided by the editor in consultation with senior executives. An outline plan is initiated at an editor's conference, held early in the day on a morning or evening paper or midweek on a Sunday or weekly, and thereafter adjusted, through informal discussions with executives, in the light of copy and picture input.

Editorial space which, as we saw, can vary day to day in response to the amount of advertising, is shown at the start of each day or week in a *dummy* of the paper prepared for the editor by the advertising department. This is put out on screen these days, and it shows the number of pages (*pagination*) agreed and the placings and sizes of advertisements sold.

The advertising, over which the editor has no control, provides fixed points around which the editorial content of each page is planned. This does not mean that the placing of advertisements is entirely arbitrary. Papers have a general policy of placement; as a rule, the front page is kept fairly clear, often completely clear, and other key pages, including the back and the main features page are kept 'light' to accommodate known editorial needs.

Beyond this, the number and shapes of advertisements, and where they are booked for, can vary a good deal. Some trading of space might be possible between editorial and advertising departments but, on the whole, advertising once placed cannot be shifted. Many positions have been bought at a premium. Advertising also has to keep its own balance in the paper to avoid clash of product or having cut-out reply coupons that back on to each other.

Format

All newspapers cultivate a visual format which is distinctively their own, and by which they are recognized, and page planning adapts to this. By format, in this case, we mean the consistent use of the same typography and style of presentation, and the placing of things such as sport, editorial opinion, women's pages, TV

Figure 12 A Sunday paper in parts: how the logo identifies the *Sunday Times* sections

programmes and late news in the same part of the paper in each issue so that the shape is familiar to the readers. This familiarity is important in page planning.

A newspaper's format is its visual brand image. While it can be modified in various ways, both in content and in typography, it is not usually subject to drastic change unless the paper is being relaunched in the face of falling circulation, or is seeking for some reason to change its market.

In all papers specialist areas such as financial news and sport, and sometimes foreign news, have their own part of the paper. The quality dailies and Sundays give separate sections to finance, sport and arts and leisure (in what used to be called the American pattern) with each section having its own pagination and masthead logo. Some provincial papers bring out separate sections on certain days, and might sectionalize their advertising features or holiday or Christmas shopping promotions. In all the sections the broad type style and presentation is in accord with that of the paper (Figure 12).

Balance of contents

Within the broad format it is necessary to achieve a balance of subject on the pages and a visual balance of text, headlines and pictures in relation to each other. It would be unbalanced, for instance, to run all stories of gloom and doom, or death and destruction, on one page, to put all human interest stories on one page, or to fill a page with stories without pictures. Account is also taken of the advertisements on the page so that the editorial part does not clash with it either visually or in content.

The editor might occasionally vary the usual balance of space allocated to news, features and sport to suit special circumstances – an election edition or a heavy weekend sports programme, for instance.

> Each newspaper arrives at a general contents balance to suit its market. Evening papers give more space to news than Sunday or weekly papers. This is because they are exposed to the main daily news breaks whereas Sunday papers, produced on Saturday nights, mop up and explain the background to the week's news and run more weekend leisure features. Morning papers, too, tend to have more features than evening papers because of their tradition of giving in-depth explanation to the day's news. Town evening and county weeklies are careful to gather together pages of area news which their readers come to expect.
>
> However, newspaper markets are by no means fixed and there can be subtle shifts in the balance of contents and news coverage over a period.

No matter how the balance is arrived at it is achieved within a total editorial space which remains at about the same percentage of the whole in relation to the advertisements, whatever the number of pages. Advertising is at its lightest, around 30 per cent or less, in town evening papers which have relatively low overheads; around 40 to 45 per cent in national popular dailies, which have high overheads but a high circulation revenue; and 60 per cent or more in the quality Sundays, which have high production and distribution costs coupled with less circulation revenue.

You can say, then, that the essential points in planning an issue of a newspaper are:

1 Balance of editorial items in relation to each other – i.e. news, sport and features.
2 Balance of subject content, including pictures and advertisements, within each page.
3 Preservation of the general 'shape' of the paper's format.

Who does what

Editorial manning varies according a paper's size. Big national dailies have a battery of executives, some with precise editorial functions, some with managerial, administrative or liaison roles, some with general overlord responsibilities for areas. While there is usually only one deputy editor who actually deputizes in the editor's absence, there can be a number of assistant editors with titles such as assistant editor (news), assistant editor (features), assistant editor (special projects). At departmental level (akin to middle management) there are more defined roles. The titles of news editor, features editor and sports editor mean that they are head of these respective departments, each with a deputy.

Producing a big daily or Sunday paper is the responsibility of the night editor, who is the senior production executive, usually equal in status, and sometimes senior, to the assistant editors. To the night editor is delegated the physical editing functions of the editor once the departmental heads have gathered the material and the production cycle begins. From the night editor flow the delegated roles of the chief subeditor, picture editor and art editor, and thence the subeditors and page editors who carry out the actual editing and make-up (Figure 8 on page 16).

On smaller papers some of these roles are merged. On weeklies and on some evenings the deputy editor, and even the editor, take a more active role in page planning. On such papers there is seldom an art desk, the chief sub and senior subs originating the page schemes. Subs might scan in and correct pictures as well as edit text and make up the pages (Chapter 3). Similarly, the subs' table might combine the news and features functions and even that of sport, although sports production on most papers is carried out separately under the sports editor (see Figure 40 on page 71).

Whatever the scale, the role of the chief sub is the fulcrum of the operation. Into his (or her) electronic basket land the copy, pictures and ideas that have been ordered and discussed, and they leave it, checked, edited and corrected, to take their place in the pages being made up on screen. Through the long production shift this important executive, aided by a deputy and supported by the copy taster, works through the material of the day, page by page, edition by edition, roughing out pages, briefing subs on the handling of stories, accepting or rejecting headlines, solving problems that arise, checking the finished work until the last edition has gone to press.

The deputy chief sub, or an assistant, might take over the revise function, an important role in computerized systems where there are no longer proof readers to check for mistakes missed – or created – by busy subs, and to see that house style is adhered to.

You could say that the job of the chief sub combines a piece-by-piece planning operation with quality control of the material being processed. It is an arduous and unrelenting task. On a small paper it might include the planning and scheming of most of the pages and a major share in decisions about the balance of the paper. In a big national paper with the back-bench system this part of the work is covered by the night editor and assistants, leaving the chief sub to give more time to polishing the material and controlling the pages being put together.

Designing the pages

Once the overall plan of the paper is agreed, the presentation of the contents becomes an exercise in design. Now takes place the *scheming* of the pages, of which the end product is the page design or *layout*.

On a big morning paper the night editor and assistant night editor roughly scheme the main news and features pages, with the chief sub and features chief sub, if there is one, usually scheming the others. (On small papers, as we have seen, the chief sub plays a bigger part, with some pages being given to senior subs to scheme.) Layout artists under the direction of an art editor draw the schemed pages in detail directly on to screen, call down any computer graphics needed, and prepare artwork such as blurbs, headline-picture composites (*compos*), and *logos* called for in the design.

The layouts, with artwork, page and advert boxes and story boxes precisely shown, then go on screen to the chief sub who puts them out with type instructions to the sub or page editor chosen to handle the page. According to the production method used, the stories are then subbed to length, the headlines written and pictures (see Chapter 3) and adverts called down into their boxes. The page editor adjusts the items to fit until the page is judged to be ready. After being cleared by editor and lawyer, it is sent electronically to the darkroom where it is turned into a high resolution negative from which the printing plate is derived. Under the latest page-to-plate systems, as we have seen, it can be sent at a keystroke direct to the platemaker thus dispensing with the darkroom.

Important note: the chief sub, or the production supremo by whatever designation, must not neglect an important task where a tabloid-sized newspaper is being produced. Since the pairing of pages at printing means that each page goes on the press with its printing pair (i.e. in a 36-page paper page 36 pairs with page 1, page 35 with page 2 and so on) the making up on screen of double-page spreads must be carefully checked so that text levels, and headlines and print borders crossing the page, match their partner page accurately.

It is possible to formulate some general principles about page design without contradicting what has been said about format, or stultifying the use of new ideas. But first it should be said that to succeed, the design must project successfully the sort of content in which the paper specializes to the sort of market that it seeks. In other words, content governs projection. Design, therefore, must look to content and readership market for its inspiration.

The pages reproduced in this and the previous chapter (Figures 9, 10, 11, 13, 14 and 15) demonstrate the sort of content and projection to be found in a varied selection of British newspapers, each depending on its market.

Focal points

The examples referred to show how newspaper design is harnessed to do a job. What works for a popular tabloid paper (Figure 13) would be as unsatisfactory for a county weekly paper with many area editions (Figure 9) as it would be for the *Sunday Times* (Figure 15), while for the *Financial Times* (Figure 11) to be projected as self-consciously artistic as a quality Sunday paper would mystify the readers accustomed to its simple authority. Each approach has to be judged by how far it achieves what it sets out to do.

If you draw boxes to represent the areas to which the eye is first drawn on each of the pages referred to, you will see that they all have one thing in common. They form asymmetrical patterns in which the pictures and main headlines are the focal points.

These focal points, by their location, first demand the reader's attention for the page as a whole. Then, as they guide the eye round the page, they lead from larger focal points to smaller, alighting on the things that first attracted the eye and, once attention is secured, taking in the lesser items. The design has succeeded in claiming the reader.

The location of the focal points around which the page design is constructed depends upon the material chosen and the position and content of the advertising. The shape of the editorial space being worked on will determine whether the pictures need to be horizontal or vertical, the stories short or long. What the advertising consists of – illustrations or mainly type – has to be taken into account. A picture should be kept clear of pictures in an adjoining advertisement, while headline type should not be alongside advertising type of a similar size. The page examples show how these problems have been tackled.

It is because of this combination of circumstances under which pages are schemed that layouts vary so much in design (though remaining within the type format) in any one paper. In describing newspaper page designs as asymmetrical it should be said that a symmetrical layout is impossible on pages with adverts because of the varieties of editorial shape left by the advertising space. Symmetry also tends towards visual monotony and is seldom tried even on the occasional page without advertising.

(a)

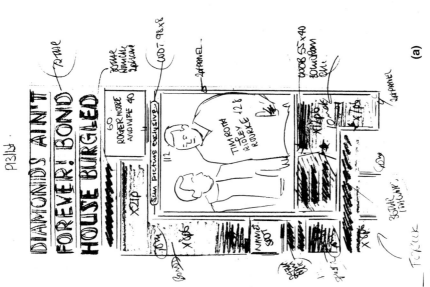

(b)

Figure 13(a) How a layout becomes a page: this example from *The Sun* in the run-up to full screen make-up still carried written headline, intro and picture instructions for the subeditor. **(b)** *The Sun* news page as it appeared.

Figure 14 How a leading provincial morning paper covers its territory: place names flag the stories in this busy *Western Mail* news page

Figure 15 All-serif lower case type, standard column measure throughout, and thick-and-thin-cut-off rules, produce elegance and readability in the *Sunday Times's* news pages. Note, in this one, the use of a cut-out, which are easier to achieve in screen make-up programs

It can be argued that the focal points in the examples given above are bolder in the tabloid pages, both national (Figure 13) and town evening (Figure 10) than in, say, the *Financial Times* example (Figure 11). This is an indication of differences of approach to the readership market rather than of fundamental difference in design philosophy. News is more pictorial in a popular tabloid, while boldness in picture and headline is less required in a paper such as the *Financial Times* and in some of the quality broadsheets. Yet the purpose and function of the visual pattern is the same, each in its market.

Order

The order in which headlines appear on a page, and their size, signify the relative importance of the text they cover in relation to the other items. In all pages there is the main or *lead* story, which has the biggest headline and sometimes, though not necessarily, the longest text. The second most important story is the *half lead*, with the second biggest headline. Then there are the intermediate *tops* (the term which used to signify top of the page is now applied to stories of intermediate length in any part), and a number of one or two-paragraph stories, usually down page. These are called *fillers*. Sometimes they are schemed into the page; other times they are kept handy to fill spaces when bigger stories fall short. In some papers they are gathered into a column of news in brief, or *nibs* (see Figure 25 on page 46).

The reader, drawn to a page by a picture or bold headline, might have time only to scan the main items, but if the reader has more time the initial impact might draw the eye into reading the whole page. A picture with its caption, for instance, can act as a taster, persuading the reader to run through the story that accompanies it.

A way of looking at modern newspaper design is as a form of packaging by which the contents are commended to the reader. In this sense it signifies a breakaway from earlier days when newspapers had columns of unrelieved small type with little or no illustration before display was discovered as a means of targeting readership.

Type character

Looking at successive issues of a newspaper you will become aware that there is a consistent use in the pages of one or two stock types with judiciously placed variants. It would be easy to work right through the book choosing typefaces, since most modern systems offer a wide range of types, but this does not happen. If it did it would produce a hotchpotch effect on the eye and make pleasing design hard to achieve.

Yet the consistency, which is common to all newspapers, is not just a question of arriving at a design. It is a way of giving a newspaper its visual character. It is a major item in its format by which it is differentiated from other newspapers. This is demonstrated in the examples in this chapter.

Summing up in this section, we can say that there are three purposes in newspaper design:

1 To draw the reader's eye to a page by creating an attractive visual pattern.
2 To signpost the items and signal, by placings and typesizes, their relative importance.
3 To give the newspaper a recognizable visual character by the consistent use of chosen types.

Typography

It will be seen that page design is made up of four elements:

Text ⇨ headlines ⇨ pictures ⇨ advertisements

Since the content and positions of advertisements are decided before the editorial material is placed, the designer – the person who schemes the page – can only note them. The emphasis on design is therefore on text, headlines and pictures. In dealing with the first two a knowledge of typography is needed.

By typography we mean the arrangement and appearance of printed matter and, for this, some awareness of the uses and purposes of types chosen is fundamental.

There are two main type families by which the Western, or Roman alphabet is rendered in print: the *serif* and the *sanserif* (or sans). The serif, of which are examples in Figures 16, 17, and 19, is characterized by letters in which the strokes are of varying thickness with the ends finished off with a decorative flourish or tail which is called the serif. This style dates back to early Latin inscriptions and from it has sprung many designs of which a number are still widely used today.

The sans family has letters of mostly even strokes without the decorative flourishes or serifs, hence the name sanserif. Sans types, of which there is a vast and ever increasing number, appeared in modern times in response to the demand from advertising and newspapers for types with boldness rather than elegance. Figure 18 gives a popular one currently used in newspapers.

In referring to type, the word *face* is used to mean the appearance of the type as it prints, while *font* (formerly *fount*) means all the characters – i.e. letters, figure, punctuations marks etc. – of any given type face in any one size.

Many of the thousands of types in the two main families are used only for advertising and publicity purposes. Newspapers adopt a conservative approach, choosing one or two readable stock types which they use in various *sizes* and

abcdefghijklmnopqrstuvwxyz
ABCDEFGHIJKLMNOPQR

abcdefghijklmnopqrstuvwxyz
ABCDEFGHIJKLMNOPQR

abcdefghijklmnopqrstuvwxyz
ABCDEFGHIJKLMNOPQR

abcdefghijklmnopqrstuvwxyz
ABCDEFGHIJKLMNOPQRSTUV

Figure 16 Examples of different weights in a well used stock type. Caslon in four of its variants (top to bottom): light, regular italic, extra bold, black

weights through the paper, with perhaps another quite different face to give variety or special emphasis on occasions, or for use on the features pages.

Of the two serif types illustrated in Figures 16 and 17, Times New Roman is the stock type of *The Times* and the *Sunday Times* and several other newspapers, while Caslon bold is popular with many regional and some Continental papers. Other popular serif faces are Century bold, Bodoni and Cheltenham. The sans face illustrated in Figure 18, Helvetica, has gained in popularity in recent years over older sans types such as Gill sans and Grotesque. Other sans types widely used are Tempo, Gothic, Futura and Univers.

abcdefghijklmnopqrstuvwxyz
ABCDEFGHIJKLMNOPQRS

abcdefghijklmnopqrstuvwxyz
ABCDEFGHIJKLMNOPQR

Figure 17 Two variants from the Times New Roman range: extra bold and bold italic

abcdefghijklmnopqrstuvwxyz
ABCDEFGHIJKLMNOPQRST

abcdefghijklmnopqrstuvwxyz
ABCDEFGHIJKLMNOPQRST

abcdefghijklmnopqrstuvwxyz
ABCDEFGHIJKLMNOPQRSTU
1234567890 &?!£$ (.,;:)⅝«/‿‘’¨

Figure 18 Helvetica (sometimes bit-mapped as Geneva) in three of its guises. Top to bottom: light, medium and bold

There is also a variation of the serif family referred to as *slab serif* in which the serifs or tails are squared off, giving a characteristic chunky look. An example is the Rockwell range, used in the *Daily Mail* features pages and in many American newspapers (Figure 19).

Under bit-mapping conversion into computer faces many of the traditional newspaper types, including some of the above, where very minor changes of shape have been made, are presented under new names.

It is usual for a newspaper to opt either for a serif or a sans type style and stick to it. Sans is more popular with tabloids, especially national dailies such as *The Sun* (Figure 13(b)) and *The Mirror* and many town evenings (Figure 10), while a mainly serif style is used in the more traditional broadsheet papers such as *The Times* and the *Daily Telegraph* and in some provincial morning papers.

abcdefghijklmnopqrstuvwxyz
ABCDEFGHIJKLMNOPQRST

abcdefghijklmnopqrstuvwxyz
ABCDEFGHIJKLMNOPQRSTUVW

Figure 19 Taking variants to an extreme: the slab-seriffed Rockwell light and its partner, Rockwell extra bold

Using type

Page design has to take account of the stock types in use in a newspaper. Fortunately, within these there exists plenty of scope for variety and a type style can be evolved by using the variants within a type range.

For example, types exist in *capital letters* (caps) and in *lower case* (l.c.), and a noticeable modern trend is for newspapers using stock serif faces such as Times Roman, Century bold or Bodoni, to have all headlines in lower case (see Figures 9, 11, 14 and 15). It is generally agreed by type experts that lower case type with its more flowing contour and variety of stroke is easier to read than capitals. To judge for yourself you can carry out a simple test by printing out this paragraph first in lower case and then in capitals.

Yet some tabloids using sans type have many of their main headlines in capitals (Figures 10 and 13(b)) on the ground that the boldness of sans caps has the sort of impact they seek. Titling Gothic, used for some of the biggest headlines, is an example of a type that exists only in caps.

Some types offer *italic* (the slope being top right to bottom left) for use along with the *roman* or upright face. Most italics in newspapers are in the sans ranges, although italic type generally is becoming less favoured.

There also exist variants based on the thickness of the letter strokes. The standard roman letter is accompanied by a thicker *bold* version and sometimes by a *light* and an *extra bold* (see Figures 16, 17, 18 and 19). Century is an example of a type that exists in all thickness variants. Other variants within ranges are based on the width of the letter. Gothic has variants ranging from *extra condensed* and *medium condensed* to *bold* and *square*, while many types are designed with an *expanded* version.

Condensed faces are useful in the narrower columns of tabloid pages, with lower case the more favoured, especially in single column, for better readability and easier eye traverse down the lines. A condensed face enables a bigger type to be used without limiting too much the number of characters (i.e. letters and figure) on a line. Condensed faces are not much used across wider measures where they are less readable, especially in caps. Expanded faces are noticeable in the more horizontal pages of the quality press. See Figure 15, top headline.

An oddity about type faces is that the *ascenders* and *descenders* – the bits that stick above and below the body, or x-height, of lower case letters b, d, f, g, h, j, k, l, p, q, t – can very in length from type to type (see Figure 20). This produces

Figure 20 A line of Bembo lower case showing the x-height of the characters in relation to the ascenders and descenders – in this type their length results in a type 'small on its body'

the phenomenon of types that are 'big on their body' or 'small on their body' (as the typeface Bembo in Figure 20).

> In computerized setting the characters in any type can be stretched or squeezed to produce condensed or expanded forms at the stroke of a key, or even tilted to give italic. Yet the need for precise control over the typography of a page has resulted in newspapers programming their typesetting with shapes that correspond with fonts as designed by the typefounder which they use rather than risk a hotchpotch of variations. Only with awkward text problems as in the crossword clues (Figure 21) is the squeeze facility used. Another attribute of the computer is that it will deliver headline type tinted with a screen tint or reversed as white on black (or on colour).

Points to watch

★ In designing pages, give the greatest number of headlines to the stock type in appropriate sizes. Too many variants can confuse the eye just as much as too many different types.

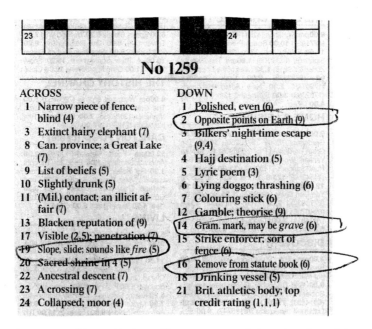

Figure 21 A space problem with these *Times* crossword clues has forced the subeditor to squeeze four of the lines to keep them within the measure.

★ In introducing a different typeface into the pages for special effect, choose one opposed in shape and character – i.e. a light sans against a bold serif or a light serif against a bold sans. Two sort of sans or two sort of serif used together invariably clash.

Typesizes

The main variation in type use is by size. Type which, as we have seen, can vary greatly in width, is measured for size by its height, using a 250-year-old system of *points* of which, as a guide, there are approximately 72 to the inch and 28 to the centimetre.

To simplify typesetting, typefounders in western and most other countries from the early 18th century designed type to a series of set point sizes which have long been accepted as the basis of print design. These traditionally had names such as minion (7pt), brevier (8pt), long primer (10pt) and pica (12 pt). Today they are simply referred to by their point sizes. The series runs:

5½, 6, 7, 8, 10, 12, 14, 18, 24, 30, 36, 42, 48, 60, 72, 84, 96, 120, 144

Sizes up to 14pt are used for reading text (see Figure 41 on page 76). Standard reading text, or body type, in most newspapers is in 7pt or 8pt, with the opening paragraphs set 10pt or12pt or even 14pt in the case of the page one lead or *splash* story. While body type of up to 14pt is available in serif and sans ranges, serif is more commonly used on the well tested theory that, as with lower case headlines, it is easier to read as the eye travels across the contours of the letters.

From 14pt upwards are the headline sizes. Papers of more traditional appearance seldom go beyond 72pt for their splash story. Headlines of up to 120pt and more can be found on the front and back pages of the popular tabloids.

Choosing the right type sizes is important not only to give certain items prominence but, as we have seen, to give visual balance to the page. It is for this reason that the computer, although it can vary sizes by intervals of a quarter point right through the range, is programmed through command keys to deliver type in traditional print sizes. A facility remains to override the programmed size to get a wanted headline to fit but, to protect type balance, it is used sparingly to vary sizes by seldom more than 5 per cent.

Setting widths

As with the points system of typesizing, so with setting widths (measure) have old printing terms been retained in computerized systems. Page widths and column widths are calculated in Britain in *ems*, an em being the width of a standard roman 12pt lower case letter *m*, which is as wide as it is deep. An em is equivalent to a pica, which is the old name for type of 12pt size. In US practice, ems, in fact, are called picas. An 84-em page would be an 84-pica page, and a 9-em column a 9-pica column. In typesetting systems of American origin measures are commanded in picas and this is now the normal practice in this area in all systems. Since an em equals 12 points it is useful to remember that 6 ems equals approximately an inch (25 mm).

Ens, based on the width of the standard 12pt roman lower case *n*, are half the width of an em. They are used particularly to denote measures that are indented to give white space either in front or on both sides – i.e., indent 'en each side', or more commonly 'nut each side' or 'nut front', all of which setting is programmed on to keys

Newspapers usually have a standard number of columns. Most broadsheet pages have columns 9 or 9½ ems wide, and tabloid pages 8 or 8½ ems, although these can be varied, especially for features display. In scheming pages the column measure of text and headlines is nominated as well as the type size. In the case of standard single-column, two-column or three-column measures it is only necessary to nominate the measure in columns, which is programmed setting in the computer.

Any setting less or greater than single-column or its multiples is called *bastard measure*. A variety of bastard setting, such as around cut-out shapes (Figure 35 on page 65), can be easily achieved in modern systems by mouse controls. These days there are more and more automatic setting formats for given story boxes on pages so that the sub can concentrate on editing to fit rather than on arranging the setting.

Design workshop

Within the established format of a newspaper there exists a selection of typographical devices that can be used to give variety and emphasis to a page. Subs and page editors, as well as page designers, should familiarize themselves with them because of their use in the editing and page building stage.

Most papers give the first one or two words in capitals to signal the start of a story. Some, more particularly on features pages, make the first letter of the intro a 24pt or 30pt *drop letter* as a form of decoration. This can be set into the first paragraph, or it can line up on the first line and stand clear, making a *stand-up drop*. Where used, two-line or three-line drop letters are programmed on to a key as a setting format but drop letters of up to six lines are used (see Figure 22).

A subeditor might use selected *bold* or *italic* paragraphs (never both) within a story to give an eye-break or to highlight a point; they should be used sparingly (if allowed by style) to avoid bittiness.

Breakers

Crossheads, usually single lines of 12pt or 14pt to style, are used to help the eye cope with long texts and also prevent greyness in display. If set flush left they are called *sideheads* (or *shoulders* on some papers). In features display, crossheads can be more ornamental, often deriving from the main headline type being used. See Figures 23, 24 and 25.

Figure 22 Giving emphasis to lists: black blobs and squares are used to separate as well as emphasize these connected items. Bold caps in a roman context have similar function in the horoscope setting, bottom right

While crossheads are principally eye-breaks in the text, they should occur in natural breaks in the story and not interrupt the sequence. Full lines should be avoided since they cut off text from text and halt the eye. They should have at least 4pts of space above and below.

In some features display, and in magazines, words are dispensed with and breaks achieved by using a piece of ornamental *print rule*, or by dividing off sections by the use of selected stand-up drops (see examples in Chapters 11 and 12) with attendant white space. These can sometimes fall badly, or result in repeated use of the same letter. One way to locate eye-breaks tidily in a long features spread is to use *quotes* from the text in, say, three lines of 12pt, and locate them around the spread where they can usefully act as tasters to the story as in Figure 24.

Figure 23 Six-line drop letters give style to the *Daily Mail* feature, left, as well as acting as eye-breakers in place of crossheads in a long text. Drop letters are used as guides for the reader in the *Western Mail's* question-and-answer medical column above

Figure 24 Another device used in place of crossheads to break up a long text: poignant quotes have been taken from this news feature and used between thick-and-thin rules as breakers. They are located in mid-paragraph to avoid halting the eye above the rule

Merseyside TONIGHT

Pensioner's theft ordeal

ROBBERS forced their way into a Liverpool pensioner's home, pushed her on to the bed and stole her bag. The 82-year-old was confronted by a man in her Mulliner Street home in Edge Hill.

Police would like to trace two men and a blonde-haired woman who flagged down a taxi at the junction of Smithdown Road and Mulliner Street in the early hours of Saturday.

Arson attack: Police are investigating an arson attack by burglars on a house in Bagot Street, Wavertree. No-one was hurt in the incident.

Safety drive: Six-hundred St Helens children will be learning about safety awareness during a week-long event starting today at Parr High School. They will hear advice from more than 10 agencies.

Gems raid: Burglars pushed a 73-year-old disabled woman to the floor and stole jewellery and foreign currency from her home in Eaton Road, West Derby.

Pub facelift: A Liverpool pub is being given a £1m refit including the construction of a Wacky Warehouse. The Allied Domecq-owned Queen's Drive at Stoneycroft is being converted into a pub for families which will include a children's play area.

Chelsea jobs: Chelsea FC is holding a recruitment day at the Adelphi Hotel, Liverpool, tomorrow between 11am-6pm in a nationwide search for hotel staff. The club's new luxury Village Hotel opens on December 1.

Speke lecture: Julian Treuherz, Keeper of Art Galleries for the National Museums & Galleries on Merseyside, is giving a special lecture on *William Morris and the Pre-Raphaelites* at the National

Figure 25 Run-on sideheads in 18pt italic are used under a stock logo to tabulate the items in this column of news brief from the *Liverpool Echo*. Note the text setting – set left, ragged right

Indicators

Initial words in *bold caps* are a useful way of introducing 'news in brief' paragraphs or items in commodity reports or market prices. These can be preceded by a *black blob* or *open square*, often included as standard 'furniture' in a type range (see examples in Figure 22). *Stars*, black or open, are useful on short showbiz items – but beware of using too many of these things on the same page.

Figures in lists can be set bold up a size – or even as *drop figures* – or reversed as white on black. *By-lines* and *sign-offs* can be give a special style, perhaps a simple 10pt Metro line on news stories and something more decorative (reflecting the writer's eminence) on the features pages (see Chapter 11 and 12).

Headlines

Headlines can be delivered to the page as white on black, or type on tint or colour – a much used device on the popular tabloids when a page is thin on pictures and the display demands bold highlights. Underscores can give headlines extra boldness but are less used these days. They should break around the descenders on lower case headlines to avoid excessive white between underscore and type.

Special setting

While pages, particularly news, are generally schemed within their columnar format, setting widths can be varied for design purposes. A rectangular space clear of adverts can be divided into equal widths of bastard measure, as in Figure 51 on pages 198–9. 'Colour' can be give by setting a whole story in bold, sometimes inside a ruled panel to provide the page with a *kicker.* The computer enables time to be saved by being programmed to deliver setting formatted into panels of nominated size to fit page slots.

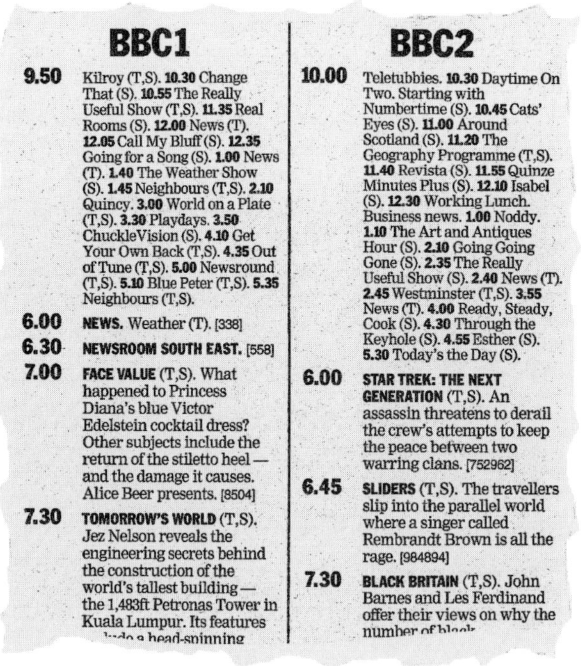

BBC1

9.50 Kilroy (T,S). **10.30** Change That (S). **10.55** The Really Useful Show (T,S). **11.35** Real Rooms (S). **12.00** News (T). **12.05** Call My Bluff (S). **12.35** Going for a Song (S). **1.00** News (T). **1.40** The Weather Show (S). **1.45** Neighbours (T,S). **2.10** Quincy. **3.00** World on a Plate (T,S). **3.30** Playdays. **3.50** ChuckleVision (S). **4.10** Get Your Own Back (T,S). **4.35** Out of Tune (T,S). **5.00** Newsround (T,S). **5.10** Blue Peter (T,S). **5.35** Neighbours (T,S).

6.00 **NEWS.** Weather (T). [338]

6.30 **NEWSROOM SOUTH EAST.** [558]

7.00 **FACE VALUE** (T,S). What happened to Princess Diana's blue Victor Edelstein cocktail dress? Other subjects include the return of the stiletto heel — and the damage it causes. Alice Beer presents. [8504]

7.30 **TOMORROW'S WORLD** (T,S). Jez Nelson reveals the engineering secrets behind the construction of the world's tallest building — the 1,483ft Petronas Tower in Kuala Lumpur. Its features ... a head-spinning

BBC2

10.00 Teletubbies. **10.30** Daytime On Two. Starting with Numbertime (S). **10.45** Cats' Eyes (S). **11.00** Around Scotland (S). **11.20** The Geography Programme (T,S). **11.40** Revista (S). **11.55** Quinze Minutes Plus (S). **12.10** Isabel (S). **12.30** Working Lunch. Business news. **1.00** Noddy. **1.10** The Art and Antiques Hour (S). **2.10** Going Going Gone (S). **2.35** The Really Useful Show (S). **2.40** News (T). **2.45** Westminster (T,S). **3.55** News (T). **4.00** Ready, Steady, Cook (S). **4.30** Through the Keyhole (S). **4.55** Esther (S). **5.30** Today's the Day (S).

6.00 **STAR TREK: THE NEXT GENERATION** (T,S). An assassin threatens to derail the crew's attempts to keep the peace between two warring clans. [752962]

6.45 **SLIDERS** (T,S). The travellers slip into the parallel world where a singer called Rembrandt Brown is all the rage. [984894]

7.30 **BLACK BRITAIN** (T,S). John Barnes and Les Ferdinand offer their views on why the number of

Figure 26 The use of white space and bold setting for times and titles is important in giving the reader easy-to-follow TV programme details

Fine *rules* normally divide item from item, but 2pt or 3pt rules can be used to enclose a spread of pictures or related items. Some papers have abolished dividing rules and rely on *white space*, a popular ploy in *The Guardian* (Figure 52 on page 201). White space remains an important element on features pages and, if used properly, can give designs of great elegance (see Chapters 11 and 12).

Special setting for such things as television programmes, race cards and football and election results needs devising and putting into the system with great care so that it is instantly readable despite the weight of information it has to carry (Figure 26). Abbreviations and the use of bold and roman, caps and lower case should be consistent and meaningful, and several dummy runs should be tried before settling for a style that is informative and at the same time easy on the eye and not too space-taking.

An advantage for the subeditor is that such setting can be formatted on to keys, thus cutting out laborious and time-consuming keying at the subbing stage. Agencies provide ready-formatted material of this sort for direct input into the system if called for.

3 DEALING WITH PICTURES

Dealing with the illustrations, as with text and headlines, is a crucial part of page planning and editing. Photographs of the right subject, size, shape and quality have to be selected and presented to the reader; where appropriate, graphics and diagrams have to be provided.

Subeditors working on pages cannot detach themselves these days from the picture content. Selection and quality assessment might begin at the picture desk but, having been chosen, a picture is still subject to editing. Editing begins at the art desk, or at the scanning studio. Here, pictures are cropped, sized and retouched in the scanner, colour corrected where necessary, and imaged onwards into their page boxes (Figure 27). On screen they are further adjusted in shape and size by the sub, using mouse controls, until they best fit the space and ideas of the page design.

Figure 27 A *News of the World* page on-screen awaiting two pictures

There can be variations of this routine. Where pages are being built on master screens, the art desk might carry out the picture function, not only scanning, colour correcting and delivering pictures and graphics to the page but adjusting them to fit, while the subs deal separately with text editing. The art desk, working with the back bench, remains responsible for page design on bigger papers, preparing detailed layouts, either directly on screen or from paper to screen, and passing them down to the editing screens for the pages to be made up by subs or page editors, where so designated.

Smaller papers make greater use of multi-skilling. A sub might be given responsibility for choosing the pictures, cropping, sizing and scanning them, designing the page and subbing the contents. There are miniaturized scanners for worktop use by subs for this purpose. On such papers multi-skilling in editorial production has always been accepted. The computer and the make-up screen and modern scanners have merely made it easier and faster.

Whichever the route – and systems are constantly being updated – pictures and the captioning of them (see pages 171–4) are very much the concern of the subeditor.

Role of pictures

The notion that a good news picture is worth a column of words does not altogether hold true. There are few pictures that can stand without text whereas the text regularly stands without pictures, although there are occasions when it badly needs them. Famous news pictures such as St Paul's Cathedral against a wartime background of flames, the shooting of President Kennedy, and the frigate *Antelope* in the midst of a fireball in the Falklands War (Figure 28), remain in the mind long after the words have faded. This is what really tells the story, the picture enthusiast will say. But on their own such pictures cannot, and do not. They have to rely on the context of words, on explanation, in the same way as tele-film relies on the commentary and the presenter's guidance.

The better and more dramatic the picture the greater is the danger of readers (or viewers) being misled by their own heightened reaction. Shorn of its context of words and explanation a picture can, in a real sense, lie or at least fail to deliver the truth.

A national paper reporting some years ago on the horrors of the Biafran war in Nigeria carried a picture of an emaciated pot-bellied child as a pictorial indictment of the perpetrators of the fighting. The child was not identified but it transpired that the picture was from another African country. It achieved its objective in bringing home its message to the reader, one might say.

This is true but the picture was nevertheless lying. Placed as it was, it misled the reader into thinking it arose directly out of the war, for it did not have the necessary explanation of its origin. If, because the intention seems to be worthy, this sort of practice is condoned, where does one draw the line in planting pictures to condition reader response?

With the digital 'correction' of tone and colour in pictures by which the pixels representing the screened dots of the image can be moved about in the scanner, the danger of misrepresentation in picture content is much greater. The growing number of complaints to the Press Complaints Committee about image manipulation and some celebrated recent cases have demonstrated this. The Commission's Code of Practice for the Press does not specifically mention image manipulation but it does say: 'Newspapers and periodicals must take care not to publish inaccurate, misleading or distorted material including pictures.'

Yet notwithstanding the possibility of misuse, a newspaper would be less informative, less complete and less attractive without pictures. They not only supplement the text; they enhance and extend it by highlighting and pressing upon the reader important parts of it; they make it easier for the reader to build up a picture of what is being read.

Figure 28 A photograph that made news: the famous Reuters picture of the frigate *HMS Antelope* exploding into a fireball after being hit by an Excocet missile in San Carlos Bay in the Falklands War

News pictures in a newspaper have a permanency and graphic effect denied to television film, which has a fragile grip on the senses and a low level of recall. Colour is now widely used, and mostly very effectively, but being in black and white can often increase the drama and tension in news pictures. It has to do with the basic unreality of the colour range that systems give compared with the nuances of tone and texture in real life. Black and white plays upon the imagination and reconstructs reality in the mind whereas colour can be bland, although it can have visual impact when used for the right pictures.

Pictures also serve another function. They form distinctive eye-catching elements that trap the readers' attention. The position of pictures in relation to the contents of a page is thus part of the balanced visual pattern by which the newspaper content is projected. We can say, in short, that a picture performs two functions:

1 It illustrates the text.
2 It forms an element in the page design.

Picture sources

Taking, collecting and providing pictures is organized on similar lines to the newsroom operation. It revolves around the picture desk, which works closely with the newsroom and the picture library. Directing this task is the picture editor or (on small papers) the chief photographer (see Figure 29). The picture editor

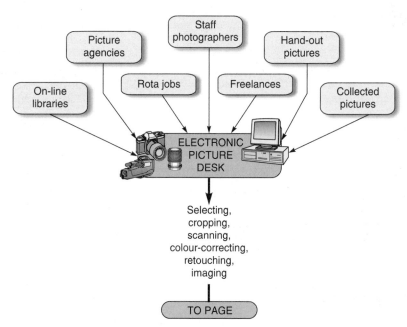

Figure 29 How the pictures flow: the part played by the electronic picture desk in routing pictures from their source to the page

51

keeps a schedule of pictures that are wanted or expected and briefs photographers about the paper's requirements and deadlines. The photographers might work alongside reporters on a job or act independently, depending on time and the sort of job. If a staff photographer is not available the picture editor has to look to other picture sources.

> In handling stories that have pictures, whether colour or mono, you should make clear their relevance to the text in a caption if the reader is to be correctly informed. No picture should be left without explanation or clear identification. Even a specially taken 'mood' shot accompanying a feature can raise doubts or misconceptions in the reader's mind if it is uncaptioned (see Figure 30).

Staff photographers

Staff photographers working from head office or branch offices, or sometimes operating independently in a district, are the main sources of exclusive pictures and can be more easily deployed alongside reporters on jobs where on-the-spot pictures are wanted. They are journalists by training and definition and their approach and job briefing are in line with that for reporters. They share the same deadlines. Their numbers might vary from four or five on a small paper to perhaps twenty or more on a big national daily.

> This is an area in which technology has brought about huge changes both in cameras and picture transmission. Says Martin Keene in his book *Practical Photojournalism* (Focal Press): 'Print transmitters have been replaced with negative scanners and laptop computers. It is possible to transmit pictures from almost anywhere in the world into the network of computers used to make up a newspaper. Some newspapers no longer have darkrooms; once the picture has been selected [from a transmitted set] the negative is scanned into a computer and the first time it is seen as a print is when the newspaper comes off the presses.' (See Photo briefing, page 55.)

Staff pictures become the newspaper's copyright and syndication or reproduction fees are earned if they are used in other papers. Photographers, even when working with reporters, are responsible for their own caption information and fact and name checking.

TERRORISED: Gillian Johnstone was haunted by a stalker for nine years. Stalker picture posed by a model

Figure 30 Even a mood picture needs a caption, especially where a model has been used in setting it up. The caption on this *Birmingham Evening Mail* picture of a girl plagued by a stalker makes it clear that the person shown is a lookalike

Freelance photographers

Freelances provide some picture input but, except for high-fee exclusive work for which they hold copyright – such as the much criticized paparazzi who snatch pictures of the famous or specialist areas such as glamour – their contribution is usually by daily, weekly or holiday relief arrangements, or for one-off jobs. In provincial areas local newspaper photographers might work as regular accredited freelances for bigger papers, being paid an annual retainer fee and a fee for each picture used.

In the more specialist areas of glamour, sport, animal and technical photography there is a good income to be earned by freelances who become known and to whom newspapers, and more especially magazines, turn to at times of need.

Picture agencies

Picture agencies provide a great range of photographs for use and stock, especially from overseas, on a contractual basis to subscribing newspapers. Such 'service' pictures, though lacking exclusiveness, usefully fill gaps in coverage. Agencies, specializing in such areas as sport, political or celebrity portraiture, usually charge a fee for each occasion of use. Occasionally they will part with British or other reproduction rights for a higher fee.

Rota pictures

Agencies are sometimes relied upon where only limited picture coverage of an event is allowed. Royal or certain political occasions, or even celebrity photo-calls where a large influx of press photographers is not convenient, are sometimes on rota. The arranging is by a committee drawn from picture editors of the various newspapers and agencies who subscribe to the rota, and it has a permanent secretary who keeps a list of those entitled to camera facilities. From this list newspapers and agencies take it in turn to cover rota jobs, on which anything from one to maybe seven photographers are allowed. The resulting pictures are made available for use to the newspapers contributing to the arrangement.

Collected pictures

In some news and features jobs pictures might be supplied by the subject or organization concerned. Permission is needed to use such material and any possible right investigated.

Hand-out pictures

A good deal of the material used on TV programme pages and showbiz stories is supplied free to newspapers from film-making and programme companies. Free pictures often accompany hand-out material where the aim is to seek publicity in a newspaper or magazine.

Picture libraries

Pictures libraries and archives, now mostly on line, supply pictures for a usage fee, and sometimes also a research fee. The main library source is usually the newspaper's own indexed picture files of news events or people who have been, or are likely to be in the news, going back as many as twenty or thirty years. These sources are used where 'head shots' or recent likenesses are needed with stories, or when an event comes back into the news, or if 'flashbacks' are need of similar events. The office's own picture files are also a useful check source for identification and personal details.

The photo briefing

The picture editor knows from the daily news schedule and the editor's conference the nature of each picture job and whether there is a need for a specific shape or sort of picture, or the inclusion of certain wanted detail.

Technology has leapt ahead in press photography and has helped to make some formerly difficult assignments easier. Long, heavy telephoto lenses for which the help of an assistant was needed are a thing of the past. The use of mirror lenses for press work, by enhancing the image magnification, has effectively halved the length and weight. They also increase the amount of light reaching the film, making for a better quality picture. The focal length of telephoto lenses can be doubled by the attachment of a powerful supplementary lens, while the use of an electronic booster between the lens and the film, by picking up the light at the red end of the spectrum, makes it possible to take pictures in almost total darkness.

The automatic pocket-size 35-millimetre cameras used for rapid clusters of shots in varying conditions are now being replaced by filmless digital versions, while the electronic picture desk (EPD) (see Figure 29) has become the normal interface between incoming pictures and the newspaper's production process. With advances in miniaturized transmitters, films can be developed on location and transmitted by telephone line by means of a modem, including in colour, so that they reach a newspaper's EPD in minutes. Modern transmitters transmit directly from the negative, reversing the image so that the picture is received in positive. It is possible with another device to take good prints from video film which make acceptable pictures for newspaper use.

Today's trend is for greater use of telephoto lenses of up to 400 mm, and occasionally up to 1000 mm, in order to concentrate on people and actualities, and there is less scope for the composed mood shots beloved of Robert Capa, Henri Cartier-Bresson and, in recent decades, Don McCullin. With today's equipment comes the opportunity of exploring the unusual angle which can enliven the page – what Harold Evans calls 'the yawn in the crowded political meeting rather than the candidate in the centre of the waving crowd.'

In news pictures it is people and actualities that hold the attention of readers, with animation and a good likeness rating high. This is nowhere more important than in the scenes and faces photographed for a local paper (see examples on pages 19 and 22).

News pictures are usually of two sorts:

1 The action shot which helps tell the story.
2 The picture that shows people, which might simply inform.

The first is more prized and is harder to catch since there might be only one chance. The second can be set up simply by the photographer asking people to take up positions. Here, the danger of a cliché picture arises, especially if the photographer is overworked or rushing from job to job. Yet ingenuity can produce an out-of-the-ordinary composition.

In big events such as State funerals, Trooping of the Colour and festivals, pre-arranged shooting positions and the lack of mobility make timing of the essence in getting the wanted picture. In indoor work the effect of the flash on the subject is the perennial hazard, plus the problem of shadow and small room perspective. Here a wide-angle lens is useful.

The skill of the picture editor lies in taking account of the various hazards when briefing for special requirements. It is from the set of contacts produced that the picture editor, looking for sharp detail and good composition, selects the frames for enlargement so that the best pictures are available from each job for the pages being planned.

Here again, technology has stepped in by devising programs that digitize and store incoming pictures on magnetic disks from which they can be recalled on a monitor screen and examined for choice. A picture chosen need not even be printed; it can be cropped, sized, colour-corrected, electronically retouched and imaged straight on to the make-up screen.

Choosing pictures

Even without stock sources, newspapers get many more pictures each day than they can use and a selection process takes place similar to copy tasting (see Figure 31). This is usually done by the picture editor but it can fall to the subeditor dealing with the page, particularly on smaller papers. In such a situation, you should take the following points into account:

Content

Does the picture show the right people and scene? Is it a good likeness? Does it capture the action, and is the background right? Does it properly complement the story and extend its content?

Composition

Do the grouping and position of the people in relation to the elements of the picture form a pleasing shape? Is it the most eye-catching of the pictures that have the required subject content?

Balance

Will the content balance visually with the rest of the page, including the advertisements? For instance, 'head'shots should not look out of the page or away from their story. Also, clashes with other picture content should be avoided. A picture of an ocean liner will look superfluous against an advert also showing a picture of a liner. A picture showing the heads of a man and a woman would lose effect against an advertisement with the same sort of picture.

Tone

Has the picture good tonal values? Is there sufficient contrast between dark and light tones so that it will reproduce adequately, bearing in mind that more parts of newspapers are in black and white than in colour, and newsprint is nowhere near as kind to detail as glossy bromide or gravure. A lack of dark or light tones can result in a grey effect which blurs detail on printing.

Stock pictures

A temptation in using stock pictures is to condition the reader by selecting one that shows a person in a particular light – the grim face of a strike leader, the smug or triumphant expressions of politicians, or pictures that send up well-known people by catching them in an unguarded moment. The choice might seem fitting for the accompanying story, but there is a line beyond which the display of foibles and character can become bad taste or propaganda, or even libel if a person is really made to look stupid, as lawyers are willing to demonstrate. Subeditors selecting pictures from stock should beware of this.

Editing pictures

Few photographs are used in a newspaper exactly as they are taken. A picture might have detail irrelevant to the story it accompanies. This might be because of difficulties in taking the picture. Perhaps it includes people who have nothing

US Navy bows out
Sadness as Stars and Stripes lowered for last time

to do with the story, or maybe the page visualizer wants to accentuate part of the picture, or exclude part of it for reasons of news value or legality. This selecting and excluding parts of a picture in the course of achieving its required shape in the page is called *cropping*. Cropping is an essential part of editing a picture – but first a few words about this contentious subject.

> Cropping can arouse violent disagreement and much pontificating by experts who think it should have been done differently, or not at all. A good picture, it is said, is its own advocate. This is true if the picture is being used for what it is and not for what it is required to do, as for example in publishing a new royal portrait. Not many pictures fall into this category.

A newspaper is not just a vehicle for the camera. The requirements of picture display, however attractive to the eye and justified by picture quality, have to be balanced against the demands on space by the news and features coverage to

Figure 31 Choosing for the page: what makes a good picture

★ The *Aberdeen Press and Journal* photographer went for mood in the shot, opposite, of an American sailor and his Scottish wife at the lowering of the Stars and Stripes at a Scottish base

★ The shot a sports photographer hopes for. The theme is action in the *Western Mail's* Allsport picture of Juventus scoring a goal against Manchester United in the European Champions' League

★ Expression is the theme of this well-caught picture in London's *Evening Standard* of Prince Charles and his son Prince Harry about to fly off on a Royal tour

which the paper is committed by its style and market. It is in detail of information that a newspaper scores over picture-dominated television both in editorial content and in advertising.

An experienced photographer knows when he (or she) has got a good picture in terms of light, composition and content. The way the picture is cropped and used on the page and the significance with which it is imbued has to obey additional parameters such as the words of the text, the space available and the requirements of page planning.

The aim is to avoid wasted grey areas while at the same time emphasizing required detail (see the crop in Figures 32 and 33). Thus in a picture showing a group of houses in which context is of no concern, a house might be selected because it is the one with which the story is concerned. A person taken from a group picture might be cropped from the waist upwards because that is what the visualizer wants. The same agency news picture might appear in rival papers cropped in different ways because of different ideas in projecting a story.

Figure 32 As taken at the ringside: *News of the World* cameraman Brian Thomas captures the moment of triumph in a big boxing match

Figure 33 The picture as it was cropped and used to show the two fighters in close-up

The editing of pictures to prepare them for the page has been both simplified and speeded up under modern systems. There are four stages in the process, although on smaller papers some might be merged:

1 Assessment for quality and suitability.
2 Cropping and sizing for shape.
3 Retouching.
4 Fitting into the page.

Here is what happens on a typical well-staffed national paper.

Assessment

The picture editor – with the benefit of an electronic picture desk (EPD) these days – examines on a monitor screen the contacts transmitted digitally from the photographer or from other on-line sources, and shortlists a selection of the input for the back bench or other executives. The picture editor does this by reference to the quality and composition of the pictures and their suitability for the requirements of the pages. A final choice is made, either from the material showing on screen or from printouts of it, after discussion involving the picture editor and those responsible for the various parts of the paper.

Cropping and sizing

This is usually done either by the art desk or the executive in charge of the page. The picture, having been chosen, is called up from the picture desk computer and is cropped and sized at the same time on the scanner screen to give the required image. The wanted part is enlarged or reduced so that the size and shape of image produced fits exactly its pre-selected box on the page. Where the task is left to a scanner operator, the cropped area and size required are usually marked for the operator on a printout of the picture or of the contacts.

Cropping and scaling was formerly (and still is under paste-up) done manually on the back of the print by the diagonal method as shown in Figure 37 on page 66.

The shape resulting from cropping (anything other than a rectangle is not normally feasible; even a cut-out or oval would be developed from a basic rectangle) is governed partly by the composition, partly by the intentions of the visualizer and partly by the space available. Composition predominates; it is not usual to force a picture of naturally horizontal shape into a vertical. In such a case it is either the wrong picture or it is on the wrong page.

Cropping should be creative. It is a method of editing a picture for emphasis. Bad cropping occurs:

1 When the position or attitude of the subject person becomes distorted or meaningless because of the exclusion of detail.

2 When the cropped area is too small, causing a dispersal of detail on enlargement and printing.
3 When lines and perspective are thrown out by 'tilting' in an effort to get a wanted shape.

Retouching

Inevitably there are problem pictures. A picture of inferior, or even poor, quality might be used because it is the only one available and is vital to the story. Another example is where, despite cropping, a picture has unwanted detail such as someone's head which has nothing to do with the story, or heavy tones of wallpaper which clash with a person's features.

This used to be the area where a retouching artist with an airbrush was called on to 'improve' the picture, occasionally with indifferent results. Today, programs such as Adobe PhotoShop are achieving, with electronic retouching in the scanner, effects far better than the best possible results produced by the old retouching artists. The method, however, entails changing the 'pixel' structure of the picture's image, which can lead to 'image manipulation' and even invention of detail. This has led to tighter editorial control over retouching to avert lawsuits that can follow tampering with pictures.

In some cases a picture might be *reversed* (i.e. printed from the negative back to front), so that people are not looking out of the page or the story. This is a dangerous practice unless the detail is carefully studied. Readers are good at spotting coats buttoned the wrong way, wedding rings on the wrong hand, or hair parted on different sides in different papers. More bizarre results are right-hand drive cars turned into left-hand drive and number plates reading back to front.

Fitting in to the page

In full screen make-up it falls to the sub in charge of making up the page to check and adjust, and even if need be to enlarge or reduce the image, after the picture has been imaged into its box from the art desk or scanning studio. By mouse controls the box size, and therefore the picture size, can be varied on screen, and even tilted, if layout changes demand it at make-up stage. The reaction to the mouse click is instantaneous, and the speed and degree of control give the page sub great flexibility at edition changes, or if the layout or space has to change during page make-up.

The pace and ease of page building with mouse controls has widened the role of subs on smaller papers. On tight staffs, and with formula-based pages it is common, as we have seen, for a sub looking after a page to design it, choose, crop and scan the pictures required, sub all the stories, and build the page on screen up to plate-making readiness. On the bigger national papers the greater specialization practised in editing precludes the use of this degree of multi-skilling.

The design function

The needs of page planning can influence the choice of a picture and its shape and size. Since pictures, as we have said, form part of the visual pattern of the page, it is usually desirable to have one main illustration with perhaps a number of small ones, or maybe no others at all. The choice of the main one has to be made at the start for it governs the design.

The best available picture for visual effect may not go with the main story. It might be with one of the minor items or be covered by a self-contained caption, and be chosen in the absence of any usable picture with the main items. The visual balance of the page thus becomes a factor in picture choice. The main picture is a focal point in this balance, its position being influenced by the relative visual mass of advertisements, main headlines and text. Newspaper pages reproduced in chapters one, two, eleven and twelve of this book show this factor at work.

Taking our explanation further we can say that the inclusion of a story on a page can be because it provides a picture which helps give visual balance as well as illustrating the story. It is not usual to have two stories with good picture coverage, leaving none for another page. An exception would be a page of news-in-pictures. Only where the editorial space left by the advertisements is very small would the page executive not bother with illustration.

> Visual effect can become an obsession with tabloid newspapers, including some provincial ones, where display can starve the pages of reading matter if pushed too far. A balance should be struck between pictures and text so that the functions of illustration and visual balance performed by pictures are utilized and a newspaper, while making itself attractive, does not become a slave to its design and short-change its buyers of reading matter.

Uses of pictures

Where a certain type or shape of picture is expected to be used it is usual for the picture editor to brief a photographer with such advice as 'a strong double of this,' or 'go for a wide shot – it's the heads that matter.' The worldly camera-person, who is planning a cluster of shots using a digital automatic, will probably go for a variety of shapes and angles for good measure so that there is a choice should the advertising department leave the editorial an awkward space to fill, or a story and its picture be moved to a different page.

Nevertheless, the picture finally chosen will determine by its composition, and what is required to show, the shape it takes in the page. In fact a picture that is considered to be worth a good space, whatever pre-conceived ideas might have been held, will be given a page where this is possible. Its shape and size will govern the disposition of stories and headlines around it. It will become a fixed point in the design to which the other elements adapt, although it still has to fulfil its function of informing the reader since it is part of the day's input of news.

If a number of pictures are used together on a news page, a *sequence* (Figure 15 on page 34) is better than a *montage*, the coupling of pictures into a display pattern, with complicated cutting in (Figure 34) since it is less troublesome and time-taking. It also looks less contrived. Screen make-up – and even paste-up – has made a great variety of display ideas possible but for news there is nothing faster or more urgent than a well-cropped, good-sized, perfectly toned rectangle.

Found more often on features pages is the *cut-out* in which part of the picture is highlighted by being cut away from its background to reveal the outline of a head or building or other salient feature (see Figure 35 and examples on pages 198–9). Display advertisements often make good use of cut-outs, with bastard measure text spilling round strange outlines, an effect produced effortlessly with mouse-controlled computer setting.

Pictures are also used as parts of a *compo* (or composite illustration) along with headline type, sometimes reversed on to colour, and occasionally line graphics. This is a fussy, though eye-catching, device much favoured for *blurbs* (examples on pages 62 and 212) used in features pages and often in colour on page one to signal inside page contents.

On news and features pages a simple but significant picture subject might be used as a small *bleach-out*, in which the image is over-exposed in the processor until it loses intermediate tones and takes on the hard black and white of a line illustration. The technique is used where a motif, or series of repeating motifs

Figure 34 Eight diverse fashion shots are imaged together into a montage in this women's page presentation in London's *Evening Standard*

EVENING STANDARD

First
Chapl

Life Story of Charlie Chap
by ANDY GARDNER

IN 1928 Charlie Chaplin was at the height of his powers, a colossus in the Hollywood film industry. The Little Tramp, distinguished by a battered bowler and a twirling cane, had made it to the very top.

The comic calamities, unsteady gait and bumbling persona of his comic creation had ensured Chaplin a place in 20th century film history and a Beverly Hills mansion. Life was sweet.

That was u ntil the great man discovered a film-maker in his native London had documented his rags-to-riches life. The trauma of his childhood was about to be played out on the big screen.

Chaplin, it seems, was not happy to be the subject of one of the first ever warts-and-all celebrity documentaries. He is said to have ensured the black and white silent movie was never released.

Now, almost 70 years later, the film ~~~~urfaced after gathering dust in ~~~~ ~~~ account of

Figure 35 Cut-out pictures and bastard setting are easily achieved in modern page make-up programs. In this *Evening Standard* example the setting spills round the bent cane in a typical Charlie Chaplin look-back picture

Figure 36 Successful blurbs, especially those at the top of the front page, are best achieved by a composite of boldly presented pictures, headline type and cross-references printed in colour. In this example from *The Express*, attractive girlie cut-outs, one extending into the masthead area, take the eye. Headings and cross-references are here reversed on to red and blue

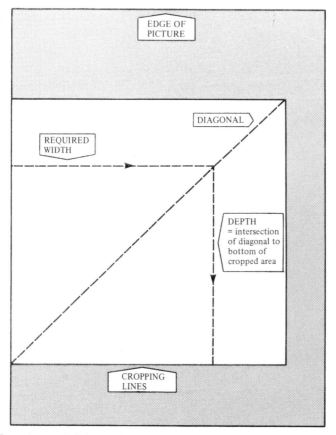

Figure 37 Cropping and sizing a picture on the back of the print by diagonal method before shooting it for the page. Nowadays, under full-page composition, photographs are cropped in the scanner at the outset. The crop and size can be further adjusted on screen, if need be, by the page editor

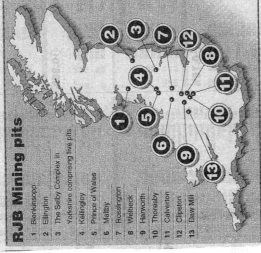

Figure 38 Jobs that graphics can do:

Top left: In this working graphic, a *Daily Mail* artist shows the method by which a man survived in the sea by turning his waders into a lifejacket. Also included is the time scale and geography of the man's rescue

The Guardian's map pinpoints deep coal mines threatened with closure in an accompanying story about problems in the power industry

Right: Symbol graphics – an example from the *Western Mail's* horoscopes column

(examples on page 196) is wanted to flag a long-running or special story. Examples might be the outline of a jet fighter in an air war story, Big Ben on a parliamentary column, or a winning post in a classic race report. Bleach-outs, if chosen wisely from a sharp but simple original, can have a drama a drawn motif lacks.

Reproduction of photographs by the half-tone process, in which the tones are rendered by means of tiny printed dots of varying density, still applies in web-offset printing used with computerized systems both in colour and black and white. Pictures are printed, in effect, through a fine screen (as they were in the hot metal process), though with the use of smooth polymer printing plates on web-offset presses an even finer screen is possible, giving greater clarity of reproduction in the modern newspaper.

Graphics

Graphics, in newspaper and magazine parlance, means any drawn visual aids as opposed to photographs. It was originally limited to the use of design symbols to explain statistical material – little people and half people signifying voting intentions, petrol consumption, Budget benefits, etc. – and examples of stylized 'idiot' graphics have been available for years in Letraset and other stick-on types.

The greater use of trained layout artists in recent years on the bigger newspapers as well as on magazines has led to a boom in in-house graphics as illustration, especially on the quality Sunday papers. There are occasions when a drawing can get closer to a story's actuality than a photograph. Tabbed diagrams can show methods used by an escaping convict, the infiltration of terrorists, or the opium trail from Thailand, in a way denied to the camera. Family trees can come alive out of the routine searches of geneaologists, the range of capacity of inter-Continental missiles and battle layouts demonstrated, and football moves and golf strokes shown in detail.

Graphics can combine with half-tones by juxtaposing tabbed identification panels alongside a picture, demonstrating with arrowed lines the path of a bullet or the route of a careering vehicle, thus extending the text.

These examples are what might be termed working graphics (see example in Figure 38). Symbol graphics still have their place. Drawn or bleached-out motifs are used to label a column or flag a long-running story such as an election or a big strike. They abound on holiday supplements, the logos of well-known columnists, TV programmes and racing cards – a silhouette here, a pair of sunglasses there, the scales of justice, and so on. They give easy recognition to regular features and looked-for parts of the paper. They are part of the paper's visual character, part of its familiarity

The computer has greatly increased the use of symbol graphics (see also Figure 38), although graphics drawn in-house can be entered into the computer as stock for use as needed and will be more exclusive to a publication.

4

HANDLING TEXT

Subeditors edit all the text that goes into a newspaper, the broad areas of news and features and sectional specialisms such as sport and financial.

Advances in technology have broadened the subs' role. We have seen how, from the start, the computer allowed them to turn their material into type for the page, thus cutting out the old-style composing room, and finally how to control the whole edited product by making up the pages on screen.

It is easy to exaggerate the effect of all this on text editing. The computer has proved a marvellous tool, leading to cost-saving and greater speed and efficiency, to say nothing of better looking pages, but one needs to remember that in its editorial guise it is still a tool. Traditional skills in the handling of text, and its projection in the page and targeting on the reader, have never been more necessary. It is to these skills that we now turn.

The subs' table

Subs vary in number from three of four on a small weekly to maybe a dozen on a town evening paper and perhaps twenty or thirty on a national daily. Because of shift systems and holidays not all work at once.

The ubiquitous keyboard and screen have greatly altered the layout of the old subs' table. There is a growing stress on multi-skilling with subs on some papers being designated as page editors, handling stories and pictures for a given page and seeing it through from screen to plate, with other subs carrying out specialist editing, rewrite or revise functions. On small papers, page design and picture editing can be included in the subs' or page editors' brief.

Subs' table layouts thus vary from office to office. There remains a good deal of compartmenting in the bigger quality papers, with enclaves of subs and a designer working on specialist parts of the paper. Home or foreign, sport or general, the subs' job in terms of handling text is the same, however, although the more mechanical aspects of typesetting and casting off to a length have been simplified by the computer. This chapter will look at the techniques involved by examining the role of the general news subeditor.

The editing function

Your job as a news sub, in terms of text editing, is to:

1 Check the names, addresses, figures and other facts of the story for accuracy.
2 Check and put right any errors in grammar, spelling and structure.

3 Check for legality, if necessary referring queries to the office lawyer.

4 Edit the story to the length needed for its page slot, if necessary cutting and amending it, or collating copy from a number of sources into one story.

5 Rewrite any part, or all, of the story if need be to bring it to the length and standard required.

6 Prepare the story for its page slot by setting it in the required type and measure.

7 Write a headline to the chosen type and measure.

8 Write any captions needed to go with the story and the accompanying pictures.

9 Revise the story in length and context for later editions in the light of new copy or a change in position in page or paper.

10 Ensure that these procedures are carried out to meet page and edition deadlines.

Features subediting is described in Chapters 11 and 12.

Getting it right

The amount of news and the sheer accumulation of facts in a newspaper, coupled with the speed of production, make inaccuracy a daily hazard. People are quick

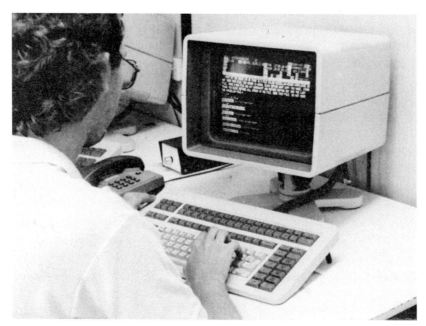

Figure 39 Subbing at an editing screen: the text rearranges itself and gives a line count in response to cuts and adjustments made by the cursor

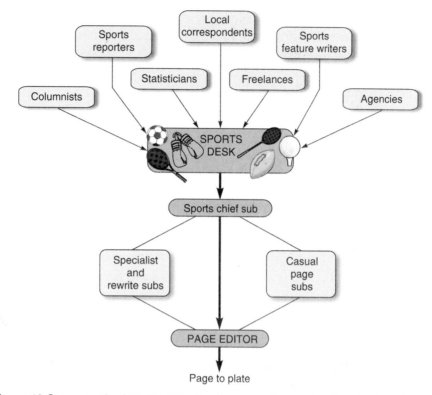

Figure 40 Sports production: the copy flow from reporters and writers is filtered through the sports desk to the chief subeditor, specialist subs and page editors in a replica of the news and features operation. On most papers sports writing and production is independent of the rest of the paper

to condemn when a newspaper gets things wrong and the graver errors can get an editor into serious trouble.

A vital part of your job as a subeditor is to *check*, *check*, *check* everything that is checkable. In the days of hot metal production the system of proofreaders often helped in correcting editorial errors. It is now down to the journalist. If avoidable mistakes get into the paper, it is the subeditor who edited the story who is deemed to be at fault, and who needs almost a sixth sense to detect hidden traps.

Error can arise in many ways. No two eyewitnesses see things in the same light so discrepancies can occur in different reports of the same incident. Reporters have to be relied upon to cross-check information on the job. There is not much you can do about this aspect except to check back with the reporter any fact or figure that is suspect.

Checking with the reporter should be a regular practice where there is the slightest doubt about anything. Even if the original source of information cannot be contacted, your query might reveal an error in telephoning or keyboarding. A nought might have been added to a figure, or left out, or a sentence misheard. An unlikely age, an unusual spelling of a name, or a figure or sum of money that seems disproportionate to the facts, should alert a sub to possible transmission errors.

'Attractive blonde model Jenny Jones, aged 43 . . .' would write in angrily if she were only 23.

A man fined fifty pounds for a minor theft would regard it as damaging if the newspaper added a nought to the fine by mistake.

> *Misreadings* can lead to mistakes when you rewrite reporters' copy. Check all rewrites against the original story (usually kept in the system), especially names and addresses, ages, dates, figures and quotations. It is annoying if the reporter gets the facts right and they turn up wrong in the paper.

'*Quoted speech*', where meanings have been changed or frustrated through vital words or sentences being left out in the editing, is a particular source of complaint to the Press Complaints Commission. The reporter's note or tape is no protection if the quotation has been altered by the subeditor in shortening a story so that the speaker is held up to ridicule or appears to have said something he or she did not say. This does not mean that quoted speech cannot be edited or shortened, only that it should be done with care, especially in sensitive circumstances.

A common danger is the *paraphrasing* of quotes in the opening, or intro, to a story where the sub, in an attempt to grab the readers' attention, pushes the meaning of a quotation beyond its limit. If a councillor tells a reporter, 'It is likely that the Council will consider demolishing three blocks of substandard flats,' and the first sentence of the edited report says, 'Bromley Council is to consider demolishing three blocks of substandard flats', the subeditor has gone too far. Sources of information to a newspaper can dry up if they get this sort of treatment.

In the offices of competitive papers, a high degree of polishing and rewriting and striving for effect goes on the subs' table in the battle to outdo rival papers. The subeditor who combs his or her brains for the telling phrase, the eye-catching introduction and words of the right length for a difficult headline count can be in as great a danger of doing damage to the facts as the reporter rushing to get the story into the paper by the deadline.

Cases of *mistaken identity* are another cause for complaint. In captioning stock pictures to go with a story you must make certain that the person is identified beyond all doubt. There was a well-known case in a British newspaper where a perfectly law-abiding citizen opened his paper at breakfast time to find himself staring out of a gallery of hoodlums at the top of the page just because he happened to share the same name as someone. Mistakes like this can be expensive.

Picture files, even electronic ones, can finish up containing more than one person of the same name. It is no defence for you to say the picture came from the file. If there is the slightest doubt about it being the right person you should not risk attaching a caption to identify to it until it has been checked.

Likewise, with pictures of groups, it is not enough for the cameraman to say that he thinks the fourth person from the left is so-and-so. It is down to the sub handling the story, by whatever means, to identify the right person. When you are building a page on screen – for example, if you are the page editor – you must ensure the right captions get on the right picture. The *News of the World* once had the President of the Board of Trade playing in midfield for Chelsea.

> Picture captions and mistaken identities are two of the biggest traps a subeditor has to deal with (see previous chapter, pages 49 and 57). There is no calculating what damage might be being caused to someone's reputation or business by a simple mistake. Even where, through no fault of the paper, a person is mistaken for someone else through having the same name and similar address or description as the person in the page, editors will publish a short *disclaimer*, if asked, if they think damage might be caused. Mistakes which cause annoyance and irritation to a person or organization, rather than actual damage, can be put right by agreement with the editor, by a simple *correction* in a later edition. More serious mistakes can lead to an action for *damages* or, more frequently, the paying of an agreed sum out of court and the publication of an apology.

Needless to say, editors do not like having their mistakes aired in public and look to their subeditors to protect them from trouble.

Check sources

There are a number of routines which should be followed by subeditors to ensure accuracy. You should check all stories against files in the *cuttings library*, electronic or otherwise, even though the reporter might be presumed to have done this. This will show what publicity the person or subject has had and may supply useful background detail. It will also tell you if the story is, in fact, new or has already been published. The cuttings might contain names of people who can be used as check sources and can give biographical facts to flesh out sketchy details supplied by the reporter, or to correct actual errors.

It is always worth checking the *names, titles* and other references to people in the public eye. Peers, judges and lieutenant-generals can be touchy about their description, particularly the next time you want to talk to them. And beware about their marital state. Be up to date (through cuttings) on divorces and remarriages and whether people really are married or are only thought to be married. The real wife can be annoyed to find a mistress masquerading in her place in print.

Fortunately, in this area, checking is not difficult. Titles, heirs, family arrangements and even hobbies of the famous can be found in *'Who's Who'*, while *'Debrett'* and *'Burke's Peerage'* can keep subs up to date with peers, knights and baronets. It is the nature of the titles minefield that Lords Astor, Douglas, Russell, Cohen, Lloyd and Balfour (to name but a few) seem to come in pairs and even threes, and the right one must be identified.

Sorting out the Revs, Right Revs, Vens, priests, pastors, rectors, abbots, archdeacons, canons and rabbis becomes possible in individual cases by reference to such works as *Crockford's Clerical Directory, The Catholic Directory, Free Church Directory, Baptist Handbook, Jewish Year Book* and others. The word priest is particularly misused in stories about religion.

Whether or not a school is a public school can be gleaned from the *Public and Preparatory Schools Year Book*, and the names of MPs, their titles, and qualifications, from *Dod's Parliamentary Companion* and *Vacher's Parliamentary Companion*.

For military people and military matters there are:

The Air Force List
The Army List
The Navy List
Jane's Fighting Ships
Jane's All the World's Aircraft

For the Arts there are:

BBC Year Book
Oxford Companion to Literature
Oxford Companion to Music
Oxford Companion to Art
Radio and TV Who's Who
Who's Who in Music
Who's Who in the Theatre

In business, Government and other areas at home and abroad there are:

Civil Service List
The Directory of Directors
Foreign Office List
International Who's Who
The Stock Exchange Year Book
Who's Who in America

Quotations from the literary greats can upset readers, especially of upmarket papers, when rendered wrongly. Is it 'all that glitters is not gold'? or 'all that glisters is not gold'? Which homely English poet described tea as 'the cup that cheers but not inebriates'? Is 'Get thee to a nunnery' from *Hamlet* or *King John*? And was it Sir Toby Belch who said: 'Dost thou think because thou art virtuous there shall be no more cakes and ale?' Memory plays false and the safest thing is to resort to the *Oxford Dictionary of Quotations* or to its *Everyman's* or Penguin equivalent.

Despite all these prestigious and accessible volumes there are four reference works that are inseparable from any subs' table: *Whitaker's Almanack*, which has the most comprehensive information about governments at home and abroad, trade unions, economies and geographies; *Bartholomew's Gazetteer of Great Britain*, which can settle every dispute about the spelling and location of towns and villages; a modern dictionary and a full set of telephone directories. Add to these a good international gazetteer and a selection of national year books and you are factually set up.

Making it fit

Casting off is an old printers' term for setting a piece of copy or headline in type to fit its space. It is still used in subbing for editing a story to the length required. To cast off a story, the subeditor must know first how many words it contains. This is now easy for a word count comes up on screen when copy is entered.

The sub must then know how many words in body setting can be contained in a given space on the page. Here a knowledge of the newspaper quickly provides the answer since setting of whatever size works out at a given number of words per column inch. A new subeditor will find it useful to stick examples from the paper across single column and double column on a card until familiar with the requirements of various column depths. Figure 41 shows some examples of column width setting by the inch.

At its simplest, cutting an over-long text to fit a given space is achieved by two means:

1 Leaving out unnecessary facts.
2 Leaving out unnecessary words.

1-inch   I hated it but there wasn't much I could do about it. Just before we got together again he told me this woman only had a year to live and   10 pt Roman lc × 8½ ems

1-inch   The new passion in Jim's life, who has rescued him from the depths of despair, is his own daughter Sarah, from his first marriage.

    Before their recent reunion they had not   8 pt Roman lc × 8½ ems

1-inch   and when he said he might take up a permanent suite he got the real red carpet treatment."

    In fact, the cunning count was broke—but he even conned the Ritz into letting him take out £500 cash advances saying he could not be bothered to   7 pt Roman lc × 8½ ems

Figure 41 Column width setting by the inch: a useful guide in text editing for new subeditors

Keep in the facts and details needed for intro and main sequence and delete the rest as necessary, beginning with the ones of least importance to the story. Then work through the copy, carefully paring down the text, rooting out repetition, ambiguity and redundant words, shortening wordy phrases, checking the grammar as you go, so that every word that is left does a job.

There is a good deal more to good subbing, however, than cutting a story to fit, as will be explained in the rest of this chapter, but the problem of long texts is one that frequently has to be faced. We have seen from the way news is selected and from the variables at work in news origination that a great deal more copy enters a newspaper than can be used. Even after copytasting, much remains to be done to reduce the amount to the size and shape needed to project in the pages. You as the subeditor are the catalyst for this.

The main task of subbing, after checking for accuracy, is the cutting and collating of copy so that a story is given an orderly shape within the space chosen for it. There can be hard feelings between reporters and subs over this. Here you invariably have the advantage of having worked as a reporter beforehand, whereas the reporter is more concerned with the two hard days spent on gathering a story than with questions of balance on the page, and often has had little or no subbing experience.

It is not always possible to give reporters a precise length to which to write because the factors governing space – the number of pages and the volume and quality of news stories available for them – is not known in time. Some story lengths can be decided in advance come what may. Some favoured news stories, however, might in the end get less space than expected, or be dropped altogether, because of some unexpected development. Space on pages can be lost as a result of late changes in picture and advert sizes.

Stories can grow. Extra copy might come in from other sources or a story might become important because of unforeseen happenings. Thus the length and shape might be decided hours after the reporter has finished writing it, by which time he or she has gone home or is on another job.

Editing for the page

The editing process begins (unless you are working for a paper that still uses cut-and-paste – see pages 4 and 10) when the sub or page editor receives on screen the schemed page and, as they become available, the stories required. Each slot will indicate the story catchline and the body type and headline setting. The chief subeditor will brief you on the handling of any special aspects of a story and you will then commence shaping it to its place in the page.

A quick reading of the text will reveal by how much it needs cutting, if at all. Some stories can be placed at almost their original length. Others might be the work of several reporters with important aspects embedded in accompanying agency copy or with the promise of 'more to follow' from the reporter still covering the job.

Some *running stories* may continue right through a day's editions with '*add copy*' and pictures arriving from various sources and several revisions for the page necessary (see Chapter 10). Throughout this job of checking, cutting and revising, not only of one story but of several during the shift, your job is to assess and update the material for the reader in the light of the latest information and the space available.

The editing process ends, when, having got the story to the right length and the facts in the required order, you type it up with its headline into the page slot, these days using coded setting formats. You might need to trim it on screen if it is still slightly over. If it is only a line short it is possible, using a command key, to level up the text by distributing the line space – eight points, say – evenly through the text.

Order and shape

In text editing, your assessment of the story, upon which you base its order and shape, comes from a close reading of the copy and an informed judgement about what it is 'saying'. Newspapers are often accused of formularizing news into stereotypes. Some criminal court cases, marriage-and-divorce situations and show-biz stories seem to come typecast with the order of events and even the things people say, being recognizably similar. Such stock situation stories are not common enough to make life easy for the subeditor. Sometimes the crux of a story in terms of news has to be pulled out of the middle of a long account, or it comes to light from a query raised or an idea from a senior executive. The simplicity and directness of the final version can conceal a lot of work.

Order and shape are needed in editing a news story to get the maximum benefit from the space it occupies. The essence of what the story is about has to be identified and made into an attractively-worded introduction, or *intro*, so that the reader's attention is aroused. Thereafter the facts must be unfolded so that the intro is justified and the story fleshed out. It has failed if the supporting facts fail to justify the intro, or if they leave the reader asking questions.

The facts should be presented in order of importance, those most connected with the intro being given first, irrelevant ones removed and the least important left to the end. The notion that a reporter should include a potent end paragraph is an attractive one but in the heat of late copy and quick edition changes the story might have to be cut from the end. It is also true that the least read paragraph in a news story is the last one so that a pearl of information could be wasted.

Attempts have been made to impose a neat formula on news subbing but none is watertight. There are always stories that require a different approach, and some of these approaches will be examined later. Perhaps the most useful way to look at story structure is to say that a well-subbed news story should have:

1 *A statement*
2 *Explanation*
3 *Corroboration*
4 *Qualification*

These categories, as will be seen, apply only in the most general way as do most teaching slogans. It is perhaps easier just to say that the story should have a logical sequence in which the facts drawn to the reader's attention in the intro are explained in the body of the text so that the story is as clear, complete and as up to date as the subeditor can make it in the space and time available.

Let us now examine the various stages.

The intro

Your opening paragraph must catch the eye at first reading if the brain is to be persuaded to read on. This introduction, or *intro* as it is called, is a contrived device in which attention is gained not by starting at the beginning of a sequence of events, as in the first chapter of a novel, but by giving first the highlight or most important or most interesting part of the story.

Fashioning a good intro is a skill you must learn since it is the cornerstone of the method by which news stories are presented and edited. Experienced reporters are made aware of this requirement in their training and in an ideal world they will produce copy that requires little editing. There are always reasons, however, why a new intro is required. The vital news fact, despite the reporter's efforts, might be stuck somewhere down the story. Later information or the arrival of copy from other sources, or the more experienced judgement of a night editor or chief subeditor, can result in the story being treated in a different way. The arrival of news pictures to go with it can require a shift of emphasis.

Whatever the state or the amount of copy, an experienced subeditor will know what the intro should say after a first reading, and most certainly after a second. With a running story, or with several copy sources, or with changing news angles for different editions, some preliminary tasting and editing is usually necessary. With a big running story – say an air crash or an election – the intro is sometimes the last paragraph to be written since it has to contain the most up-to-date facts. In such cases stories are edited and given their typesetting, and maybe a standby intro, or a space is left in the on-screen page to await the intro.

Guidelines to help a young sub to master the art of intro writing are best demonstrated by examining examples. Let us see how a big provincial evening paper, the Bristol *Evening Post* writes its intros:

> Four families with brain-damaged toddlers were taking court action in London today over an inquiry into a heart surgery unit at Bristol Royal Infirmary.

It is a simple sentence but it gets straight to the point. The fact, referred to in the next but one paragraph, that two heart surgeons are facing a disciplinary hearing by the General Medical Council, is already known; the new fact is that the families are pursuing civil claims against the local Healthcare Trust. Therein lies the intro.

The story is, in fact, a follow-up and it demonstrates two rules about an intro:

★ *It should highlight the salient and most newsworthy point in the story.*
★ *It should not try to say too much within its space.*

And another punchy example from the *Evening Post*:

Teenage runaway Kirsty McFadden has revealed how she earned an astonishing £600 a week begging on the streets of Bristol to feed her heroine habit.

Again, 25 words encapsulate the vital fact of the story – how a girl of 16 made the money she needed to stay on hard drugs while living rough for a year. The fact that she has kicked drugs and is back with her family is covered with a heart-warming picture alongside, but the subs' headline, £600-A-WEEK BEGGAR, confirms that the intro point is correctly chosen.

This demonstrates another useful rule about an intro:

★ *It should seek out the point that makes the story special.*

Here is an intro from another paper which is less effective:

A total of three hundred and five thousand children will have their education disrupted next week when the National Union of Teachers stages the fourth in its weekly three-day selective strikes in support of the teachers' pay claim.

This is not a bad intro because it gets to the heart of what is to happen but it uses too many words. It would be better to say '. . . stages a fourth three-day selective strike over pay.' That would have used nine words instead of sixteen for that part of the sentence, and would have avoided using the word 'teacher' twice. The rest could be explained in the second and third paragraphs. This brings us to another rule about an intro:

★ *Every word should count in making the intro readable. There is no room for passengers.*

Now look at the facts in the following story:

In Salford yesterday afternoon a five-year-old boy, Kevin Jones, was knocked down by a reversing lorry outside his home and died later in hospital.

Here is an example of the right information in the wrong order, with the result that the effect is weakened. The intro should relegate the time and place to the end of the sentence and get straight down to the news fact:

Five-year-old Kevin Jones died in hospital after being knocked down by a reversing lorry outside his home in Salford yesterday.

The intro rule:

★ *It should not begin with the place and time.*

The delayed drop

One type of intro that does not follow the above rules is the delayed drop. Here the substance of the story is deliberately kept from the reader to create a feeling of suspense. It can work well in offbeat humorous or human interest stories or in atmosphere stories in which the effect depends upon how the facts are presented rather than upon their intrinsic importance. For example:

Yesterday was Vera Jones's 46th birthday. It was a day she is not going to forget for five good reasons.

First, she slipped getting out of bed and emptied her Teasmaid cuppa all over the carpet.

Second, the cat, not used to such behaviour, took flight and jumped out of the first floor window.

Third, when Vera struggled down to the kitchen to make another cup of tea she found it was flooded. She'd left the tap on.

Fourth, when she managed to get to her pub, the Rose and Crown, in time for the birthday drink she'd promised herself she found them fighting a fire in the bar.

Fifth, when she returned home for lunch, fed up to the back teeth, she found a letter on the mat saying she'd won £50,000 on the pools.

Vera, of Culrose Street, Bolton said last night . . . etc.

Delayed drop intros are effective on the right sort of story, but like many special devices they become tiresome with over-use. The story structure must be contrived with great skill – a job that usually falls to the subeditor – so that the reader is 'hooked', and the denouement must make the slow-burning effect to have been worthwhile. On no account should this treatment be used on hard news, nor should more than one delayed drop story appear on the same page. It has to be kept for a special sort of material.

Story sequence

Once you have settled the intro you are ready to tackle the main body of the text, which means presenting the facts in sequence so that the story has shape and pace as the reader moves through it.

The first point to remember is that your intro must not be left unsupported. The paragraphs immediately following it must explain any incomplete references it contains, even if this means changing the order in the reporter's copy. If it describes a boy of seven, then you must quickly give his name and details, if known. If it contains a general reference to a group or organization then you must identify it fully as soon as possible so that the reader is not left guessing. Any device or generalization used to make an intro short and pithy – references to leader, boss, court, team, minister etc. – requires a fuller description in the next two or three paragraphs.

If, for example, a story says, 'A Labour councillor told a delegation of young mothers at the Town Hall today that the party supported their demand for more crèches . . . ' the councillor and the composition of the delegation should be quickly identified.

Having supported the intro, you should unfold the remaining facts in order of importance. Facts touched upon in the intro should not be repeated as if they were new facts but should be referred to and amplified as they occur in natural sequence. Quotes should be introduced and attributed in corroboration of what the story is saying.

If the story has several 'ends' (information from different locations, or writers, or enlargements of specific aspects of the story) you should connect the segments by linking phrases so that the reader knows that the narrative has diverted from the main story, even though the material still relates to the facts in the intro.

The skilful unfolding of a news story in this way should have a natural rhythm of its own whether it consists of three paragraphs or twenty-seven paragraphs. Here from *The Express* is a six-paragraph story that vividly demonstrates the sequence of *intro, explanation, corroboration* and *qualification*:

A British climber was recovering yesterday after he was swept 2000 feet down a mountain by a rockslide.

His two companions died in the fall from the East Wall of the Matterhorn.

Martin Hood, who was dragged after them on the same rope, suffered only fractures and was later rescued after other climbers raised the alarm.

Six other climbers have died on the mountain in the past week, and 56 since the climbing season started in June. Mr Hood, who works in

Zurich, was with an American woman and another man. Police said, 'He was well kitted out. It was just another tragic accident.'

Across the central Alps, another seven mountaineers fell or were crushed to death in snow avalanches, bringing the number of deaths in the region to more than 150 since June.

Many accidents are caused by night snowfalls followed by high daytime temperatures, says the Swiss Mountaineering Association.

Notice that the intro is correctly focused on the amazing survival of the one mountaineer rather than the death of the other two, however tragic.

Here are some special points about story sequence:

Using quotes

In stories based upon eyewitness interviews short telling quotes can energize the text. For instance a story of a train being struck by lightning might begin:

A hundred people were injured when an express train ran off the lines north of Watford after being struck by what a witness called 'a ball of fire.'

It is does not matter if the quotes do not all entirely agree. After the main facts given in the first couple of paragraphs the above story might go on:

Jane Watkins, of North Road, Rickmansworth, who was in the third coach, said: 'There was a great flash as we passed over a bridge and everyone screamed.'

Her friend June Smith, of Long Lane, Welwyn, Herts, said: 'The fireball – it was more than just a flash – seemed to land right in front of the train.'

A word of warning: a story based on a contentious statement someone has made is incomplete and could lead to trouble if the person's quoted views are not included as they were said. If a story starts, 'Boomtown's Labour mayor said the Tory Opposition group on the council were "preying" on people's misfortunes to make political capital . . .', then it should have a qualifying paragraph such as, 'The Mayor, Coun. Thomas Jones, declared: "The Opposition on this council are like vultures . . . etc."'.

In introducing quoted statements beware of misrepresenting what a person is saying by using in intros and headlines words such as 'criticized', 'insisted' or 'demanded'. Such verbs require strong views to sustain them. If a local councillor said, 'I think housing tenders should be advertised over a wider area to try to bring in cheaper quotations,' he could be aggrieved to find on opening his local newspaper that he had 'denounced' his council's house-building programme.

Some adjectives and verbs describing what people say have a loaded or emotive effect which goes beyond the objectivity required by a good news writing. There is nothing wrong with the neutral 'said' or 'told' or 'added.' Let the person's words speak for them.

Mixing quotes

Some subeditors, in an attempt to get everything of interest near the top of the story, break up interview quotes used by the reporter, using first those of one person, then another, and even a third, in the first few paragraphs. This might seem a good idea for the order of facts the sub has in mind but it can confuse the reader.

In reporting discussion – at a meeting, say – mixing of quotes and speakers might seem justified but in the run of the story it is better to deal one at a time with the things people say rather than break up and shuffle their words. If comments are detached and used in the same part of a story as other people's words, not only the context but the meaning of each speaker's words can be lost.

Other points in quoting speech:

★ Where a person is quoted as criticizing someone, the other person should be allowed an opportunity to give their view. If the reporter has failed to do this, the sub should go back and ask for it to be done. Even if the person criticized tells the reporter, 'I have no comment,' it is worth using this to show the newspaper is trying to be fair.

★ Whether quoted or paraphrased, statements in a story *must* be properly attributed.

Here, from the *Western Mail*, is a report of a political speech in which quoted and paraphrased statements are interspersed to keep the report to a length while still giving the salient points:

The welfare state will be modernized to support work and not dependency, Social Security Secretary Harriet Harman declared yesterday.

The new welfare state would be based on work, savings and honesty, she told the Labour conference in Brighton.

'We will modernize the welfare state so that all the children in Britain grow up with a decent standard of living, so that it helps people into work rather than leaves them on benefit, modernize it to give our pensioners the dignity they deserve,' she said.

Ms Harman said one of the Government's test projects to get lone mothers back to work had proved an early success.

'In one of our pilots, as many as one in every three lone mothers has got a job – sometimes after years on benefit – after their very first interview.

'This is what we mean by reforming the welfare state. Tough decisions on benefits, yes, but always determined to help those on benefits get into work and become better off.'

Ms Harman said the Government's New Deal for the long-term sick and disabled would tackle discrimination and put people into work.

The Government had put £200m into the New Deal. 'Now I can announce I'll be inviting employers, disability groups and voluntary organizations to bid for funds from our New Deal to give real job opportunities to people with disabilities,' she said. 'The point is not the amount we spend but how we spend it.'

The juxtaposing of paraphrase and quoted speech presents a rapid unfolding pattern of the substance of the speech where quotes alone would have slowed it down. Political speeches do not normally present their most potent points in the first few minutes.

Geography

The local connection of a story is important in a paper serving a local or regional area and is a valid ingredient in the intro and even the headline. In a national paper, geography is less important and is often relegated to the third or fourth paragraph or even later. Readers can become annoyed, however, if the location of a happening is kept almost to the end when they find to their disgust that what they are reading about happened not in some nearby town or even in England but in Ulan Bator, Outer Mongolia.

Even in national papers, geography in a national sense matters, and foreign stories are often used because of their British connection. A person involved in a story in Saudi Arabia would be a Briton in paragraph one, while he would be from Halifax or wherever in paragraph six or seven. In Halifax his local connection would merit the first paragraph.

Time

The *yesterday* or *today* should be made clear in the intro and followed through in the story. Any changes in time sequence should be introduced by a linking phrase (sometimes in italic) such as 'earlier in the day' or 'speaking last night.' Once the sequence has changed the story should not revert to the original time or the reader will become confused. Other 'ends' to the story should be introduced after the main explanatory text by a similar device such as 'a spokesman at the town hall said later,' or 'Mr X's former wife told reporters by telephone from New York last night.'

Background

In giving background material, especially from press cuttings, records and reference books, subs should beware not to use it to slant a story or influence the reader's reaction.

A person's career or achievements can often be filled out usefully in the editing, but if a person appointed to public office has been found in cuttings to have been put on probation for theft when a teenager many years ago, this could be actionable if used, even though true. It could be construed as malicious (see Chapter 9).

Any background material worked in should be relevant to the story and not be used to support a point of view.

FAULT-FINDER'S GUIDE TO ENGLISH

In editing text you need to be able to spot a variety of errors and misuses that can crop up in copy. Some of these faults are grammatical – even the best writers go through life with blind spots from when young – and others are to do with the use and meaning of words.

Newspapers respond to new usages that are part of a growing world use of English. These usages reflect popular expressions and vogue words and the subtle shifts of meanings that stem from the spoken language and the influence of commerce and technology. To pick a way through this minefield and decide when a new usage of phrase or word is acceptable is more difficult for the grammarian than for the journalist since the grammarian acts as the custodian of the language. The journalist is merely using it to an end.

Even so there has to be consistency and acceptability in the way language is used if the journalist is to communicate properly with the reader. This is important where copy, even though well written, has to be condensed without loss of meaning, words and phrases substituted to save space, ambiguity excised and order imposed on stories that might have a variety of copy sources and a changing slot-length in a page.

This selection and condensation can lead the unwary sub into error when time is short. Stories cannot be left with difficult sentences, misleading punctuation or words that do not make clear the writer's intentions. The subeditor must ensure not only that the text gets through to the reader in a readable form, but that the best use is made of the space given to it. The following guidance on language is given with this purpose in mind.

The sentence

Good sentence structure is the key to good writing. All sentences must have a *subject* and a *verb*. The verb, if need be, can be qualified by an *adverb*:

Subject	*Verb*	*Adverb*
The policeman	walked	quickly.

The sentence can also have an object:

The policeman walked quickly towards the boy (*object*).

Newspapers, and some fiction writers, allow the subject to be implied in certain cases, and sometimes even the verb. This can work provided the sense makes the subject clear to the reader:

The policeman walked quickly. Too quickly (*he walked*).
They did everything to give him a day full of activity. How full a day (*they gave him*).

The use of an *implied subject* is a device that can give pace to a narrative provided it is clear who or what is the subject. It is best used to produce a special effect. If over-used, or used without justification in place of conventional structure, it becomes a tiresome mannerism.

Where a verb is inactive (where it expresses a state of being or feeling) it takes a *complement* in place of an object. For example:

Subject	Verb	Complement
The girl	felt	happy.

It is important to know which is the subject of a sentence because the verb must agree with it in person and number. In person the verb changes only in the third person singular:

I *move*   He, she or it *moves*   They *move*

Agreement in number, however, can cause problems. Where a sentence has a double subject the verb must be plural, as in:

Oil and water *do not* mix.

Where words are joined to the subject by a preposition the subject remains singular as in:

Iron, with copper, *is* the most important metal.

In neither–nor or either–or sentences the verb agrees in number with the subject nearest to it as in:

Neither John nor his brother *is* a member.
Neither Helen nor her sisters *are* going.

Beware of pitfalls with numbers and quantities. Use *fewer than* for numbers as in:

There *were* fewer than fifty copies left.

Use *less than* for amounts or quantities.

There was *less than* a quorum so the meeting was abandoned.

Generally numbers used as terms of measurement are singular:

There *was* ten pence in the hat,

but:

there *were* ten pennies.

None as a subject generally means *not one* and should be treated as singular.

Thirty years ago there *were* many fishing families in the village. Now there *is* none.

Agreement in person and number with the subject is most difficult in the case of *collective nouns*, the term given to collections of things such as a herd, a class, a bevy, a gathering etc. Grammatically, they should be treated as singular.

The class *was* too lively for the new maths teacher.
The Government *has* decided to scrap *its* proposed wealth tax.

This is a useful rule on the whole, but sticking to it pedantically can lead to stilted structure, and some newspapers allow collective nouns such as the Cabinet or football and cricket teams to be treated as plural subjects to make for ease of reading. In such cases consistency should be the rule. It would be wrong for a subeditor to allow this sentence through:

The Government *has* decided to scrap *their* proposed wealth tax.

Words like politics, mumps, graphics and acrobatics should be treated as singular despite ending in an *s*.

Participles

Participles such as having, going, running, turning etc. are said to be left dangling in sentences in which the writer has failed to identify the subject. For example:

Having addressed the meeting for two hours, an interval was then agreed.

The subject is the person addressing the meeting, but who was it that agreed the interval?

Passing quickly through the agenda it was then the turn of the treasurer to give his report.

Was it the treasurer who passed quickly through the agenda?

A *dangling participle* is a certain cause of confusion to the reader and a fault that crops up in the copy of inexperienced writers.

Pronouns

The main fault in the use of pronouns occurs in constructions in which the writer has failed to relate them properly to their antecedents. For example:

Helen cooked for *her* sister *her* favourite meal.

Whose favourite meal?

The general looked at *his* aide grimly. *His* eyes were half closed.

Whose eyes?

If there is any doubt about the identity of possessive pronouns (*his*, *her* or *its*), or personal pronouns (*me*, *you*, *him*, *her*), reshape the sentence or split it in two.

Confusion of *me* and *I* is a pitfall. Broadly the rules are these: where the first person pronoun is the subject of the sentence it should be *I*. Where it is the object of the sentence it should be *me*. Thus 'It affects you and me,' is correct; but you would say '*You* and *I* are good friends' because *you* and *I* become a double subject – *you* are a good friend and *I* am a good friend. *I* should be used and not *me* following a conjunction, as in:

'He is as baffled as *I (am)*,' not 'as baffled as *me*.'
'He is younger than *I (am)*' not 'younger than *me*.'

Confusion between *who* and *whom* is more deeply ingrained. As a very loose guide, one says *to whom, from whom, by whom, of whom* and *than whom*, using *who* in most other cases. Thus *whom* is used in a sentence when it is preceded by a preposition. A trick is to substitute *he* for *who* and *him* for *whom* in your mind and see how the sentence works out. 'I did not know *he* was the one' would indicate that 'I did not know *whom* was the one' could not possibly be correct. And so on.

A difficulty with pronouns is highlighted by the following passage: 'When a young journalist starts his or her first job it is necessary that he or she should learn to take a competent note. If any problem crops up, especially over court hearings, he or she will be asked to substantiate . . . etc.'

The glaring fact shown here is that the English language lacks a singular pronoun of common sex for use where the references are to either sex.

Otto Jesperson, in *Growth and Structure of the English Language*, refers to the three available makeshift alternatives – using *he or she*, *they*, or just the universal *he* in general references. Sir Ernest Gower, in *The Complete Plain Words*, is not happy with *they* or *them*. 'Each insisted on their own point of view, and hence the marriage came to an end.' He says this usage is not defensible, though he concedes that 'necessity may force it into the category of accepted idiom.'

Strunk and White, in *The Elements of Style*, say boldly: 'The use of *he* as a pronoun for nouns embracing both genders is a simple, practical convention rooted in the beginning of the English language. *He* has lost all suggestions of maleness in these circumstances.' They go on: 'The furore recently raised about *he* would be more impressive if there were a handy substitute for the word. Unfortunately there isn't.'

Quite. Meanwhile this writer and others do all they can to recast sentences so as to ward off the dreaded choice.

> The personal pronoun *one* can also be a problem. *One* should follow through, once having started, though *one* can quickly find *oneself* wishing *one* had used a different pronoun, however much *one* feels that *one* should stick to *one's* guns.

Which or *that* – an old bogey in sentence construction. A general guide is that *which* must be used in a commenting clause. Example: This should go to the news desk, which deals with these matters.' In a defining clause *which* or *that* is correct as in, 'The committee *that/which* dealt with the matter has been disbanded.' (See under Punctuation, pages 100–6.)

'The man *that* deals with the matter' and 'the man *who* deals with the matter' are equally correct in a defining clause.

Sir Ernest Gowers favours the use of *that* where the choice is justified in making for a smoother sentence. He also says that either should be dropped in sentences that sound right without, the ear being the guide. This is useful advice. Thus you could trim the sentence, 'I think that the record which he wants is the one that is in that box,' to say, 'I think the record he wants is the one in that box.'

The above sentence reminds us of the awkward fact that the word *that*, unlike *which*, can serve as a conjunction, a relative pronoun and an adjective.

Tenses

The necessary thing is to be consistent in the use of tenses. Beware of captions that are in the present tense. Try to avoid:

Elizabeth Taylor *arrives* at London Airport when she *came* to attend the premiere of . . . etc.'

If an interview is in the present tense, do not allow *she says* in one part and *she said* in another.

Do not mix past and perfect tenses in one sentence:

'I went there because I have been thinking that I should like to see her.'

A muddle of tenses like this is best resolved by recasting the sentence:

'I went there because I thought I should like to see her.'

The verb *to be* can cause complications in the lesser-used tenses. Note that *I was* and *he/she was* in the simple past tense becomes *(if) I were* and *(if) he/she were* in the past subjunctive. Reserve the *were* in this sort of usage for unlikely or conjectural situations, for example: 'If I *were* the Prime Minister . . . ' The *if* is not necessary in a sentence such as, 'Suppose he *were* the Prime Minister.'

A good tip is that tenses should relate to the tense of the governing (introductory) verb of a news story, which is usually in the past tense. Allow for differences in tense in quoted speech but, at the end of the quoted passage revert to the governing tense. An exception to this would be any reference to a permanent truth. For example, 'He said that the world *is* round,' is preferable to, 'He said that the world *was* round.'

On the whole, try to keep tenses simple. Recast sentences where there are complications.

Verbs

The worrying thing about verbs is the rate at which new ones are being formed from nouns. A story full of containerize, hospitalize, civilianize, servicize, anathematize and peripheralize can mesmerize. Many of the *ize* or *ise* verbs enable complicated things to be said briefly and should not be rejected but writers should guard against using so many that the text becomes jargonized. It is up to the grammarians to decide how many of these creations are accepted into the language, but the subeditor could strike a blow for sanity by, for instance, substituting *moisten* for moisturize, *complete* for finalize and *curse* for anathematize.

News stories have more pace and immediacy if verbs are used wherever possible in the active voice rather than the passive – 'The policeman saw the boy,' not 'the boy was seen by the policeman. For use of verbs in headlines see pages 126–7.

Two constructions seem to give some writers trouble: the use of *shall* or *will* in the future tense of verbs, and the use of *lay* or *lie* in the verb to lie (down).

Shall is normally used in the first person singular and plural as in 'I shall' and 'we shall,' while the second and third person singular and plural take *will*, as in 'he will,' you will,' and 'they will.' This order can be reversed in emphatic statements such as 'I will go!' or 'You shall win through!'

In the verb to lie (down), say 'He lay down . . . ' (intransitive) but 'He laid down rules . . . .' (transitive). Say 'You should *lie* down,' not 'You should *lay* down,' unless the use is transitive, as in 'You should lay down rules.'

Split infinitives

The infinitive of a verb is its basic form: to be, to go, to take, etc. Splitting the infinitive means inserting an adverb between the particle 'to' and the verb, as in to quickly go, to quietly take, to always be. People are no longer scandalized by the breaking of the old grammatical rule that infinitives should not be split in this way as when H. G. Fowler first suggested it in his *Modern English Usage* in the 1920s.

Conveying the correct meaning is the important thing, yet this can usually be done without splitting the infinitive. 'To further improve the working of the engine,' makes just as much sense and makes for a smoother sentence if worded, 'to improve further the working of the engine.' If we mean there is a further intention to improve the working of the engine, then 'further' must go before the infinitive as in 'further to improve.'

'The purpose of a drug is to better deal with hay fever' would sound and look better by not splitting the infinitive and saying 'to deal better with hay fever' or even 'to deal with hay fever better'.

There is also the question of stress and scansion. 'For man to boldly move towards his future' has a metrical ring absent from 'For man to move boldly (or boldly to move) towards his future.' On these grounds, although they are unlikely to affect most newspaper writing, the infinitive might reasonably be split. In the vast majority of sentences the separating adverb can be placed outside the infinitive, as shown above, with little or no damage to the sentence or danger of ambiguity. R.W. Burchfield, editor of the third edition of *Modern English Usage* (Clarendon Press, Oxford, 1996) supports this view when he says, 'Avoid splitting infinitives whenever possible, but do not suffer undue remorse if a split infinitive is unavoidable for the natural and unambiguous completion of a sentence already begun.'

Qualifiers

These are words that vary or extend the meaning of the noun or verb and they are of two sorts: *adjectives* and *adverbs*.

Adjectives, which qualify the noun, are frequently the most expendable words in a text since an excess of them slows down the writing and takes up space. Many, such as in luxury flat, stunning blonde, staggering sum, hush-hush inquiry, vital clues and burly policeman are among the most tired and overused words to be found in newspapers. Many, as in surprise swoop, brutal murder and secret hideaway, are tautological as well as brain-lulling.

> Another section of popular and over-used adjectives are those based upon nouns such as *miracle, shock, model, terror, horror* and *love*. The more popular national dailies are awash with miracle babies, mums, dads and granddads; shock reports, disclosures, results and endings; model babies mums, dads and granddads; terror flights, terror drives, love nests, love children; unquantifiable numbers of people in terror, and horror stories of many types.

It is in the use of adjectives that newspapers, instead of expanding the frontiers of language, seem to be shrinking them. It is a useful exercise for a subeditor, as well as a writer, to cast out all the above listed adjectives and go for some that more precisely qualify the noun or, if nothing comes to mind, go without. Twenty adjectives saved in a column of type will make room for a one-paragraph news item. Over the page this amount of word saving could allow in an important extra news story.

Here are some usages that could be pensioned off with little loss:

considerable difficulty	serious danger
all-time record	grateful thanks
cherished belief	track record
psychological moment	broad daylight

I leave the reader to add to this list, but you see the idea.

A fault to look for is the tendency of some writers to limit or extend absolute adjectives. You cannot qualify absolute, basic, essential, final, ideal, unique and ultimate. Almost unique or partly ideal are a nonsense. You cannot be more basic than basic.

Adjectives/adverbs such as *very, rather* and *quite* can be debilitating to the text and read like the extension into writing of verbal props. The high incidence of *quite* is (quite) extraordinary.

Beware of *non* as a prefix. Non-essential, non-cooperative, non-aligned and non-active invariably mean inessential, uncooperative, unaligned and inactive, while non-professional usually means amateur. The shorter alternatives also have no intrusive hyphen.

Adverbs qualify the verb and other adjectives by words such as occasionally, rightly, severely, half-heartedly, simply, implicitly, purely and finally. Be certain to put the adverb in its right position. 'You can quickly teach dogs to do tricks,' is not the same as, 'you can teach dogs quickly to do tricks.' Be certain of what you are trying to say.

Nouns

These offer fewer problems than do other ingredients of a sentence. The use of collectives nouns is covered above under 'subject,' and of possessives later under 'punctuation.' Plural forms of nouns can give difficulty. The *ey* endings as in valley and money take an *s*; *y* endings without a preceding vowel change to *ies*.

Oes and *os* endings: the commoner two and three-syllable words such as tomato, potato and hero take oes. Long words, particularly imported ones such as archipelago and gigolo, and also proper nouns such as Lothario, all take os endings. Words with a vowel before the *o* such as cameo, intaglio and imbroglio take os, as do abbreviated words such as photo.

Foreign words: many Anglicized ones, among them sanatorium, syllabus, terminus and ultimatum, take a simple *s* or *es* ending. Some French- and Latin-based ones, however, keep their own plurals. These include:

addendum	addenda	fungus	fungi
beau	beaux	memorandum	memoranda
bureau	bureaux	minimum	minima
cactus	cacti	phenomenon	phenomena
criterion	criteria	plateau	plateaux

Beware of words such as medium which becomes mediums for clairvoyants and media for methods of mass communication; series which remains series, fish which can be fish or fishes, and folk which can be folk or folks.

A blight that afflicts current English is the growth of polysyllabic nouns derived from the new generation of *ize* verbs, themselves often derived from shorter nouns. Thus we get:

container	containerize	containerization
hospital	hospitalize	hospitalization
moisture	moisturize	moisturization

With casual, casualize and casualization comes a more advanced growth: de-casualization. We are only one step from de-containerization, de-hospitalization and de-moisturization. The space saved by using such monster words is wasted if the reader is lulled into insensibility before the end of the sentence. It is better to take up a bit more space and use a few short simple words to explain what you mean and this avoids jargonization.

Prepositions

The rule never to end a sentence with a preposition can be broken without ill-effect in sentences such as 'She's the wife he goes home to,' or 'She's dating the chap she works with.' It would sound pedantic to say 'She's the wife to whom he goes home,' or 'She's dating the chap with whom she works.'

> A good tip is that if the sentence sounds right and is free of ambiguity then the preposition can be left at the end. However, avoid collections of prepositions at the end such as in the classic 'This was the book he wanted to be read out of from to.'

Most uses of prepositions with nouns and verbs (conform to, connive at, taste of, taste for, consequent upon, etc.) are idiomatic and have to be learned.

Other sentence tips

★ Sentences can be made nonsensical through a misplaced clause or phrase: 'For the third time a baby was trapped in a washing machine at . . .' Same baby? Or: 'There was a discussion about rape in the staff room,' or 'It carried an important article about adultery by the Archbishop of Canterbury.'
★ The non-sequitur can strike: 'Injured in the fighting in Korea, Joe Bloggs retired last week.' The second clause bears no relation to the first.
★ If correcting the grammar of a sentence makes it sound stiff or pedantic it is better to re-write it until it sounds right.

Length

Because of narrow newspaper columns, short sentences and paragraphs are preferred in order to avoid an unbroken density of type. This does not mean that all sentences must be short, just that shortness is an advantage to the scanning eye. Short sentences mean generally less complicated sentences with fewer clauses and less punctuation so that meanings can be got over to the reader more quickly, so there is an advantage in comprehension, too.

Short sentences are also faster and more graphic for the telling of hard news stories. Here is an example from the London *Evening Standard*:

POLICE fought a gun battle with an armed gang in an East London square today.

It happened as a team of marksmen from the Central Robbery Squad were keeping watch on four men suspected of plotting an armed raid.

But the gang realized they were trapped and opened fire with shotguns. The police returned the fire.

Three shots were fired by police, but no one was hurt. One of the officers, however, was taken to hospital suffering from shock.

A police motorcycle was damaged during the skirmish.

It happened soon after 9 a.m. in Carlton Square, Stepney. Police later recovered three shotguns from the scene of the shooting.

Four men were this afternoon being questioned.

Note how short words, as well as short sentences and paragraphs, give pace to the action-filled story. Of 117 words, 74 (or 63 per cent) are words of one syllable.

It would be boring, however, to have nothing but short sentences in news stories. It can fall to you, as the subeditor, to decide in wordier texts when longer sentences are justifiable or when – for the reasons just given – a sentence should be split, with a little recasting, into two or more sentences.

Here, from *The Times* (see Figure 42), is a story in which a slower pace is needed and into which longer sentences and paragraphs fit naturally:

A puff of wind and the ingenuity of an Australian inventor may have produced the answer for amateur golfers who dream of shaving a few strokes off their handicaps. Roy Halle, a 55-year-old mechanical engineer from Sydney, claims that the answer to millions of golfing prayers lies in a weighted hat.

Even better news for those familiar with the disappointment of yet another false golfing dawn is that Mr Halle's Inertia Golf Hat contains no hidden catches. There is no need for a new grip, deep breathing or positive swing thoughts: just pop the hat on and, as Mr Halle promises, the strokes will follow.

The idea for the invention came about partly by accident, when Mr Halle was playing golf on a stormy day on a course in New South Wales, one of the finest in Australia.

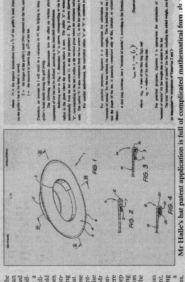

Figure 42 Style and pace in writing: an example from the world of golf see page 97. (Courtesy *The Times*)

'It was blowing a gale and my hat kept flying off,' he said from his home in Sydney yesterday. 'So the next day I attached some solder wire to the brim to weigh it down and keep it on my head. Before I knew it, my game started to get better by quantum leaps and I realized it could only be my hat.'

Flushed with his discovery, Mr Halle, whose handicap has dropped from 14 to 9 in 12 months, took his idea to a patent lawyer. Six months ago, after carrying out detailed research, he founded the Stability Golf Company and started selling the hats at A$40 (£15.50) each, etc.

The gentle pace and slow telling is totally acceptable in this type of news story and allows the writer a touch of self-indulgent humour, while keeping to the facts.

Where the pace of a story demands shorter sentences, or where the sentences are just unacceptably long, you should avoid the easy option of splitting a sentence by turning its clauses into sentences beginning with an *And* or a *But*. Recasting will produce a better flow as well as better grammar. It is considered acceptable in newspaper journalism to begin sentences with *And* or *But*, but it should be done sparingly to produce a particular effect of continuity within the context of sentence pauses, rather than as a device to break up long sentences by replacing commas with full stops.

Paragraphs

This is a thorny subject in newspapers. H. W. Fowler (of *Modern English Usage*) was right when he said: 'The paragraph is essentially a unit of thought, not of length; it must be homogeneous in subject matter and sequential in treatment.' But he also said: 'The purpose of a paragraph is to give the reader a rest.' With narrow columns to fill, newspaper editors tend to give more stress to the second function, and paragraphing has come to be used to break up the text into readable nuggets rather than to mark thought and fact sequences.

With more display in modern newspapers has come a reaction against the style of only a few decades ago of columns of unbroken reading matter with few paragraphs. This has become exaggeratedly so in the popular tabloids where it is assumed readers are as allergic to long paragraphs as they are to long words. Taken too far on this premise, paragraphing can finish up identifying with sentences, however short; continuity of thought and fact are abandoned and the text is read in a series of quick jumps. Here, the plethora of indented and broken lines becomes as big a handicap to the scanning eye as solid text was.

The middle way between the desiderata of Fowler and the projection requirements of modern newspapers is to try to relate the visual breaks as closely as possible to breaks in the sense of the text. This is not usually difficult in the economic style of newswriting common to most newspapers, though bad breaks will still occur if excessively long paragraphs are to be avoided.

Worse than breaking a paragraph in mid-thought is connecting two ill-matched thoughts or sentences into one paragraph, or ending a quotation and starting a description or a new quotation in the same paragraph. This can happen during page make-up when the page editor might run two paragraphs together so that a story carried in a number of legs across the page can show a full line at the top of each leg and not a 'widow' or jack-line.

The idea is to give a neat printed effect so that the eye does not turn to the top of a leg on to a broken line. Yet the yoking together of two unsequential paragraphs for this purpose frustrates the intention of the writer and can damage the sense of the text.

As in the examples quoted, the length of paragraphs can be varied to suit the text. Action-based stories can be given pace through short paragraphs as well as short sentences, while more leisurely stories such as accounts of ceremonials, royal occasions, functions etc., or those requiring explanations, can give the descriptive writer the benefit of longer paragraphs for a slower telling.

Punctuation

Many ambiguities and misunderstood sentences are caused by faults in punctuation, particularly in the use of *commas*, either wrongly placed or removed. To say, 'The people who arrived because of the rain were accommodated in tents,' is not the same, for example, as saying, 'The people who arrived, because of the rain, were accommodated in tents.' In the first sentence the arrival of the people was brought about by the rain. 'Because of the rain,' is a defining clause. In the second sentence, 'because of the rain' is incidental. It is therefore called a commenting clause and is bounded by two commas. These commas make all the difference to the meaning.

Take a sentence that might occur in a murder story; 'Jones killed his son because, he said, there was nothing to live for.' Then write it without the commas. Immediately the phrase 'there is nothing to live for' is transferred from Jones to his son. The meaning has totally changed.

Punctuation in newspaper texts is more concerned with clarifying meanings and avoiding ambiguities than in providing natural pauses, although the two purposes can coincide in longer sentences.

The old rule that commas should not precede the conjunctions *and* and *but* is generally worth keeping but the subeditor should be on guard for cases where the sense of a sentence requires a comma. In some cases *but* introduces new information or a new thought and a comma pause can mark this helpfully as in,

'Yes, I think I ought to go, but I must be certain to get permission first.'

A comma is not needed in these sentences: 'It was not only the colour but the texture that turned her against it.' 'He reached the top of the steps and turned to the left.'

Yet here is a case where the meaning hinges on the placing of a comma: 'They gave the prize to Jones, and his wife and the family were delighted.' Without the comma the reader would be at a loss to know whether Jones or Jones and his wife had won the prize.

Commas can be used to give stress to words and adverbial phrases. 'This was, evidently, the truth,' gives more stress to an important adverb than 'This was evidently the truth.' They are also used to separate items in a list, but their use to separate strings of adjectives is becoming less common and is not essential.

> The best attitude towards commas is to use them only if, without them, the meaning is in doubt. This will avoid a tedious excess of them. If a sentence has many commas marking out many clauses it is a potential source of misunderstanding. By splitting it you will help the reader.

If a sentence contains an ambiguity because of the bad use of commas (or for any other reason) that cannot be resolved by reference to the context, for your own good you should refer back to the writer. A guess could land you in trouble.

There is no need of a comma between a house number and a street. Thus: 14 Coronation Street.

Full stop

Its use to indicate abbreviations as in Feb. and the Rev. is generally accepted but not in abbreviations where the first and last letters of the full word appear, as in Cpl, Mr, Dr etc. (For abbreviations see under 'house style.')

A full stop is not used at the end of captions or in headlines (except in rare cases where a long quotation becomes a headline).

Semi-colon

It denotes a pause longer than a comma but not as long as a full stop. In books and in feature writing there is still room for the semi-colon by stylists who know how to use it and have scope for polishing a sentence, but in news writing there is not a lot of call for it. It is sometimes used when a comma or a full stop would have been adequate and its presence can be sign that a sentence is getting too long.

A semi-colon serves a useful purpose in subdividing lists as in '. . . east wing: three bedrooms, two with bathrooms; three dressing rooms, one with balcony; two staircases, one at either end, and a staff rest room . . .'

Colon

This is a necessary but not often used punctuation mark in newspapers. Use it to introduce lists of names, objects, qualities etc., and in front of a quotation or explanation. It is pointless to have a colon followed by a dash for this purpose. Its use in a sentence to indicate a pause longer than a semi-colon but shorter than a full stop is now so rare, even outside newspapers, as to be almost extinct.

Dashes and brackets

Dashes are much overused and misused in newspapers on the assumption that they jolly up the text, and their rise in favour is in contrast to the decline in the amount of punctuation used generally. Here are some actual examples in newspapers of how dashes were employed:

'A bungling bandit robbed a bank – and left his chequebook behind.'

'Across the country heavy rain washed out the end of the Bank Holiday – and downpours were blamed for a series of crashes. Twenty-nine day-trippers were hurt – one seriously – when their coach hit a truck in Leicestershire.'

'When you crash-diet, your body reacts as it would do in an emergency – it burns muscle for energy and starts storing fat for long-term energy use. In this way, a person can lose almost half a stone in one week – but it's the wrong sort of weight you are losing.'

'Three more were arrested at Blackpool – one of the seaside towns named in the IRA 'hit list'. The new arrests – they bring the total now detained to 16 – came after a police swoop at a house in James Gray Street, Glasgow – less than a mile from the tenement raided at the weekend.'

The first example shows the dash being used to draw attention to the telling part of the sentence. This is the most justifiable in these quoted. In the second example the three dashes should clearly have been commas.

The third example appears at first sight to have a 28-word parenthesis taking up more than half the paragraph. Not so. Using a colon instead of the first dash would have made it clearer that an explanation was following. This then liberates the second dash in the paragraph to draw attention to the concluding point being made.

The worst misuse of dashes appears in the fourth example. Here the punctuation in two consecutive sentences consists of two full stops, a set of inverted commas, one comma and four dashes. The result is almost unreadable. The first dash should have been a comma. The second pair encloses an unnecessary parenthesis. The words could have read '. . . arrests, which bring the total now detained to 16, came . . .' without taking up any more words. The final dash in this sentence comes so quickly that the reader is in doubt as to which dash ends the parenthesis. Here a comma would have been sufficient, although of the four dashes used it is the one most justified by the sense.

Using dashes for commas is not only grammatically wrong, it is confusing to the eye, space-taking and it devalues the dash as a significant text mark. It has resulted in the use of dashes being banned by some editors.

You can reasonably use dashes to enclose a parenthesis, though they are more space-taking than brackets. Grammarians are divided as to whether dashes or brackets signify the greater interruption. Whichever method is used, the words contained in the parentheses should be a comment or fact outside the flow of the sentence, but which the reader needs in order to digest its full import. Office style should insist that you stick consistently either to dashes or brackets for parentheses (some newspapers, in fact, shy off brackets, although they are shorter). In any case it is best to use parentheses sparingly. They impede the flow of the text and often indicate that writers have not got their thoughts properly together.

Ellipsis

This much misused punctuation mark is supposed to show that letters or words are missing. Missing letters: 'According to the gamekeeper the man shouted,' You f. . . pig,' and vanished.' Missing words: 'There could have been a different ending had Helen only . . . but that is another story.'

It might be deduced from these examples that there is little use for ellipses in newspapers, yet they have become as pervasive as dashes. Here are some that appeared:

'A pony runs free through a meadow...dramatically reprieved from death at the eleventh hour.'

'"Oh Gawd . . ." said Geldof when I cornered him.'

The first example seems to show an ellipsis being used in place of a dash to point a sentence since there are clearly neither letters nor words missing. The second seems to be in place of an exclamation mark.

Some newspapers even use ellipses to enclose a parenthesis instead of dashes or brackets. There are four points to be made here:

1 It is inconsistent to use a dash *and* an ellipsis to point sentences in different parts of the same newspaper.
2 An ellipsis is not suitable for this purpose in any case since it is supposed to denote missing letters or words.
3 Ellipses print badly on long print runs and sometimes the dots disappear from the page leaving mysterious blanks.
4 An ellipsis is the most space-taking of all punctuation marks and should be avoided for this reason unless needed for its correct purpose.

Exclamation mark

Sometimes called a screamer, the exclamation mark used to be a favourite of tabloid headline hacks and blurb writers who treated it as the magic cypher readers wouldn't be able to resist. Overuse has debased it. A recent edition of *The Sun* had only two headline screamers and the *Daily Mail* on the same day none.

There is a simple rule about an exclamation mark which should save a lot of trouble: it should be used only after an exclamation. It is unlikely that a phrase more than four or five words long could qualify as an exclamation by reason of the simple mechanics of delivery. Generally it is couched as warning, a demand, a brief instruction or an ejaculation.

Apostrophe

These should be used *before the s* in singular possessives and *after the s* in plural possessives ending in s:

boy's   boys'

A common mistake is to fail to add an *s* after the apostrophe in proper noun possessives of names ending in *s*:

James's   Peebles's
Francis's   Lagos's

Note that the plural form of James and Jones and similar proper names adds *es* as in Jameses and Joneses.

Some well-known place names containing possessives drop the apostrophe, for example St Albans and Earls Court. A gazetteer should be consulted for these.

The apostrophe's original purpose of denoting missing letters is shown in use in don't, won't, can't and it's (it is). In the case of possessive pronouns it has fallen out of use in his, hers, yours, theirs and ours, but is retained in one's.

There is no justification for using an apostrophe in plurals such as MP's, all the three's, or in expressions such as ten years' imprisonment or three weeks' leave, which are best regarded as adjectival phrases. If there is doubt as to whether an apostrophe is needed, be guided by the sense. If the meaning is intact without it, leave it out.

Quotation marks

Inverted commas enclosing quotations can be single or double according to style. Most newspapers use double, although allowing single in headlines. The usual style in text is to have double inverted commas for main quotes, single ones for quotes within quotes, and double again for quotes within quotes within quotes (an extremity to avoid).

Check quotation marks carefully in copy to see that statements are properly attributed and so the reader knows where a quotation begins and ends. This is especially important in quotes within quotes where sloppy editing can leave bugs. Use a colon to introduce main quotations. For short ones in the run of a sentence or paragraph a comma is sufficient at the beginning and end. For example: The constable said he heard a voice say, 'Come quickly,' as he walked past the building.

Question mark

A fault to look for is a misplaced question mark in a sentence containing a quoted passage. If the quotation itself is a question, the question mark must come inside the closing inverted commas. If the question lies in the main sentence, then the question mark must come outside the inverted commas as in: 'Do you think it wrong to say, "No children will be admitted"?' The correct position can make a difference to the sense.

Hyphens

This maligned punctuation mark should be used sparingly but is sometimes crucial to the sense. In line with the move towards less punctuation newspapers have discarded it in familiar compounded words such as lowline, overuse, boyfriend, checklist, wartime, gasfilled, nosebag and handbag, but have kept it for co-operative, co-pilot, co-ordinate, ill-used and other words where its absence might confuse.

Use hyphens:

★ To avoid ambiguity in some adjectival phrases, as between 'a model-manufacturing technique' and 'a model manufacturing technique', and 'a lost-business file' and 'a lost business file.'
★ To indicate a compounded adjective as in 'an up-to-date-method' or 'an away-from-it-all holiday,' but not in 'the method was up to date.'
★ To distinguish different meanings of words as in re-formed and reformed, and re-creation and recreation.

Hyphens, as with other punctuation marks, are discouraged in headlines to preserve visual neatness, but have an important use in typesetting systems to break words at the end of lines when justifying setting widths. It is not typographical style (or easy to read) to break a word in mid-syllable to justify a line, or to break proper nouns if avoidable.

6 WORD TRAPS

Your subs' table has a well-used English dictionary and a gazetteer of place names because of the need to get words and locations right. Only the foolhardy, however splendid their vocabulary, would do without a dictionary since it gives not only spellings but also meanings. It should be the most up to date containing the very latest shifts and nuances in meaning or, better still, there should be two dictionaries in order to compare definitions even though your computer has a spell-check. The gazetteer, provided it has the latest boundary changes, is the ultimate arbiter where there is doubt or argument over geography. Armed with these authorities you are ready to deal with the words.

The right word

The demands on space, especially in daily papers, mean that there is no room in news stories for a long word where a shorter one can do the job as well. Ten long words excised in a story three column inches long can make room for an extra sentence, which might allow you to bring in another useful fact (see headline words in Chapter 8).

Yet where you substitute words take care to ensure the writer's meaning has not been changed. The right word is the one that is likely to be instantly known to the reader and that makes the writer's meaning clear beyond all doubt while at the same time being no longer than it has to be. A general guide is that foreign words should be avoided where there is an adequate English equivalent. It will be found that English words of Anglo-Saxon origin such as house, bite, grip, flight, bold, sharp, bright and evil are shorter than their imported equivalent. Excise words that have more than one meaning with the same spelling, along with abstruse or academic words, circumlocutions and officialese of all types.

Technical words

Finance, computers, space, weaponry, sociology – these are just some of the areas of science and commerce that have developed their own vocabularies. Many words from these areas that are accepted in specialist publications would mean little to the general newspaper reader.

Technical words should be introduced sparingly on the news pages and only in contexts where their meanings are clear. Yet in each of the special areas just listed, and in other similar ones, there are words that have begun infiltrating the general vocabulary to win growing acceptance among readers. The space programme has provided lift-off, splashdown and hardware (a new use for an old word now meaning the machines and equipment). Economics has provided upturn, downturn and throughput; industry, blueprint, bottleneck and spin-off; the Forces bombshell, blockbuster and broadside. The examples could be multiplied: image, model, reading, programme, strategy, ceiling and target have all taken on new meanings through their use in technical fields.

Should such new words and new uses for old words be accepted? Certainly, if the context makes their use clear and they extend the meaning of the text for the reader better than any other word. Bottleneck, blueprint, blockbuster and spin-off, for instance, are colourful, metaphorical and almost 'visual' words that project an immediate mental image; but guard against applying them to situations where they are not justified. Is a plan really detailed and precise enough to be called a blueprint? Is a new book or film really a blockbuster in the effect it will have on the public; are such words becoming stereotypes to be reached for from the shelf out of laziness? Are they in danger of and sinking into clichés?

Beware also of using too many at once. A piece of writing peppered with downturns, upturns, spin-offs, lift-offs and 'go' situations has descended into jargon.

Foreign words

There is little point in using foreign words that have obvious English equivalents such as: rendezvous (arranged meeting), carte blanche (blank cheque, free hand), melee (mix-up, skirmish), cul-de-sac (blind alley, close), ad infinitum (indefinitely) and per annum (yearly). The following words of foreign origin are more generally acceptable on the ground that they are not easy to substitute:

ad lib	cortège	fiancé
aide	coupé	fiancée
aperitif	crime passionel	negligée
attaché	debut	nuance
blasé	de facto	premiere
bourgeois	de jure	protegé
brochure	elite	regime
carafe	entrée	repertoire
cliché	exposé	status quo
clientele	facade	sub judice
corsage	fait accompli	venue

Circumlocutions

Journalists with any experience are not given to using long-winded phrases. Many circumlocutions (strictly bundles of words) that grammars warn against are speech props such as 'as I stand here before you today' or 'in this day and age' or 'to all intents and purposes', or are examples of officialese. A subeditor, while ever vigilant, would not normally expect to encounter such phrases in written copy, although some might enter via quotations, particularly from tape-recorded material. Some quaintness of phrase is reasonable in quoted speech to preserve the flavour of the speaker's words, but take out the really space-wasting ones. Their loss will not damage the meaning.

Nevertheless, because of their lulling familiarity, some circumlocutions can tempt even subeditors into a trap. Here are some examples, with the recommended usage on the right:

adjacent to	*near*
prior to	*before*
as yet	*yet*
as a result of	*because*
in consequence of	*because*
currently	*now*
at this moment	*now, today*
as to whether	*whether*
he is a man who	*he*
in order to	*to*
tighten up	*tighten*
fill up	*fill*
in the first instance	*first*
owing to the fact that	*because*
sound out	*sound*
check out	*check*
rest up	*rest*
try out	*try*
start up	*start*
meet up with	*meet*
meet with	*meet*
consult with	*consult*
inside of	*inside*
he himself	*he*
personally, I	*I*
all of	*all*
end result	*end* or *result*
at the back of	*behind*
in front of	*before*
at the side of	*beside*
join together	*join*
in terms of	*as*
acid test	*test*

each and every	*each*
extra special	*special*
face up to	*face*
horns of a dilemma	*dilemma*
out and about	*out* or *about*
true facts	*facts*
absolute truth, lies etc.	*truth*, *lies*, *etc*.

Synonyms

To avoid long words or repetition of words within a sentence or paragraph, or when seeking words for a headline with a limited type count, the subeditor searches for the alternative or shorter word that means the same. Beware here of the word that means *almost* the same but not quite. The main danger of this lies in headline writing (see Chapter 8) but meanings are at risk in the text too.

To say that a man *claimed* or that he *asserted* is not the same as saying he *said*. A change of verb for the way in which things are said can give undesirable colour or emotion to a speaker's words. To call a discussion or an exchange of words a *row* invests it with a suggestion of violence. An *alibi* is not the same as an *excuse*.

Study not only the spelling and number of letters in the synonym you choose but its precise meaning.

Clichés

The term cliché is given to a wide range of hackneyed expressions, over-used phrases, tired adjectives, worn-out metaphors and current vogue words. Any word or combination of words if used excessively, is in danger of becoming a cliché.

Under this general umbrella are a lot of words and phrases that are unlikely come your way since they remain in the limbo of their own environment. They are part of the jargon of their field and consist of what, by newspaper standards, are tedious circumlocutions. Commerce has its own special ones: 'in this connection'. 'for your information', 'it is considered that', 'at the end of the day' and 'somewhere down the line.' Everyday conversation has its own matching verbal props: 'as I was saying,' 'if you see what I mean,' 'I mean to say,' and so on.

The danger of contamination from these sources is instilled into young journalists at the start. What is sometimes not instilled is the danger from journalism's own shifting world of clichés. Keith Waterhouse, in his book *Daily Mirror Style*, pointed out the changing fashion in newspaper clichés, some of them drawn from popular lore, others entirely invented by subeditors.

In the 1950s and 1960s the favourites (some still with us) were:

burning issue	dropped a clanger
cheer to the echo	and that's official
clutches of the law	the absolute gen
crying need	speculation was rife
fast and loose	monotonous regularity
red letter day	last but not least
just like the blitz	out and about

By the 1980s and 1990s a new raciness had begun to imbue clichés:

alive and well and	pinta
Billy Bunters	cuppa
fashion stakes	taken to the cleaners
knickers in a twist	fairytale wedding
purr-fect (of cats)	sweet smell of success
clown prince	the end of the road
writing on the wall	sir (of teachers)
love child, nest etc.	wait for it!
don't all rush!	to zero in
tears of joy	the name of the game
using your loaf	what it's all about

Commentators have good chortle when they point these out in writing about press style, yet there is, in my view, a case to be made out for the cliché in certain controlled circumstances. A journalist writing for a popular readership can use the newspaper cliché, like its relation the proverb, as a way of addressing the reader in familiar terms, provided:

1 It is not wastefully wordy.
2 It does not gloss or misrepresent the facts.
3 It is not used too frequently.

To refer to Billy Bunters in a piece about overweight schoolboys, or to a love child for a baby born out of wedlock, or to knickers in a twist in a funny story about charwomen, can strike a rapport with the readers of a popular daily where words like obese, bastard and muddle-headed might fail.

The term fairytale wedding, provided it does not exaggerate the nuptial splendour, conjures up an instant picture to the reader which any other two words would find it hard to equal. 'The sweet smell of success' and 'the writing on the wall' can sum up particular human situations evocatively, provided they also sum up what is in the text.

It falls to you, the sub, to decide when a cliché is justified. In fact, there are clichés and clichés. It is the more specifically subeditors' gimmicks such as 'Don't all rush' or 'Wait for it', purr-fect (in cat stories), pinta for milk and cuppa for tea that become most tedious by repetition.

> The danger with cliché words and phrases in unthinking hands is that they can blur the facts of a situation by over-simplifying things for the reader, turning stories into stereotypes. They should be used only when they are apt within in the context of the story and when they can make a point to the reader better than any other word or combination of words. In short, the odd cliché or two is acceptable provided it earns its keep.

In dealing with writers' favourite metaphors, beware of mixed ones, as in 'She was an angel of mercy pouring oil on troubled waters,' or 'He preferred to paddle his own canoe and cock a snook at authority.'

Over-used adjectives are particularly objectionable in a language as rich as English. Stunning, staggering, sexy, super, sizzling, terrific, luscious and amazing should be consigned unmourned to the waste bin along with superstar, megastar, zap! and phew!

Phew!

Vogue words

Writers on the use of English generally devote some space to what they scornfully call vogue words. These are words or new uses for words which have taken the fancy of speakers and writers and are being used a lot. It is difficult to generalize about them. Some, like *parameters* and *arguably* have a lulling polysyllabic charm for speakers with academic pretensions. Others, like *clinical, interface* and *syndrome* have a scientific ring about them which makes the speaker or user feel up to date. Some are useful and new ways of saying things without the need for lots of words, and appeal to the busy. Some seem to have no justification at all.

What should you do when encountering such words? The best advice is to accept them and use them where they help clarify a meaning and communicate a point of view to the reader, but (unless they are claimed as sacrosanct by a prestigious by-liner) do not allow them where a simpler or more direct, or more accurate, word would be better.

You should look for the nuances of meaning that new words bring, accepting them as a broadening of the language rather than a restricting of it. You should be certain, however, about what they mean. If there is any doubt or ambiguity about their use, leave them alone until the grammarians have sorted them out. And pounce on them if the context shows they have been wrongly used.

Here are some examples of current vogue words, one or two of which will be found usefully deployed in the text of this book. They should be treated on their merits. Some could be the Queen's English of tomorrow.

Accord Agreement. Began popular life as a headline variant. Not much justification for it in the text.

Aggravate Has subtly added to its meaning to annoy or cause trouble as well as to make worse. The usage dates back to its vogue in the abbreviated form *aggro* during the Teddy boy period in the 1950s and 1960s – hard to reverse a trend like this; best left to quoted speech.

Ambience Once an encompassing circle or sphere, now an aura or atmosphere. Useful for descriptive writers but not a good word in a hard news story.

Arguably 'Capable of being argued as' but mostly wrongly used as 'more likely to be' or 'almost certain to be.' A perfectly good word that has become astonishingly popular in its wrong use. It deserves a rest.

Axiomatic Used to be used only in scientific proofs; now in vogue as conferring certainty on a statement or conclusion on the lines of 'it goes without saying.' A silly misuse.

Basically A tiresome prop with which to begin an explanation, often used by the less-than-articulate. Very expendable.

Charisma Formerly a unique or God-given grace or talent. More recently a special quality or aura displayed by someone. An overused word, but there is no other that says precisely this.

Chauvinism Exaggerated and bellicose patriotism; now adapted to mean glorification of the sex – i.e. male chauvinism – and seems to have taken root. It is doing no harm used with the word 'male' and describes an attitude that is recognizable.

Clinical Pertaining to the sick bed (as of clinics). Has mysteriously come to mean *coldly* and *detachedly* (as in action). Best avoided.

Concept Used a lot where the word *idea* used to be used. Has pseudo-scientific ring. Use *idea* – it is shorter and is mostly what the writer means.

Contact A useful noun-verb when one is not certain of means or method. Better, if possible, to say *meet, telephone, write* or *call on*.

Criteria Necessary requirements upon which a judgement or decision is based. There seems to be a lot of criteria about these days but the word mostly does a good job.

Dialogue A vogue word from the international political scene. Strictly it is between two people or sides and is wrongly but widely used for general discussions, meetings, talks etc.; could do with being aired less.

Ecology   Has taken over in some quarters from *environment*, meaning the natural world in which we live. It is stretched to mean anything which is natural as opposed to man-made, although originally it meant simply the branch of biology which dealt with the relationship of plants and animals to their surroundings. No stopping this one.

Escalation   Another bastard from the international political and war scene. Developed in the post-war decades as a back formation from *escalator*, a moving staircase. It means to increase or develop by successive stages. The world's trouble spots are keeping it well employed and it has carved a patch for itself.

Fruition   Plans everywhere are coming to fruition, yet the word has nothing to do with fruit or bearing fruit but means the act of enjoyment or pleasurable possession.

Hopefully   It means 'with hope' but is now worked to death meaning 'it is hoped that' or 'I hope so.' Should be given a rest along with its soulmate *arguably*.

Image   Not so much a copy of an original as a special highly glossed version to present to the public ; more a facade than a copy. But everyone who is anyone seems to have one – or to need one.

Interface   A surface separating two portions of matter or space. Became in the 1960s a region or piece of equipment where interaction occurs between two systems. More loosely it has come to mean any form of joining together. Treat with caution.

Line   A particular type of argument or set of explanations – e.g. the Marxist–Leninist line (that was), or whatever line adopted. *Argument* is more descriptive, and preferred, despite being longer. Also, *line* is . . . well . . . discredited.

Maximize   Meaning to work or pursue something to the maximum degree possible or feasible, has come to stay. Although one of the prolific new 'ize' verbs it is pithy and colourful and says it in a word.

Meaningful   A much used invention of recent decades meaning full of or replete with meaning. I can't bring myself to condemn it since it does a job – but beware of overuse. Just a whisker and we'll have *meaningfulness*.

Minimize   Handy – as with *maximize*.

Mix   A useful adman's word meaning the sum total of all the various ingredients. An insinuatingly useful word which has the extreme advantage of brevity.

Normalize   Means to cause to return to normal – akin to *regularize*. These are handy verbs although too many of them on a page can cast a blight.

Ongoing	Very popular for *continuing* or *never-ending*. It has its uses but is often used unnecessarily like a verbal prop.
Parameters	Queen of the vogue words. A scientific expression meaning qualities or factors which has caught on as a synonym for limits or boundaries. There seems little need for it in the context in which it is usually used.
Prestigious	Having or manifesting prestige (it formerly meant practising juggling or cheating). It is now cheerfully bestowed on people, jobs, property, business and sites. If only it were used a little less . . . though it is clear there is a lot of prestige about.
Proliferation	The endless development, formation and spread of things, is a useful word which does a job. One can live with its popularity.
Scenario	A scriptwriter's word which describes something more detailed than just a scene. Is sometimes the right word but is too exotic to stand much use.
Situation	We are surrounded by situations. Every decision, development, spending programme, injection of funds, order and cancellation depends on a situation. There are go situations, no-go situations, stop situations, study situations, new situations, bad situations, ongoing situations – too many situations of every sort. Even situations vacant are commoner than they were. Blame the politicians and the economists for a word that's become a canker.
Spectrum	A pseudo-scientific word for *range*, which is preferable.
Symbiosis	A withdrawn cult word used a lot by those who think they know what it means. Strictly: living or involved together in mutual support. One for newspapers to leave alone.
Syndrome	A set of concurrent things or symptoms, now used for may conditions of the body, mind and imagination. Has become generally accepted, and puts things in a nutshell even if there are more syndromes about than we thought possible.
Thematic	Having, or pertaining, to a theme (of art forms, philosophies, systems, musical movements, instructions etc.). A useful descriptive word that earns its keep.
Thrust	As of an argument or explanation. A nice phallic word much favoured by aware males. Does a job.
To host	Meaning to preside over, or sponsor, an invited gathering (of friends, visiting heads of state, knitting association delegates, etc.). An Americanism that has become acceptable.
Traumatic	It once meant pertaining to, or caused by, injury or shock but is often used instead of *dramatic*. Though it hardly deserves to, it sounds good. It really should suggest an element of shock, however.

Trendy	Used for things that are going to be 'the thing' or, these days, that were recently 'the thing'. A discredited word.
Update	As a verb or noun is a useful technical addition to the general vocabulary. It is brief and precise and no other word seems to mean quite this.

Misused words

A more general danger is a newspaper's misuse of words because of popular misconceptions about them that have stuck and have evaded the writer or subeditor. For instance *chronic*, in the case of illness, means lingering though not necessarily severe. Buildings that catch fire are not *razed to the ground* but simply razed. People are not *exonerated from blame* but *exonerated*; while in spending programmes and budgets *targets* are there to be hit and not exceeded, and *ceilings* are to set limits and not to be smashed.

Here is a list of words commonly misused or misunderstood which subs should look out for in editing text:

Alibi	Latin for elsewhere. To offer an alibi is to explain that one was elsewhere at the time. Not to be used for *excuse* in general.
All right	Spell as two words, not *alright*, except in slang text.
Alternative	Every other. Not to be confused with *alternatively* – offering one of two possibilities.
Among	Used where there are more than two people or things. Not to be confused with *between*, which distinguishes between two people or things.
Anticipate	Should not be used for *expect*. It is not the same.
Appraise	To form a judgement about something. Not to be confused with *apprise*, to inform.
Apprise	See *appraise*.
Avoid	To have nothing to do with. Not be confused with *avert*, to turn away from. You *avert* trouble by *avoiding* its likely cause.
Beg the question	Not to evade a straight answer, but to give an answer based upon an unproved or unacceptable assumption.
Between	See *among*.
Can	Not to be used for *may*. *Can* means able to, *may* means allowed to or permitted to, or has a chance or a possibility of doing. Differentiate between 'you can do it,' and 'you may do it.'
Claimed	Not an accurate substitute for *said, stated* or *declared*. It suggests an element of dispute about what is being said or stated.

Compare to	To liken one thing to another.
Compare with	To note resemblances and differences between two things.
Consensus	Not *concensus*.
Credence	Means belief or trust. *Credibility* is the quality of being believable. *Credulity* is readiness to believe.
Credibility	See *credence*.
Credulity	See *credence*.
Declared	More precise and emphatic than *said*. See *claimed*.
Different	From, not to or than.
Dilemma	A choice between two alternatives. Not to be used in general for difficulty of choice, or for weighing up a situation or problem.
Discomfit	Means to overwhelm, to defeat, to disconcert. Do not confuse with *discomfort*, lacking comfort.
Disinterested	Means not tempered by personal interest. Do not confuse with *uninterested*, without interest in.
Dissociate	Preferable to *disassociate*, not to associate with.
Due to	Should not be used in the place of *because*, as in 'he was delayed due to the weather.' Leave *due to* to phrases including 'the respect due to . . .' etc.
Economic	Was tight, sparing, careful, but now mostly associated with the (country's) economy or political economy.
Economical	Relating to economics.
Farther	Of distance (see *further*).
Fewer than	Of numbers. Do not confuse with *less than*, of quantity.
First	Say *first, second, third*, not *firstly, secondly, thirdly etc.*
Fix	Vague as a verb. Where possible use *arrange, attach, organize, set up*, etc.
Following	Do not use instead of *after* or *as a result of*. It is less precise.
Forensic	Simply means pertaining to words of law – nothing more.
Forgo	To abstain from. Do not confuse with *forego*, to precede.
Forego	See *forgo*.
Forward	Not usually *forwards*. The *s* is mostly dropped from *homeward, backward* and *sideward* but is retained in *towards*.
Further	Of time or degree. See *farther* (of distance).
Hanged	Criminals are *hanged*. Things are *hung*.
Happened	Without warning, as in *occurred*. *Took place* suggests planning.
Historic	Part of history.
Historical	Concerned with historical events or records.
i.e.	From the Latin *id est* (that is) and should be used to introduce a definition; *e.g.*, *exempli gratia* (for the sake of example), should be used to adduce an example.

Imply	To suggest without stating directly. Do not confuse with *infer*, to deduce or draw a conclusion from.
Infer	See *imply*.
Insure	To provide for damages or replacement in the event of loss. Do not confuse with *ensure*, to make certain, to guarantee.
Last	Of more than two things.
Latter	Of two things.
Leading question	Not a question that is difficult to answer, but a question that is so designed that the answer is suggested.
Lend	More correct that to *loan*, which is an obsolete Old English verb that has come back to enjoy a vogue in the US.
Lengthy	*Long* is mostly better (and shorter).
Less than	See *fewer than*.
Leave	Do not misuse for *let*. Say 'let it be.'
Loth, loath	This adjective, meaning unwilling, is correct in both spellings but is best spelt without the *a* to differentiate it from *loathe*, meaning to detest.
Militate	See *mitigate*.
Mitigate	To make less severe or serious. Do not confuse with *militate*, to be directed against or fight against.
Nice	Too vague a word now that it has lost its old meaning of *fine*, *balanced*. Use a more precise adjective.
Practical	Useful in practice.
Practicable	Capable of being carried out.
Practically	Has come to mean *virtually*. Better to use *virtually*, which has only one meaning, or *almost*, which is shorter and simpler.
Protagonist	Means advocate or champion and not necessarily the opposite of *antagonist*.
Refute	Means to prove wrong, not to deny or repudiate.
Resource, recourse, resort	A source of much muddle. *Resource* is a stock or reserve to draw upon. To have *recourse* is to return to or fall back upon (one's *resources*). *Resort*, in this area of meanings, is a place, or thing or person upon which one depends for a solution: 'A royal pardon was his last *resort*.'
Respective	Pertaining to those in question – an adjective of which *respectively* is the adverb. 'The *respective* authors,' but 'the authors were, *respectively*, etc.'
Seasonable	Suitable for the season or time of the year.
Seasonal	Occurring in association with a particular season. 'Hot weather is *seasonable* in the summer' but 'most holiday work is *seasonal*.'
Stated	More fully covered than *said* (as of a statement), not so emphatic as *declared*.
Took place	See *happened*.

Transpire	Became known – not *happened* or *occurred*.
Try	*Try to*, not *try and*.
Under way	Beginning to move. Formerly *under weigh* (anchor).
Unique	Avoid *quite*, *most* or *rather unique*. There can be no degrees of uniqueness.
Verdict	The finding of a jury. The judge gives the decision and sentence.
Whence	'She returned *whence* she came,' not *from whence*.
Wise	Tax-wise, price-wise etc. are mostly and preferably avoided.

House style

In handling text, you need to be familiar with the house style of your newspaper in order to avoid textual inconsistency in spelling, numeration, the use of abbreviations, the Anglicizing of foreign words and in other areas where alternative uses exist. Most newspapers, having opted for particular ways of doing things, guard their house style as zealously as their typographical style and can come down heavily on its neglect. Subs are expected to prevent style faults getting into the paper.

> The justification for sticking rigidly to house style is not that the newspaper's version is necessarily the right one but that spellings, abbreviations and style in numeration are confusing to the reader, untidy and also unprofessional if rendered in different ways on the same page. An imposed consistency is the way out.

You can resolve style problems by adopting recommended uses in such works as Collins's *Authors' and Printers' Dictionary* or Hart's *Rules For Compositors and Readers*. Some newspapers opt for the shorter or more contemporary or more 'English' of any given alternatives, while others go for etymological exactness (with its risk of pedantry) or follow a style because it has always been the style. Whatever the reason, here are some areas where newly trained subs should reach for the house style sheet when in doubt:

Spellings

Inquire/enquire	Authorities who try to prove these words mean different things are nit-picking.

Gaol/jail	The old Norman French legal word is giving way to the more modern *jail*.
Connection/connexion	The new *connection* is ousting the old English form.
Despatch/dispatch	It's commoner with the *i*.
Marquis/marquess	*uis* preferred.
Gipsy/gypsy	Both forms remain popular.
Judgment/judgement	The *e* is losing ground.
Swop/swap	The *a* version is growing in favour.
Transatlantic	The medial cap *A* is seldom used.

The use of *ize* endings in such words as organize and nationalize as against *ise* for merchandise, advertise, etc. (despite the advocacy of the *Oxford English Dictionary* and the *Authors' and Printers' Dictionary*) is losing ground and *ise* is appearing in all cases. The differentiation was never popular in newspapers. It is still used in some publishing houses – and in the text of this book.

American words

The use of American spelling is generally discouraged in English newspapers even in quotes from documents. Subs handling American-originated copy should see that *railroad* is railway, that a car *fender* becomes a bumper, and that *specialty* becomes speciality. Beware the use of the word *subway*. *Color, honor, rigor, glamor etc.* should have their *u* restored, and *defense* should read defence.

Yet *peddler* is often used in place of the English *pedlar* where drug peddling is the subject, and *program* is here to stay in computer contexts.

Foreign names

Wide variation exists in the spelling of foreign names, with Russian composers coming up in particularly bizarre forms. Tchaikovsky can be Chaikovski and Scriabin Skryabin. Peking (or Pekin) has become Beijing, while Hankow can turn up as Quanzhou.

More simply, Capetown and Hongkong can be Cape Town and Hong Kong. Then there are Baghdad (Bagdad), Irak (Irak), Tokyo (Tokio), Tehran (Teheran), Khartum (Khartoum), Bucharest (Bucarest) and Rumania (Romania, Roumania).

Capital letters

In the eighteenth and even nineteenth century capital letters littered writing to denote qualities, word stress, people's titles and specific references to things. Now they are the exception. The Prince or the Duke is used where a specific person has been introduced by name and continues to be referred to, and where the title is part of the name. A capital is not used where the word is simply the rank or appointment, as in judge, chairman, secretary, chief engineer, etc. A country's President takes a capital *P*. Some papers use capitals when they introduce an important official for the first time, as in 'Trevor Griffiths, General Secretary of the National Union of Teachers', thereafter referring to him as Mr Griffiths. The Royal Family is usually capitalized but other uses of the word royal are kept in lower case.

The seasons can be capitalized or lower case according to house style, specific areas like the North, the West Country, etc capitalized but points of the compass usually not. The Government takes a capital *G* but government in general lower case. Left-wing or Right-wing, or simply the Left and the Right, are capitalized to show political meaning.

Capitals used in abbreviations are appearing more without points, as in UK, BBC, EEC, and IBM, but U.S. takes points so that it does not mean *us*. Acronyms (combinations of initials pronounced as words) take no points and are usually given in lower case as in Unesco, Mensa and Nato.

Names

The usual style is 'John Jones, aged 20' but sometimes the *aged* is missed out. Street names are occasionally hyphenated as in 25 Church Street, Norwich, although house numbers are often dropped to save people being pestered. A danger, however, is that there may be two people of the same name in the street. People are referred to after the first mention as Mr, Mrs, Miss or Ms, or in some human interest stories by Christian name. In criminal court cases the style is usually by surname only.

Numbers

Most newspaper style sheets give one to ten in letters and eleven upwards in figures. Fractions can be an exception, $5\frac{1}{2}$ looking better than five-and-a-half. Figures are always used for mathematical formulae and percentages. Sentences should never begin with a number in figures: 'Three hundred years ago, a leading poet . . .' is better (see Chapter 7).

With dates, many style sheets go for the day, month, year order – 23 December, 1998, but some have the month first. Inclusive dates are best rendered 1998–9, 1915–16 rather than changing just the last digit.

With money, amounts are usually rounded down in headlines and intros, £507 becoming £500, and with an *m* used for million in headlines, as in £35m, with £35 million preferred in copy to £35,000,000. Figures are used in text where more precise amounts or numbers are required. In smaller, say, £49.07, but in 49p use the *p*.

Editor's phobias

Every style sheet has them. Few editors will tolerate *kiddie*, *hubby* and *doggy*.

An overused headline word is sometimes put under total interdict. For years the word *sex* was banned in the *News of the World*.

Cyphers

The ampersand & is little used in newspapers despite its brevity. Accents are mostly missed out and the dollar sign $ is not always in the type range. Percentage signs % tend more and more to be written as pc or per cent.

Abbreviations

Most capital letter abbreviations are written without full points, with acronyms in lower case after the initial capital (see above). In the case of common abbreviated titles as in Prof., Mr and Dr, many style sheets leave off the point if the last letter of the word is included. Headline abbreviations carry no points unless the meaning is in doubt without them. Give organizations in full at first mention so that the abbreviation thereafter is understood. In long texts it is useful to repeat the full name, even in a shortened form, to refresh the reader's memory.

With ranks there is wide divergence, as in Lieut-Cdr (Lt-Cdr), Flt-Lieut (F/Lt), Lieut-Col (Lt-Col), Con. (PC), Corpl (Cpl), etc. You need to study the house style sheet. Check the use of county abbreviations such as Beds., Berks., Bucks, Oxon. and Salop, and also abbreviations for the months such as Aug. Sept. and Nov.

Weights and measurements, where giving precise amounts, are usually abbreviated thus: 10 kg, 4 lb, 6 fl oz and are not pluralized with a final *s* or given a full point. If written out in full, as in five kilograms, the normal plural *s* applies.

> Excessive use of a variety of abbreviations in the text is tiresome to the reader and should be avoided. The space saved by them is often more than counterbalanced by the loss in clarity.

Writers should never use time-saving abbreviations such as aftn (afternoon), btwn (between), yesty (yesterday), mng (morning) or chmn (chairman) in keyboarding in case the subs miss them and they turn up like that in the paper.

Typographical style

It is necessary to be consistent in the text in the rendering of book and film titles, quoted verse, the names of newspapers and popular songs, and the style and title of MPs, church dignitaries, and so on. Some newspapers give all titles of songs, books and newspapers in italic. Others give them with initial caps. Song titles are sometimes quoted. Check the use of quoted line-set verse with the type style card. MPs can be given as John Jones (Con, Glamorgan South) in a political report, but as John Jones, Conservative MP for Glamorgan South in other contexts. Check style and titles of church dignitaries in reference works if they are not given in the style sheet.

Each newspaper has its regular style for setting tabulated work such as television programmes, racing programmes and election results, which should be followed. Look out for simple formatted setting codes in these areas. Some newspapers use page-ready setting input from agencies for this sort of material.

Trade names

Many firms take umbrage if the names of their products are used as generic names without capital letters. Angry complaints received on this subject have resulted in all newspaper offices having lists of trade names with their general equivalents either as part of house style or listed separately. These have to be learned. Some well-known examples include:

Hoover	vacuum cleaner
Kleenex	paper tissues
Fibreglass	glass fibre
Thermos flask	vacuum flask
Biro	ball-point pen
Elastoplast	tape dressing
Oxo	beef or chicken cubes
Nylon/Terylene	artificial (man-made) fibre
Martini	vermouth

Journalese

How do you recognize journalese? By its words. It is a debasement of the language caused by the stereotyped short words and short-cut phraseology used in headline writing infiltrating the text.

Words that are tolerable in headlines because of the difficulties of character count and the need for visual balance should be examined closely before they are used in the text. Here the need is for precision if meaning is to be conveyed. The explanation and justification of facts, upon which the headline leans, cannot be put at risk by ambiguous jargon words, however well these might have served their purpose in drawing the story to the reader's attention.

While the short word 'boss', for example, might get you out of a difficulty in a headline, it is a noun that must be clarified and taken a stage further in the text as manager, superviser, general secretary, chairman, or what-ever. 'Boss' is simply verbal shorthand.

The words 'rap' or 'row' in a headline might suggest criticism or disagreement but they do not have the precision the text requires if the story is to mean anything to the reader. To be 'axed' or 'probed' in a headline might put across the general idea of what happened (if there is no time to write a better heading) but the text has to back up these words with clearer, more precise ones.

Words of this sort are used in headlines not just because they are short but because they can fit a variety of stories in which more specific descriptions are too long to be accommodated, and sometimes because there is little time to the page deadline. It is this lack of precision (apart from the fact that they have become headline jargon) which limits their usefulness in the text. The fault with journalese, in fact, is not just its mind-lulling jargon but its vagueness.

We have noted elsewhere that words used in news language are rooted in everyday speech, even though the grammatical structure and thought and fact sequence are not. As a useful test of a piece of edited news try mouthing it silently to judge by its 'sound' if the words used are real demotic words or just chunks of your newspaper's home-produced headline jargon..

Would a neighbour say to you, 'I hear cops have quizzed Jones following a cash probe at the superstore he's just quit,' and would you reply,

'Yes, and I hear he's quit home in a night drama after a big rap from his wife'?

A final word for subs on this depressing subject: Winkle out journalese if it appears in any reporter's copy – and do not be guilty of it yourself.

7

WRITING HEADLINES

Writing a headline is one of the more difficult of subediting jobs. It takes a high concentration on the materials of the story – the facts and supporting quotations – to render them quickly into a few short words that will tempt the reader to read on, even though the reporter may have encapsulated the main points.

Some subeditors have a natural flair for it at first reading of the copy, but headline writing comes mostly with painstaking practice. The best ones are not necessarily quick off-the-top-of-the-head ideas; they can be the result of patient juggling with words on a copy pad after subbing on the screen is completed. Here, the morning paper routine, particularly on a well-staffed national paper, with its longer time factor, is an advantage. There might be time for discussion in the case of a big story. Many a good headline is a 'committee job' in which improvements have been worked on the ideas of others. There is thus every reason why a national paper should show polish in its headlines compared with a town evening with its tight edition deadlining.

Yet there is no room for sloppy, ineffective headline writing on any newspaper if it wants to be taken seriously and get the reader's attention.

It is useful at this point if we have a definition. We can say that the headline has two main functions:

1 It draws the attention of the reader to the contents of the story.
2 It forms part of the visual pattern of the page.

The first function has to do with words. The sub is the synthesizer, filtering the material so that its essence is refined into a simple 'read me' message. This must be achieved without doing damage to the facts by over-simplification or 'bending.' In other words, under the pressure to achieve a good headline, the sub must guard against distortion.

Here, the sub comes up against the second function of the headline. For the technique of modern newspaper design demands that some sort of type pattern be imposed on newspaper pages. On news pages, stories are allotted a size of headline type and width of setting that suits the story's relationship to the page as a whole. This limitation nominates the maximum number of letters or characters to each line. In writing a headline, the sub (except where the layout can be changed) has to accommodate the words it contains to the character count allowed by the type.

The words

To attract the eye a good headline must have *clarity* and *impact*. Clarity means that the wording conveys to the reader what the sub intends without confusion or ambiguity. Impact means that the effect of the words is strong enough to persuade the reader to read on.

It will be seen in the pages that follow that headline language, in its simplicity and immediacy, is close to everyday language – the demotic spoken tongue of a country with its familiar, generally short words. Yet in its construction a headline is nothing like ordinary speech, for to say what has to be said it has to be as deliberately composed as a metrical poem. It is language pared down to the bone, producing the maximum effect from the minimum of words, which words, in addition, must submit to a typographical discipline quite alien to ordinary speech. Every word has to be carefully weighed and measured, key words located and not left out, legality and factual accuracy considered, and a visual effect achieved with the result.

Subject

Since it is, in effect, a condensed sentence, the headline has to have a subject and a verb in the right place. The subject is what the headline is about. THE QUEEN ABDICATES would be a blockbuster of both subject and verb at work. 300 DIE IN JUMBO JET CRASH shows that it is the deaths of 300 people rather than the crash itself that is the subject. The subject comes first in an effective news headline. It is your summation of the material of the story. It is what the story is about.

While, in the text, an implied subject can sound right in a context that makes clear what it is, a subjectless headline should be avoided. I read in my local paper the headline BLAMED DRINK, and in an American paper STEALS PISTOL TO END LIFE. This is headline space badly used. There are better and clearer and more compelling ways of attracting the reader's attention than by this verbal shorthand.

Verb

The *active voice* is stronger and uses fewer words than the *passive voice*. STORM POUNDS BEACHES has more pace and immediacy than BEACHES ARE POUNDED BY STORM. BOY MEETS GIRL is better than GIRL IS MET BY BOY. But beware of distorting the headline in trying to avoid the passive voice. ROCK STAR KILLED IN SKI FALL is better than the more active ROCK FALL KILLS SKI STAR because it has the subject in the right place. A headline that relegates the subject to the last two words is a weak headline.

Yet the verb must be used as soon as possible. It is the verb that energizes the headline and gives it pace, compared to which an adjective, for instance, has a modest role.

Special words

Whatever the words, you should go for plain English. Multi-syllabic or unusual words are a put-off to the reader except in newspapers in a specialist field. They rob the wording of pace as well as impact. At the same time the sub should not try to create a special headline language by using words that only exist in terms of their headline use. (See Journalese, pages 123–4 and Alternative words, pages 152–8.)

Omission of words

A number of ploys are used to give a headline pace while containing its message within a given type and measure. Some of these, if not used carefully, can endanger the meaning.

For example, the auxiliary verbs *to be* and *to have*, can be omitted where they are implied beyond all doubt in the wording. SIEGE GUNMAN GIVEN LAST WARNING sounds right without the *is* after gunman. But JOBS PLAN HOPE FOR WORKLESS should include either *is* or *gives* before 'hope' to avoid ambiguity. 'Plan' could strike the reader first as a verb and not a noun. SICK PAY UP is tantalizingly ambiguous without the *is*.

LAB FIRES PROBE BY CID boggles the eye until we learn from the text that it means LAB FIRES *are* PROBED BY CID.

ABUSES INQUIRY IN S. AFRICA tempts us into thinking there is an implied subject with *abuses* as its verb. But *abuses*, it turns out, is a noun-adjective describing 'inquiry'. The auxiliary *is* after 'Africa' would have made this clear.

Nouns and adjectives

Nouns as adjectives, sometimes compounded, are a useful short cut in identifying the subject without using too many words. *Abuses inquiry* in the headline above, is shorter than *inquiry into abuses*, but a headline like FAN CLUB FIGHT DRAMA is baffling until we realize that it is a label headline and that *fight* is not the verb we are looking for but part of the subject and that *fan club* is two nouns compounded into a noun-adjective.

Likewise in JUMBO CHECKS ORDER we discover on reading the story (if we are tempted to read it by such a muddle of words) that *jumbo* is a noun-adjective (jumbo jet) and not the subject, and that *checks* is a noun and not the verb, and that the headline is a verbless label telling us that a check on jumbo jets has been ordered.

These faults show the ambiguity and obscurity that lurk when nouns are used as adjectives in headlines that are not activated by a verb. In all the examples quoted above (which really did appear in newspapers) the faults might have been detected had the sub mouthed the words half aloud. A good headline should sound good as well as reading right.

Here is a headline in which the subject has a compounded adjective made up of three nouns and a verbal phrase (not a recommended idea) but which is saved by an active verb following the subject, as it correctly should be:

JET CRASH GIRL'S 'WAKE UP' PLEA SAVED MOTHER

Let us look at one more actual example of nouns used as adjectives.

MYSTERY MAN FACES 'DEAD PRIEST' CHARGE shows an adjective-noun phrase being used as an adjective to describe the criminal charge in a headline in which the subeditor is trying, for legal reasons, to avoid using the word *murder*. The headline, though not ideal, is acceptable and produces a wording that makes the story clear. It also tempts us to read on to find out more.

Symbols

A metaphor or phrase that can sum up a complicated situation and signal it clearly to the reader is a subeditor's dream. It not only eases the job of containing the message in the type but can give a colourful headline.

PRINCE WOOLLIE COMES HOME, from *The Sun*, not only symbolizes a picture of Prince William swathed in woollies on a cold Spring day but is a clever play on the name. In a different market, the *Financial Times* is not averse to using metaphor and literary allusion to create a symbol headline in an unlikely setting as in:

DANISH ENGINEERS TAKE A TILT AT WINDMILL MARKET

Sport is a great area for metaphor, pun and allusion. Even *The Times* pitches in with BLACKBURN REVEL IN ROVER'S RETURN, using a popular TV 'soap' to point a football team's success. The *Birmingham Evening Mail* goes back to Laurel and Hardy for ANOTHER FINE MESS, STANLEY, while *The Sun*, a master in this field, put PAT'S JAZZ BANNED on a story about a jockey called Pat and an unlucky horse called Jazz.

The more everyday use of love nest, love pact, sex-bomb, whizz-kid. brain drain and latchkey babes as situation symbols show the extent to which headline imagery has filtered into the language. The danger at this level is that these identity flags will lose their potency through overuse.

Word accuracy

Since a headline gives a story its prominence in the page, you should be careful, as we have said, not to damage the accuracy of the facts in the search for a compelling wording. Emotive words such as hysterical, failed, regretful, ruthless, resentful, glib and cruel should be used in court cases only with care, and if they are supported by evidence given in court or in a magistrate's or judge's summing up. Verbs such as critical, attacked, condemned and scorned must be borne out in the text by attributed quotations. People's words must not be pushed beyond their meaning to stand up a headline.

Beware of devaluing words such as slashed, slammed, lashed, smashed, rushed, raced, grabbed, slaughtered and demolished by using them to pep up headlines when the material of the story does not match up. In one issue of a national tabloid paper the following headlines appeared: TELFER LASHES LIONS, POLE-AXE FOR POOR BUSTER, INTIKHAB BLASTS A WARNING, JACK FLATTENS SUSSEX CRICKET, WILLIS CALLS FOR KILLER TOUCH and SOBBING SUE SMASHED. Violence on the sports pages seems to be trying to outdo violence on the field.

Headline punctuation

A headline is a condensed sentence so as well as needing a subject and a verb it needs punctuation. A quick examination of any headline, however, will show that commas, dashes, question marks and brackets look untidy in big type. While keeping in essential punctuation, it is a good idea to write headlines that need little or none. The following guidance is offered:

Full points are not used except in wordy free-style headlines (mostly on features pages) which have a sentence break such as:

ON YOUR BIKES
YOU LAZY LOT.
THAT'S THE
MESSAGE FROM
THE MINISTER

A *colon* is a useful break in a two-idea headline:

JAIL CRISIS
LOOMS: STAFF
QUIT TALKS

But even the colon is being phased out on many papers. Instead, a second headline idea, if wanted, is given a deck on its own. A colon is still useful, however, in a headline like this:

The ultimate test
of a marketing
man: Sell Libya

Or in place of a dash as an acknowledgement:

WE'RE A NATION AT LAST:
MANDELA IN LONDON TODAY

The *comma* is sometimes necessary but avoid it if possible. It can be used to denote a missing *is* as in INVESTMENT BOOM IN COINS, STAMPS or a *that's* as in ABSOLUTELY ELEGANT, JOANNA'S NEW ROLE. It is not necessary before an attribution as in VICAR INSULTED ME SAYS VERGER. If you need a comma to avoid ambiguity, it is better to reword the headline.

Avoid *question marks* if possible. A headline should not be asking the reader a question. An exception would be in a dialogue headline such as:

A BULLY? NOT ME SAYS WIFE

Exclamation marks (or screamers) should be restricted to exclamatory phrases such Cheers! or Howzat! or Get out! Using one is pointless in the following actual tabloid paper headline:

£85,000 JET-SET CAR IS A LOCK-OUT!

A seven-word exclamation that also labours under figures, a pound sign and two hyphens. Happily there seem to be fewer of them in headlines these days.

Quotation marks are best used single. Apart from enclosing actual quotes they are useful to put round words to indicate doubt or an unconfirmed assertion as in: 'DEATH-TRAP' CAR BLAMED FOR CRASH or to show up a fact to be false as in 'DEAD MAN' TURNS UP AT WEDDING. Single quotes also get over a problem where two or more words are compounded into an adjectival noun as in 'SHARE A JOB' SCHEME TO BE SCRAPPED. Where actual quotes are used in a headline, either the name should be included or a *tag-line* should be used as attribution.

Ellipses are strictly dots denoting missing letters or words, but they are used in newspaper headlines for a variety of purposes from replacing a colon to filling out short lines. They are visually ugly, especially when accompanied by an exclamation mark as in the actual example in Figure 43 on this page.

They should not be necessary.

Headline abbreviations

Abbreviations, especially those formed from initial capitals, make a headline hard to read and can make it obscure to some readers. A number will be uncertain what EEC, EU, WEU and CJD mean, to say nothing of the ever-changing abbreviated forms of trade unions. BBC and TUC pass muster but the Electrical, Electronic, Telecommunication and Plumbing Union, the Amalgamated Union of Engineering Workers and even the National Union of Mineworkers are better referred to in headlines as the electricians, the engineers and the miners rather than by initials. The full name can be explained in the text.

Figure 43 Punctuation that a headline can do without: one that appeared

Acronyms such as Unesco and Nato (where lower case letters are used) are more memorable and easier on the eye but are still best kept out of headlines. Even the better known abbreviated forms of organizations should be avoided, or at least rationed to one to a page for the sake of eye comfort. Dr, Mr, Coun., Capt., the Rev. and Prof. are often inescapable but are more acceptable. Whether they are followed by a full point is a matter for house style (see Chapter 5).

The most unattractive abbreviations are those invented by headline writers themselves for use in a tight spot, such as 'tec, 'groom, 'quake and 'copter. It would be a blessing if all papers followed the practice of the enlightened few which ban such monstrosities.

Numbers

Multiple noughts look ugly in headlines, apart from being eye-boggling to some, and where the figures are simple it is better to say 'ten thousand', or 'three thousand' or 'two million'. With sterling amounts use £10,000 or £3,000, although with millions the abbreviation *m* can be used as in £2m. This looks better in caps in a caps headline. Odd figures are usually rounded down for the sake of tidiness, 5943, for instance, becoming 5900 and 507 becoming 500.

Figures are narrower than letters in a type range and in Old Style the 3, 5 and 7 hang below the x-height of the type, a point to watch in automatic line spacing when using capitals.

Content

Anything that is news to the reader is material for the headline. Yet there are certain points that should be kept in mind.

Taste

It should go without saying that you should not identify people by race, creed or colour unless their race, creed or colour is the subject matter. Words used to describe people should be relevant to the text. If a mother of four is evicted from her house, the size of the family is worth using in the headline. If a father of four children is made editor of a newspaper the size of his family is of no importance.

People can be touchy if certain things about them appear in a headline with no apparent justification. To say someone appointed as a magistrate was expelled from school at 15 could be regarded as bad taste, if not actually damaging. If a well-known actor is homosexual it is no concern of a reviewer or headline writer. It becomes of concern to the newspaper only if the actor is involved in court proceedings in which homosexuality is an issue.

Vital facts

It follows from the above that relevance is important in considering a fact for a headline. Not everything that a reporter gathers is vital to the story. Take ages. Lists of offenders due to appear before courts usually give everyone's age. It might concern police records that a motorist accused of dangerous driving is aged 53. It matters little to the headline.

Yet if a woman of 53 becomes a Wimbledon tennis champion or even is chosen for a hockey international, her age would be the headline point. Likewise, if a man of 89 becomes a father it is a headline point. Age, like other facts, is important only in its relevance to the story. Effective headline writing lies in you identifying vital facts that bring a story alive.

The personal touch

The *who* of a headline is important. Opinions and quotations derive their strength from the reader knowing whose they are. There is nothing wrong in having a person's name in a headline – in fact, the abstract *he* or *she* should be avoided. If what a person does for a living is the important thing, then give that. For instance: FIREMAN SAVES GIRL WITH KISS OF LIFE, or TOWN'S BUTCHERS GO ON STRIKE OVER MEAT PRICES.

Headlines should avoid giving offence by skimping on the name. 'Maggie' might have saved useful headline space in the Thatcher days, but people encountering such diminutives of their name in headlines could take umbrage. Princess Margaret dislikes being called Meg in American papers. Remember that the Queen and the Pope take the definite article.

Man, girl, baby, mother and pensioner are acceptable words but the headline should flesh out who or what they are. For example MOTHER GETS BACK LOVE-TUG BABY, and COWBOY BUILDER WRECKS PENSIONER'S HOME.

'The man who . . .' is a useful way of personalizing a headline, and getting away with a label, as in THE MILLIONAIRE WHO LIVED IN A COUNCIL FLAT.

Time

With the *when* of a story, there is a natural assumption that the news on the page has just happened or is still happening. The use of the present tense in headlines confirms this as in TOWN'S BUS DRIVERS STRIKE OVER TOLL PLAN or TEENAGER SHATTERS LONG JUMP RECORD. Even with a football game the night before, the headline would read LIVERPOOL WHACK BOLTON STRUGGLERS. BRITAIN MOVES INTO THE BLACK is used in the present tense even though the trade figures it refers to are for a quarter that ended three weeks previously.

The future can be specified if it is relevant to the story, as in MUCH-MARRIED MP TO WED EIGHTH, or AT LAST – IT'S A SUNSHINE WEEKEND.

Location

The *where* of a news headline is most used in an area or regional paper anxious to show the spread of its coverage. Thus a county weekly in Cumbria might refer to the towns of Silloth, Aspatria and Whitehaven to assure these widely-scattered places that it is looking after their interests. Where an area has its own page of edition news under an area label, the need for place names is less important. In a tightly-knit urban evening paper a few place names are useful where they are relevant to the story but a rash of names on every little filler is tiresome (see pages reproduced in Chapters 1 and 2).

In a national daily or Sunday paper, place names are not common in headlines unless their relevance is inescapable, as in: WEST RIDING POLICE CHIEF LINKS CRIME RISE TO DRUGS, or WINDSOR 'RUINED BY NOISE POLLUTION' SAY PALACE.

Composing a headline

In composing a headline it is possible to reduce the approaches to two:

★ The direct approach
★ The oblique approach

The direct approach

A headline taken directly from the facts of the story is the commonest method. It conveys the 'hardness' of the story. By hardness we refer to the particular quality of stories that are rooted in facts – a Cabinet reshuffle, a rescue of a person or animal, a rail accident, a Test match, a by-election, a political speech – rather than stories that are based upon the words, reaction, behaviour and oddity of people.

What people say and do can be an integral part of a news story. 'News,' Harold Evans has said, 'is people.' Yet in the coverage of 'hard' news, which occupies the principal part of a reporter's job, the quotations from people with whom the reporter has spoken tend to be used in justification, description or corroboration of the facts of the story. It is the facts for which the reporter has gone in search, and it is the facts the reporter has gathered and checked that form the bedrock of the story and the material for the headline. Thus the hard news of the day might yield such headlines as:

POLICE CHIEF SUSPENDED OVER BRIBES ALLEGATION

MOTHER DIES SAVING BABY FROM SEA

SABOTAGE FEAR IN DOCKYARD EXPLOSION

ENGLAND CRASH TO AUSSIE SPINNERS

The words available to the headline writer – police, chief, bribes suspended, mother, baby, dead, sea, sabotage, dockyard, explosion, England, Aussies, spinners, defeat – are rooted in the event the headline has to cover. They are tight, informative, un-emotive, and yet they are evocative of the nature of the happening. They are the direct means by which the headline makes the connection with the reader. In selecting from such words you are making a qualitative judgement about the story and using that judgement to give it impact in the page.

The oblique approach

Scattered here and there in a newspaper, and sometimes given typographical prominence, are stories of a softer sort to which we give the term 'human interest'. These are hard to classify but they are generally concerned with the human situation: what someone has done or said, how they have reacted to something; or they concern unusual personal circumstances that have come to light. Often they are about animals and their relationship to humans. There could be an element of oddity or humour which lifts a story out of the ordinary, or a quirkiness about the personality of the people involved.

It is here that an oblique approach is useful in writing a headline, although it has to be said that the guidelines are less precise than in the direct approach. A story might inspire a headline based upon a popular song or catch phrase with which the reader is expected to be familiar, or a proverb or saying. Irony or humour might shape the subeditor's thinking. The headline could be done in the form of a quotation projected in a deliberately wordy way. Let us look at some examples that have appeared.

JUST THREE WHEELS ON HER WAGON AND STILL SHE'S ROLLING ALONG

This from the *Daily Mail*, was a bizarre story in which the motorist was seen driving along on three wheels after being involved in a crash. It both utilizes wordiness and derives its words from a song.

WHEN DID YOU LAST SEE YOUR MOTHER?

This one tweaks a famous picture title to draw attention to a news feature in *The Express* about mother and daughter relationships. It is a headline where a question mark is completely acceptable, as it is in another oblique headline from *The Times*:

What do you do if papa is a Rolling Stone?

There is greater scope and more fun for the sub in writing headlines like this, although most newspapers wisely limit their use. They can be fun for the reader, too, when they are used judiciously as 'kickers' on a page, but a glut of them can make news pages look trivial.

Headline thoughts

To be effective, a headline should express one main thought and not hedge it around with qualifications and explanations. In arriving at this thought you should be looking for what it is about the story that makes it different from any other – why this story is chosen for this particular space on this particular page. If there are other thoughts or facts to be brought forward they can be given in a second deck of headline (if one is schemed) or be put into the intro.

If there are two thoughts that are simple and complementary, however, you can compound them into one headline as in PASSENGERS FLUNG OUT AS TRAIN HITS BUFFERS or VIOLENCE FLARES IN GAZA AS POLICE GO ON STRIKE.

The *after* headline is in a similar category to the *as* headlines quoted above: MANAGER FOUND GAGGED AFTER RAIDERS SNATCH DIAMONDS, and LOOTERS STRIP SHOPS AFTER FUNERAL ENDS IN RIOT.

Label headlines

These are headlines without a verb, or in which the verb is incidental, and they are not recommended on news pages. The can sometimes work on a 'colour' or human interest story, as in BRRRRRRR . . . HELLO SUMMER! or in THE MAN WITH THE IRON JAW.

Possessives can help them work as in MOSCOW'S DAY OF SHAME. A dramatic statement such as THE BOOT FOR ENGLAND stands well because it is really an exclamation.

Some apparently label headlines such as PANTHER'S TRAIL IN SNOW gain strength from an implied verb – in this case 'is found' before 'snow'. Generally speaking, label headlines have not the pace needed for hard news and are best left to features pages.

Split headlines

The old strictures about grammatical splits in headlines – turning lines so that the subject is separated from the object, the adjective from the noun, or the parts of the verb divided – no longer have the force of taboo they used to have. Good flowing headlines were often spoiled by applying these pedantic rules. It is still best not to have the indefinite article *a* or *an* at the end of a line, but only because it is weak visually, not because it breaks a sacrosanct rule. The general scan of the words and the visual effect of the type as it comes up on screen should be the guiding principles. Does it look right? Does it sound right?

Turn heads

Where a story from Page One (or elsewhere) continues on an inside page, the inside page headline, or *turn head*, should contain a key word or phrase from the main heading so that it can be identified immediately. This does not mean that it has to be a label. If a story is about a doctor charged with an offence against a patient the Page One headline might say: DOCTOR ACCUSED OF RAPING DRUGGED PATIENT. Then the turn head could say: ACCUSED DOCTOR: NURSE TELLS OF 'STRANGE SUBSTANCE IN BOTTLE'. Thus, while the story is clearly flagged for the reader, the headline draws from the inside page material to carry the story forward. Another way would be to use a *strapline*:

> **Accused doctor: hearing continues**
> **NURSE TELLS OF 'STRANGE SUBSTANCE IN BOTTLE'**

Either way, the headline should have close to it, either reversed or as a white-on-black or preceded by a black blob, the slogan ● FROM PAGE ONE which leaves no doubt that it is the right story.

Things to avoid

★ Avoid headlines with *no, nothing* or *no one* in them. They are crying out to be passed over by the reader. If the story is worth using it must have a positive angle. For example:

NO ONE INJURED IN JET TAKE-OFF CRASH

would attract more readers if it said

90 ESCAPE INJURY AS JET HITS TREE

★ The positive angle of the escape in the unusual circumstances of an aircraft hitting a tree becomes the story. The fact that it was on take-off can be given to the reader in the intro. But beware of calling it a miracle escape. A miracle, says the *Shorter Oxford Dictionary*, is 'a marvellous event exceeding the known powers of Nature.' The reason 90 people escaped is because the aircraft had brakes and the captain the knowledge and skill to use them in an aborted take-off. This the story can explain.

★ Beware the temptation of creating miracle babes, miracle mums and miracle dads in circumstances in which the text offers perfectly rational explanations of what has occurred.

★ To get the best out of a headline word it should not be repeated in the same headline nor, if possible, in any other headline on the page.

★ The words *may*, *might* and *could* should be avoided as they leave the reader uncertain about what happened in the end, unless they keep a look-out for the continuation of the story in the next few days or weeks. This is too much to ask.

If a story is based on the possibility of something happening it is worth using only if the likelihood is very strong, otherwise the possibilities that can be written about are infinite. Newspapers sometimes have inside knowledge that something is about to happen which enables them to go a step further than *may*, *might* or *could*. Headlines such as BUILDING SOCIETIES SET TO CUT MORTGAGE RATES or 2% CUT IN LENDING RATE LIKELY are ways of writing headlines in which the possibility is almost a certainty. Even then, such headlines should be given to the readers only when the expected event is days or hours away.

8 HEADLINE TYPOGRAPHY

Modern newspaper design with its strength below the fold allows for a great variety of headline shape, especially in broadsheets. Pages these days consist of *one-deck*, one-thought headlines, as opposed to the multi-deck style once favoured, although sometimes a second deck is introduced. A *deck* of headline can consist of a number of lines of type depending on its width, or measure, and upon its shape and position in the page.

Shape

Single-column headlines are usually of two, three or four lines, although sometimes they can have as many as five or six if they have dominant end-column positions, or contain some particularly wordy phrase which the page planner wants to put across (see example on page 136).

Double-column or *three-column* headlines are usually of two or three lines and of a bigger type size than single-column heads since they are found on the more important stories on the page. The *page lead* has a headline that crosses most of the page – a *banner* or *streamer* – running into perhaps a shorter second line alongside a picture or another story (see examples in Chapter 2).

In addition to these conventional shapes there are long single-line headlines crossing the page, often down-page, and extending perhaps from three to as many as six columns in maybe 36pt or 42pt type. These cover stories carried in a number of *legs*, such as under a picture. See also examples in Chapter 2.

The more important stories both in tabloid and broadsheet layouts, particularly the page lead, might occasionally introduce a second headline thought for emphasis or for design purposes by means of a *strapline* or *overline*, as in:

Sects break truce in border flare-up
TEN DIE IN JORDAN AMBUSH

A strapline can justify a main heading which might seem bare on its own, or make possible one that might not otherwise stand at all. The *second deck* is also used on some papers for this purpose as in:

RAIL FIRMS FACE
SAFETY PURGE
Action follows
Southall smash

This method permits a bold main heading to hold the top of the page while giving needed explanation below it in smaller type.

A one-thought headline consisting of an opinion might have a *tag-line* to justify as in:

EXPORT BOOM
A TRIBUTE TO
'NEW LOOK'
INDUSTRIES
Chancellor tells City

Although it would have been better here to include 'Chancellor' in the main headline thought.

Most headlines, however, concentrate on one point in one deck. In single-column ones of this sort the character count in the bigger type sizes might be as little as 6½ characters to the line, although where an 18pt or 24pt headline is used, usually down-page, the count is easier. With wider headlines across two or more columns the count is not necessarily any easier since the typesize called for is bigger. A seven-column streamer in large type can offer the most difficult count of all. Its one advantage is that the words do not need to break into a number of even lines to satisfy a narrow single-column measure.

A headline that offers a really generous character count is the *freestyle* one which is often built around a statement or a quotation which aptly sums up a story. Such headlines are made a focal point in page design, often in conjunction with a picture, and cannot be arbitrarily imposed on a page without breaching its type balance. Here is a headline that accompanied an atmospheric picture:

Weapons at the ready, faces daubed, No 2 Platoon move off into the dawn light

The aim of this sort of headline is to give an impressionistic treatment to a news story. It succeeds by being different from other headlines. It signals that here is a special sort of approach.

To have visual balance and what newspaper designer Alan Hutt used to call 'eye comfort', a page of news items cannot be a hotch-potch of headline shapes altered at will to suit a subeditor's whims. Fitting the headline thought to a nominated shape and type is a discipline that has to be learned. It also focuses your thoughts wonderfully on the facts.

Arrangement

Within the various shapes a headline is arranged in two main ways. Either it is *centred* on the space available, or it is *set left*, sometimes indented by half a pica (a nut). Readability is usually the deciding factor, although type style can come into it where a paper opts for predominantly centred or set left headlines. A centred headline with a wide difference in width of lines has the eye jumping about to find the starting point of each line and is therefore hard to read. A successful centred headline should have fairly full lines with not too much variation in width, with the top line full to lend it strength (as below).

A set left headline is supposed to drop the eye to each successive line more easily. Yet it must still have a have a full top line to look visually right, and if the lines are too uneven the raggedness on the right leaves noticeable white on the page. This can give the outside edge a weak look if used in the right-hand end column. It is banned from this position in some papers.

A *set right* headline (or caption for that matter) is seldom used for the reason that the raggedness on the left makes it hard for the eye to pick up each line. Look at these examples:

| **POLICE HOLD LOOTERS IN SWOOP ON CITY SHOPS** | **POLICE HOLD LOOTERS IN SWOOP ON CITY SHOPS** | **POLICE HOLD LOOTERS IN SWOOP ON CITY SHOPS** |

The only other arrangement is the *stepped* headline, still favoured by some US papers:

METAL FATIGUE
IS LIKELY CAUSE
OF JUMBO CRASH

The first line should be set full left, the last full right, and the middle line placed evenly between. The lines need to be the same width to look right. It is a style now little used.

Type style

In a well planned newspaper the types conform to a regular stock range, with a variant introduced to give emphasis to a particular story or to form a display focal point, perhaps in conjunction with pictures, as we said in Chapter 2. Newspapers are careful to stick to their main stock types. If the seriffed Bodoni or Century is used for the news pages, perhaps a sans serif Gothic or Helvetica face will be the variant, with a greater but still controlled type variety allowed on the features pages. If Gothic or Helvetica is the stock news face, then Century Light or the heavily seriffed Rockwell or Pabst (see pages reproduced in Chapters 1 and 2) might be the variant.

Within most headline types, including the bit-mapped computerized clones now mainly used, there are bold, light and italic versions and condensed and expanded ones. There is thus ample variety in size and shape within a range without need to mix the ranges other than to introduce a chosen variant.

What is helpful to the headline writer is the modern tendency for newspapers to use only the lower case of a range in different sizes and weights. This might be accompanied by the occasional use of capitals in a variant type (Helvetica and Century light are popular for this) for logos or special headlines, of sometimes second decks. We have already referred to the theory that lower case headlines with their flowing outline and more varied contour are easier to read at sight, as with ordinary reading text. Along with the trend towards lower case is a decline in the use of italic type, both lower case and capitals, for the same reason – readability.

Using lower case certainly eases the letter count and is helping to free headlines from dependence on short stereotyped headline words of the sort sometimes used in tabloid papers with their narrow columns and large caps type. The other side of the coin is that bigger character counts can result in wordy headlines that lack punch and eye appeal. And no advocacy of lower case headlines can dispute the fact that the success of tabloid papers was built on the eye-catching poster effect of big sans caps headlines.

Character counts

The office type book, of which all production journalists should be given a copy along with the office stylebook, will provide you with character counts for the different standard measures. The examples should show each size in capital and lower case letters, with roman and italic, expanded and condensed versions where applicable, along with numbers, fractions, punctuation, stars, blobs and other type 'furniture' in each range. It will be seen that letters within a type size vary in width not only in their lower case form but in capitals, too. The count for a headline has to take account of these variations and also of the letter space needed between the words.

A headline count is easier in capitals. Apart from the I which counts as a half character, or the M and W which count as two, the variation in width among the remainder in virtually all types is slight enough to be self-cancelling between one letter and another. Allowing the space between words as equal to one character, it is easy enough in most types to get an accurate count. Even so, a rash of Is or Ws can lead to imbalance however carefully the characters are counted.

In lower case letters there is more variety of width, with f, i, j, l, r and t being narrower and averaging out at about half a character each, while w and m count usually as one and a half. Punctuation can vary from a half character to a full character, as between a comma and a question mark. Dashes and ellipses can take two or more character spaces.

Most systems are formatted for single character space between words, although this can be reduced to accommodate a much-wanted headline or otherwise save space. The readability of reduced word space depends on whether the letters separated by the space have upright or receding strokes, the latter giving the impression of greater white, as with the letter c or with capitals A, V and W.

Working out a headline count goes like this:

ISRAEL IGNORES
½111111½111111 = 13
UN ARMS WARNING
111112112111½11 = 16½

The second line here is too long for a headline which allows for a maximum count of 14, so 'UN' is deleted, leaving the headline as:

ISRAEL IGNORES
½111111½111111 = 13
ARMS WARNING
112112111½11 = 13½

This gives two almost equal lines with a little white each side when centred on the space.

But watch out when numerals are used. They are narrower than letters. The odd one or two will make little difference as in:

TEACHER
CHOOSES
PRISON
INSTEAD
OF 'UNFAIR'
£10 FINE

But in the following headline the last line will be a good deal shorter

SHOPLIFTER
TOLD: PAY
BACK FIRM'S
£50,000

Type, as we have seen, can be reduced or enlarged to any size within its top and bottom limits in a computerized system. Yet systems are formatted to give type in standard size sequence (see Chapter 2). This helps in visualizing and in giving pages calculable type balance and eye appeal. When writing a headline you can press a 'headline count' key to show on screen whether it fits or if it is too strong and by how many characters. It is allowed on most papers to vary a chosen size up or down by up to 5 per cent to accommodate a wanted headline.

Having a typebook around is important in visualizing, especially for a new subeditor. It gives the 'feel' of type and helps in understanding projection and page design. An editorial production staff with a feeling for type and an awareness of its possibilities is an important requirement for a good-looking paper. A paper's type character is threatened if subs are blindly writing headlines they cannot visualize or connect with the pages. It is a pity some offices use headline sizes and shapes coded by numbers or letters. Though quick and convenient, such cyphers discourage the young journalist keen to know about page design.

The type book is your introduction to the world of typography. The usages and nuances of effect of different types and variations of letter shape can convey to you a feeling for the psychology of type, an awareness that there are fast and slow types, and male and female, that some types are suited to particular purposes. If you lean towards page design and have a flair for visualizing you will learn how to give weight and boldness to a news page, authority to a leader page, and busyness to the sports section. You will discover how a condensed type used sparingly can enliven a standard format layout, and how a newspaper's visual character is maintained by cunning and consistency in type use.

Spacing

Tight character counts pose problems not only with the words in headlines but with the visual balance of the lines. White space used sparingly and creatively in a page can help the eye, but white space in a headline that was intended to be occupied by type is a waste. It does nothing for the page and, if occurring frequently, can make it look empty.

Try to get the letters, as far as possible, to fill the space allotted. If white is wanted for visual reasons the lines can be indented (i.e. set narrower than the space to be filled) or a deliberate display can be projected with planned white space as part of the pattern. Some glossy magazines are very good at this.

In headlines the use of white space is to give adequate separation between words and lines so that the message is easy to read and the visual effect satisfying. For instance a headline should not finish up looking like this:

GIRL
TEN, SAVES
CAT IN STORM
DRAIN

Nor should it become pyramid-shaped:

SPIN TWINS
SHATTER SURREY
HOPES AT THE OVAL

Or be a staircase:

SUN BREAKS
ALL RECORDS
FOR SEPTEMBER

If you find it hard to get a good shape, change the words and start again. The bigger the type the greater the damage caused by bad balance. An 84pt banner that falls short by half a column at each end weakens the top of the page and loses authority. Likewise, long single line headlines below the fold need to be full if they are to dominate as they are intended to.

Vertical or line spacing is automatic with most systems but it helps with headlines if space can be varied visually in lower case lines where ascenders and descenders clash one on to the other. Lower case type is difficult to line-space tidily. Spacing lines of capitals is matter of consistency, but beware the intrusion of the cross-line descender on the capital Q.

> Spacing through the lines of a headline at page make-up to fill out a shortfall of text in the story will result in poor visual balance and should be avoided except when time is short. It is better to extend the text.

Spacing – other than the above strictures – is a matter of visual style. There can be no universal rules for headline or columnar spacing. Some magazines make a feature of tightly spaced lines, which can be easily achieved in computer setting and can look good in gravure and in advertising display. Others go for all-round air or massive front indents. Some newspapers, as a matter of style, indent all columns by a nut each side to give more vertical separation of matter, or indent the front of the lines only. Others print the text with type that has a bigger body – 7pt on 8, or 8pt on 10 – thus marginally increasing the separation between the lines and avoiding clash of ascenders and descenders.

The golden rule is to be consistent. You will achieve a cleaner page if headline spacing is not tight here and wide there. Maximum readability demands that one line should be clearly differentiated from another and one word from another, otherwise the eye should not be aware of the white space.

The creative moment

There are two methods of thinking your way into writing a headline. One is to read the copy and try to come up with the wording before subbing the story. This is necessary if the headline is to be the keystone of the layout. The method has the advantage that the headline is written at the stage when the type and even the layout can, if need be, be adapted to accommodate it.

The other method is to sub the story, absorb the material and then work out the headline. The disadvantage here is that by now you are closer to the page deadline and time might be short.

Some stories produce a headline easily so that in reading the copy it jumps into your head; others are difficult to transmute into a few words. In human interest or 'mood' stories the hard facts can be few. The effect is in the telling or the description, as with royal visits or elaborate ceremonials.

Whatever the story, if a headline has not immediately occurred to you it is a good idea, as you sub the copy on screen, to jot down likely words on a pad. As many as half a dozen key words might emerge. You then shuffle them and arrange them in the right order to give balance and sense, as in a puzzle.

Take an imaginary situation. A teenager called Janice Thompson has gone missing from home. Her friends tell the school head that the girl has quarrelled with her mother over drugs and glue sniffing. A reporter on the local paper, which has already been told by the police that the girl is missing, hears about this and goes to see the mother. She is anxious to talk. She wants her daughter back. She says Janice, who is fifteen, walked out after being told by her that she was no longer welcome in the house if she continued to smoke pot and sniff glue. The reporter files the story and it is given a strong top-of-the-column space on page five.

The copy is late. The subeditor checks it, tightens it up a little, casts it off quickly and writes down the words: *mother, teenager, drug, quarrel, vanish* and *home*. The first effort is:

TEENAGER
VANISHES
AFTER ROW
AT HOME
OVER POT

This is no use for the fact that the girl has gone missing is not new. Also the word *after* splits the headline thought into two.

MOTHER'S BAN
ON POT DRIVES
TEENAGER FROM HOME

is better. Nearly there, in fact. How does it look as five lines of single column?

MOTHER'S
BAN ON POT
DRIVES
TEENAGER
FROM HOME

Still a bit slow. Also the second and last lines are one character too long for the type size and the size must not be reduced. Using the name would connect the story better with the readers. Try again

MISSING
JANICE:
MY DRUGS
BAN TO
BLAME
SAYS
MOTHER

Better, but too many lines, and the headline thought has again been split. Try not to use the colon. Thought: why not mum instead of mother?

MY DRUGS
BAN DROVE
JANICE
FROM HOME
SAYS MUM

fits the five lines and is just right. Fill out the middle line by making it JANICE, 15, and we're there.

In another story a foreman at the local car factory is sacked after an altercation in which he hits an apprentice and knocks him down. The apprentice had accused him of being a 'scab' (a non-striker) during a strike.

The words on the pad are: *union, sack, foreman, angry, scab, factory*. First of all, the 'scab' jibe is not new or contested. The new issue is what has happened to the foreman. The sub's first effort at a two-line double column lower case headline is:

Foreman loses job
in 'scab' jibe row

'Scab jibe row' is not liked. Also the headline needs more pace. A neat shuffle produces the answer:

'Scab' jibe costs
foreman his job

There are advantages in subbing a story before writing the headline. The sub knows thoroughly what the copy is about so that whatever headline emerges has to square with it. A headline written first could be based on a misconception acquired at a superficial reading. There is a subconscious tendency, too, where a good headline has cropped up first, to bend the story towards the headline. This is how distortion begins.

Alternative words

'If there is one outstanding fault in present-day headlines it is that very sameness with which they speak day in and day out. Much of this monotony in inevitable because of the cramping space limitations that compel repeated use of words, phrases and constructions that have been found most serviceable.'

Garst and Bernstein, *Headlines and Deadlines*

It will be seen from the examples quoted in this chapter that the limitations on word length and the search for type balance lead the headline writer to use a short word where alternatives are available. Fortunately this offers few problems. There is almost always a shorter word. The danger arises where certain 'serviceable' short words are allowed to become clichés: words to fall back on as familiar get-outs especially in those cases where the facts of a story do not entirely justify their use.

It is a favourite occupation of critics of newspaper headlines to tot up how many times in a day's issue of the national tabloid papers verbs such as *axe*, *snub*, *lash*, *probe*, *slash*, *hit*, *quiz* and *quit* can be found.

Using the same truncated words can lead to tired don't-read-me headlines, which is a pity with a language as flexible as English. As a young sub, you will find the best way out of this trap is to devise your own list of short alternative words for use in headlines. A good thesaurus of English words, a modern usage dictionary such as the *Penguin English Dictionary* and a stout exercise book are all that you need for this assignment.

Here to ease the way are some suggested alternative words, but remember in using synonyms that there can be nuances of meanings between one and another, and that a situation or statement could be misrepresented if an alternative word were used without proper thought. Also, as the list shows, some words have two or more meanings, each with its synonyms.

A

abandon
desert
drop
give up
leave
neglect
pull out
quit

abbreviate
cut
lop
reduce
shorten

abolish
close
drop
end
finish
rid
squash

abscond
flee
leave
run

accelerate
hasten
hustle
press
push
quicken
rush
speed

accumulate
amass
build up
gather
hoard
store

acquire
buy
collect
gain
get
grab
take care

adjust
alter
change
revise
shift

administer
boss
control
direct
give
manage
rule
run

aggravate
annoy
inflame
irritate
provoke
worsen

agreement
accord
bargain
bond
deal
pact
treaty

alleviate
ease
lessen
let up
lighten
reduce

relieve
soften

allocation
lot
part
portion
quota
ration
share

amalgamate
combine
fuse
join
link
merge
mix
team up
unit

amalgamation
joining
link
merger
tie-up

announce
disclose
notify
proclaim
report
reveal
state
tell

appeal
ask
call
plead

appoint
choose
invest

name
pick

appointment
job
mission
place
post

apportion
allot
distribute
divide
share
split

appreciate
enjoy
grow
increase
like
rise

appropriate
grab
loot
nick
seize
snatch

approve
agree
allow
OK
pass
permit

arbitrator
go-between
judge
mediator
referee
umpire

argument
dispute
quarrel
row
rumpus
set-to

ascertain
check
confirm
discern
ensure
find out
inquire
learn
seek

assistance
aid
back-up
help
relief

attain
achieve
get
reach
secure

authorize
allow
approve
back
favour
let
permit
sanction
sponsor

B

beginning
birth
dawn

debut
onset
opening
start

bequeath
allot
give
leave
provide
will

bewilderment
daze
puzzle
shock
surprise

business
company
firm

C

calculate
assess
estimate
rate
tot up
value

challenge
contest
dare
defy
dispute

change
alter
amend
revise
reword
shift

circumvent
balk
foil
outwit
skirt

close
call off
end
finish
shut

commence
begin
embark
open
start
take off

communicate
call
pass on
reveal
tell
write

competition
contest
fight
game
rivalry

complain
bitch
groan
grouse
grumble
moan
nag
object
protest
resent

confront
challenge
face
halt
present

congratulate
comment
praise

consider
examine
inspect
look at
mull
probe
report on
study

construct
assemble
build
erect
form
make
put up
raise

continue
extend
go on
persist
plod on

contradict
deny
dispute
dissent
gainsay
oppose
refute
reject

control
curb
limit
organize
peg
run

cooperate
help
join with
share

create
build
design
form
invent
make

criticize
assess
censure
challenge
chide
decry
evaluate
rap
rebuke
review
slam

D

damage
harm
hit
hurt
spoil
sully

deflate
contract
pinch

shrink
squeeze

demonstration
demo
march
show
sitdown
sit-in

deprecate
belittle
damn
discount
discredit
knock
run down

description
account
picture
sketch
story
tale

designate
appoint
fix
name
select

destroy
break
end
ruin
shatter
smash

disagreement
clash
conflict
dispute
quarrel
rift

row
rumpus
wrangle

discriminatory
biased
partial

distribute
circulate
give out
issue
supply

division
break-up
parting
split

donation
gift
grant
hand-out
present

E

employment
career
job
post
task
work

endorsement
acclaim
approval
backing
sanction
support

essential
key

main
necessary
vital

exaggerate
blow up
boost
distort
magnify
overstate

examination
analysis
inquiry
probe
scrutiny
study
test

exonerate
absolve
acquit
clear

expedite
hasten
hurry
push
quicken
rush
speed

explanation
account
alibi
answer
excuse

F

fabrication
falsehood
invention

lie
story
tale
untruth

facilitate
advance
ease
expedite
smooth

forbid
ban
bar
block
deny
disallow
prevent
reject
stop

foundation
base
basis
charity
grounds
origin
roots
trust

fundamental
basic
primary
vital

G

govern
command
control
direct
manage

rule
run

grievance
grouse
grudge
injury
wrong

guarantee
(noun)
bond
pledge
promise
support
surety
warranty
(verb)
endorse
ensure
pledge
warrant

guillotine
axe
chop
cut off
gag
silence

H

hallucination
delusion
dream
freak-out
illusion
mirage
vision

hazardous
dangerous
dodgy

perilous
risky
unsafe

I

illegitimate
banned
illegal
illicit
lawless
unlawful

illustrate
explain
picture
show

imminent
at hand
near
soon

important
big
great
high
key
notable
prime
top
vital

improve
better
enhance
heighten
polish
restore

improvement
advance
betterment

progress
recovery

inaugurate
begin
install
launch
open
set off
start

independent
free
impartial
neutral
unbiased

influence
colour
induce
lead
push
sway

inquire
ask
beg
look into
question
see

instigate
cause
incite
provoke
set off
spur
start

interfere
hinder
interrupt
meddle
pry
thwart

interrogate
ask
examine
grill
pump
question
quiz
vet

introduce
explain
float
launch
promote
start

investigate
analyse
check
deliver
examine
inquire
probe
pry
sift
study

invite
ask
beg
bid
call

J

jeopardize
endanger
hazard
imperil
risk

judgement
decision

finding
result
ruling
verdict

justify
back
bear out
confirm
defined
endorse
excuse
explain
support

K

kidnap
abduct
capture
carry off
grasp
seize
snatch
steal
take care

L

leader
boss
chief
head
master
ruler
guv'nor

legalize
allow
ordain
permit
ratify

luxurious
costly
lush
plush
posh
rich

M

maintain
assert
hold
keep
insist
support

management
board
company
directors
executive
firm
owners

manoeuvres
dodges
exercises
plots
ruses
tricks
wiles

manufacture
build
construct
make
produce

mediate
decide
intervene
judge

moderate
allay
control
lessen
limit

modification
alteration
amendment
change
switch

N

negotiate
bargain
confer
discuss
haggle
parley
talk

neighbourhood
area
district
environs
locality
place
section
zone

nominate
appoint
call
choose
decree
invest
name
present
propose
put up
raise

O

objective
aim
ambition
end
target

observe
check
eye
inspect
look at
note
see
spy
watch

operate
act
control
run
work

oppose
bar
block
challenge
combat
contest
counter
fight
obstruct
rebuff
reject
repel

organize
control
develop
fix
form
plan
run
set up

P

pacify
allay
calm
cool
ease
heal
quieten
settle

permanent
abiding
constant
durable
enduring
lasting

postpone
delay
hold up
putt off

prohibit
ban
bar
disallow
end
forbid
half
prevent
rule out
stop
veto

prohibition
axe
ban
embargo
end
halt
veto

proposition
idea
notion
offer
plan

purpose
aim
ambition
end
idea
plan
reason

pursue
chase
dog
follow
harry
hound
hunt
search
seek
trace
track
trail

pursuit
chase
hunt
quest
search

Q

question
challenge
doubt
point
probe
query

R

recommend
back
boost
comment
praise
present
support
urge

reduce
axe
chop
cut
lower
slash

regulate
control
govern
legalize
order
run
vet

relinquish
abandon
drop
forgo
give up
leave
quit
resign

repudiate
deny
disclaim
spurn

requisition
acquire
get
grab

seize
take

resign
abandon
give up
lay down
leave
quit

responsibility
duty
job
role
task

.

S

sanction
allow
approve
OK
pass
permit

scrutinize
check
examine
inspect
study
vet

settlement
bargain

bond
deal
pact
treaty
truth

support
aid
back
foster
help
prop
push
standby
uphold

T

terrorize
awe
bully
frighten
scare
threaten

tolerate
accept
allow
endure
live with
stand

U

unblemished
clean
faultless
flawless
guiltless
spotless
virgin

unyielding
firm
fixed
resolute
solid
steady
stout
unmoved
unshaken

undermine
belittle
impair
sap
weaken

undertaking
agreement
bargain
deal
duty
mission
plan
promise
task

V

vacillate
demur
hedge
hesitate
sway
waver
wobble

vanquish
beat
defeat
rout
scatter
shatter
smash
trounce

vindicate
bear out
justify
set right
uphold

vulnerable
delicate
exposed
suspect
tender
weak

9

FURTHER TECHNIQUES IN SUBBING

Not only must the story you are subbing be accurate, clear and readable and of the right length; it must also be legally safe to print. Production delays caused by a late decision to take a story found to be libellous out of a page can cost money and lose sales.

Subeditors and the law

All newspapers retain a trained lawyer or senior journalist versed in the law to read copy and advise the editor of potential legal traps. If a story is considered unsafe to use, the legal person, after consulting the editor or chief subeditor, will issue a *legal kill,* which means it must be thrown away or removed from the computer. Any legal alterations to make a story safe are passed to the sub or page editor who amends the text.

Electronic editing causes no particular problem to the legal reader. While security of text means that computer access is limited in certain areas to those performing editorial tasks, the legal reader has access to all incoming texts, which can be called up file by file and read on screen. Even so, it is necessary for the legal overview to extend to the finished pages, which can also be called up (or printed out) to ensure that no legal danger has resulted from editing, captioning or headline writing.

The overview of the lawyer or legal reader is a general one and varies in efficiency from office to office and it does not absolve the subeditor from watching carefully for legal dangers in copy. If there are any doubts about a story that you cannot resolve in the editing, refer it in good time to the legal reader before consigning it to the page. The difference between a safe story and an action for damages can turn on a phrase or a sequence of words at a critical point in the text.

Lessons in law for newspapers are included in all journalism training courses but it takes time for a young sub to develop the sixth sense a senior colleague uses to spot legal traps that can lie behind innocent-seeming words. Rewrites of stories are an obvious danger when facts are being rearranged and quotations paraphrased or perhaps keyed in wrongly. Yet a 'tick-marking job' – a well written story that needs little editing or cutting to fit – can hold as great a danger because it may lull the sub into a state of false confidence. Read a story through again carefully if it seems to have needed little attention.

Legal traps

Keep two thoughts in mind when considering legal problems in editing: one, a mistake or damaging statement gains much more currency with the public than by any other means of dissemination and therefore can cause greater harm; two, newspaper companies are regarded by litigants as rich and a good target. Editors are thus sensitive to those laws of which newspapers are most liable to fall foul.

Two sorts of law affect newspapers in Britain:

1 The general laws of the land to which editors are liable in the same way as the ordinary citizen. These include laws covering defamation of character or libel; contempt of court, trespass, confidentiality, and the various provisions of the Official Secrets Act which restrict the passing on or circulating of certain information.
2 Laws aimed more specifically at the press and broadcasting media to restrict the publicity given to court cases. These are, in effect, a form of censorship. They include the laws forbidding publication of evidence in divorce and other matrimonial cases, the identification of offenders in youth court cases, the publication of evidence given at lower courts against people committed for trial to higher courts, and the details (and names in some cases) of people involved in sex offences. Also included are some provisions contained in the race laws.

While all these laws worry editors since they restrict what a newspaper can say and do, some are of less immediate concern to the sub. The laws restricting the coverage of court cases, for instance, are accepted and applied by newspapers. While you as a subeditor should be aware of the types of restrictions, you are not likely to be presented with a blow-by-blow account of the evidence in a steamy divorce case because reporters know such evidence is not allowed to be reported. Only the names and the judge's summing-up can be used.

Nor are the laws covering youth court cases flouted. Names and identities can be reported only if the magistrates direct that they should (which they seldom do) in the case of very serious offenders who put the public in danger. Here the magistrates' direction becomes an important part of the story. The provisions of the various Criminal Justice and Sex Offenders Acts from 1967 onwards, which forbid publication of evidence against people committed for trial from lower courts (except in special cases), although disliked by editors, are universally applied.

Yet legal traps can still lurk in copy. Chief of these is the perennial danger of libel in which the threat of being sued can cause a timid editor to shelve a story which should have been published for the public good.

Libel

A newspaper is guilty of libel when it can be proved that a person's character or livelihood has been damaged as a result of statements made in the paper. A successful action can result in substantial damages being paid out. While some well-known cases get much publicity, many more are settled unknown to the public by out-of-court arrangements in which quite large sums of money change hands, accompanied by a printed apology. This method at least avoids heavy court costs where a newspaper feels the judgement might go against it.

Defence against libel is difficult. An editor might plead the truth of the statements, or contest that they are not defamatory, or that the story was 'fair comment made in good faith and without malice about a matter of public interest.'

While the decision on whether or not to publish is the editor's, the sub needs to be careful in the arrangement of words and facts in a story in which there is a known danger of libel. This is particularly so in stories where the editor, having taken legal advice, is ignoring a letter threatening libel action if the story appears. Such threats are used by people to try to stop publication and are ignored only if the editor has good legal grounds – or good legal advice. In such a story the office lawyer should be allowed to vet the edited version at an early stage to avoid late changes which would delay pages.

A persistent litigant or a wily lawyer can find libel in the most innocent statements and no paper is ever free of writs. Some, however, are just attempts by unscrupulous people to make money and a newspaper learns how to deal with them.

In stories of known legal danger you should make sure that risky statements are corroborated in the text; that people against whom accusations are made have space in the story to in which to make their reply, and that background details are not chosen out of malice or to make people look small or ridiculous. Check back any obvious danger points with the reporter.

People with criminal records are particularly sensitive about having them mentioned in stories that have nothing to do with their murky past. Actors can stand criticism of a particular role but could sue if their professional competence were being questioned. People in public life would expect to meet opposition and criticism but it would be actionable to say that they are not fit for public office. Likewise, suggestions that people are drunks or take drugs can be dangerous, or suggestions that they have been less than honest in their handling of public or shareholders' money.

Contempt of court

This means broadly any conduct or spoken or written words or printing of pictures which might impede the working of a court or bring justice into disrepute. This is a law aimed at everyone, not just the press. Yet the press, because it reports court cases, is particularly exposed to the danger of being in contempt.

Here are some things that a subeditor, or anyone else involved in editorial production, should watch for:

1 No picture should be published of persons accused, or expected to be accused, of an offence until they have been identified in court. An exception is where the police have issued a picture of a wanted person. Here the caption should avoid accusing the person and should contain words such as 'is wanted by the police for questioning in connection with . . .' etc.
2 A newspaper must not publish new facts or evidence about people being tried while the trial is in progress. The people charged are not in a position to refute them, the defence or prosecution case might be damaged by them or the jury influenced.
3 A newspaper should not interview any witness or person involved in a trial. Printing such an interview can put the paper in contempt.
4 Criticism of the judge or the court proceedings during a trial is considered serious contempt.
5 A newspaper must not try to get in touch with a member of the jury during a trial.

These are the main points concerning news stories about court proceedings, but there is a wide area beyond this in which, at the decision of a judge, an editor might be in contempt of court, and even be fined or sent to prison. For instance, two reporters were sent to prison in Britain for refusing to disclose to a judge the sources of information in a story about an accused person printed before a trial began. Also, judicial tribunals presided over by judges into disasters and other situations have been ruled to be subject to the laws of contempt of court, thus restricting newspapers in what they can print in the same way as with court proceedings.

The idea of the law of contempt of court is that a person, once accused, should be able to get a fair trial. To give an example, a persistent pattern of crime in an area such as attacks on women or children can produce in the public mind the shadowy figure of the marauder who becomes personalized as the Yorkshire Ripper or the Beast of Bournemouth. As long as the police search goes on and further attacks are reported the name Yorkshire Ripper or Beast of Bournemouth dominates the headlines. Once a person has been arrested and charged, however, or even if a person is being held for questioning and not yet named, the editor is in danger of being in contempt by associating the name given to the marauder with the person held. The matter has become *sub judice*. It is subject to the due processes of the law with which there should be no outside interference. A newspaper story can give only those details that are allowed under the law.

The sort of story that first appears after someone is arrested might run like this:

A man was helping police with their inquiries at Extown police station last night in connection with the deaths of two teenage girls whose bodies were found last Wednesday in the River Ex.

The next development of the story might be:

Charles Jinks, a labourer, of Caxton Street, Riverport, was charged in Extown magistrates' court this morning with the murder of Elsie Jones, of Privet Street, Extown on or about October 8.
He was given legal aid and was remanded in custody for further inquiries. Bail was refused.

It would be wrong of the local paper to introduce the death of the second girl into the story at this stage, even though they might know that a further charge is pending. It has to wait.

Eventually Charles Jinks is charged with the murder of both girls and evidence is presented and pleas taken. The paper can still publish only what is allowed under the Criminal Justice Acts, which means that, unless the magistrates direct otherwise, only Jinks's name and address, the charges against him, the names of the girls, his plea, details of bail if any, and the fact of his committal to a higher court can be given.

Not until the case comes before the Crown Court for the area and the prosecution and defence cases are given in full before a jury can the evidence be published in the press. Only after the trial has finished and judgement been given can the paper comment on the case, interview people involved and – if the evidence and result justifies it – use once more the term Yorkshire Ripper or Beast of Bournemouth. It can then, if it wishes, even comment on the way proceedings were brought and on the police handling of the case.

By observing the law of contempt of court, the editor has ensured that the paper's coverage has done nothing to impede a person's fair trial (since under British law a person is innocent until proved guilty) by publishing information or comment that might have influenced the jury or damaged the prosecution or defence cases.

Your job in subbing court cases is to check that the law has been observed by the reporter at the hearings at the various stages and not to allow anything into the newspaper that will get it into trouble – and that includes the wording of your headline.

The Official Secrets Act

This is a wide Act which can be used to cover many aspects of government business as well as security and state secrets. Controversial areas are spelt out to the press from time to time in DA-notices, which are requests to editors not to publish certain things on threat of being guilty of breaching the Act. The decision here is whether to publish an item at all and it is one for the editor.

Privilege

Newspapers would be in trouble with litigants much more were it not that under British law the need for freedom of speech in the public interest is recognized and certain newspaper reports are protected by 'privilege'. The law on privilege covers the reporting of court hearings and sittings of parliament and public bodies where serious accusations can be made about people which, if made and reported elsewhere, could lead to actions for libel.

The application of privilege needs to be learnt by journalists during training for it is a valuable guide to the protection their reports have. It must be known by subeditors. Privilege comes in two sorts.

Absolute privilege

Absolute privilege covers a fair and accurate report of judicial proceedings published contemporaneously, provided that legal restrictions on coverage in certain cases specified in law have been observed. However untrue in fact statements in court are, or however unfair, a newspaper who reports them and says who made them is safe from action for libel. An exception to this in the past has been statements involving sedition, blasphemy and obscenity, though these have become increasingly hard to define.

Points to watch:

1 'Fair and accurate' means that the report must be fair to both sides.
2 The report is not covered by absolute privilege if it includes matter taken from documents that have not been read out in court.
3 Protection does not include anything not part of the proceedings such as an outburst or scene in the courtroom.
4 The report must be 'contemporaneous'. This means it should be carried in the next possible issue of the paper after the hearing.
5 The wording of the headline must not go beyond the facts of the story.
6 Beware of wording. A charge of murder becomes a case of murder only after the verdict. If a person at a lower court elects to go for trial, do not say he or she was 'sent' for trial, which suggests the court has decided there is a case to answer. A statement made by a person before the hearing is an 'alleged statement' until it has been agreed and accepted in court.
7 Descriptions of witnesses, their dress and behaviour, are not covered by privilege.

Qualified privilege

This allows protection for reports of judicial proceedings that are non-contemporaneous, and to reports of Parliament and other public bodies over a wide field. Broadly, qualified privilege means that the reports are privileged in law provided that there is no malice or other improper motive behind publication. Where these motives can be established in court, the protection of qualified privilege is of no avail. Subs should keep in mind this important distinction when dealing with such reports.

The areas covered by qualified privilege include: Parliament, Commonwealth legislatures, international organizations and conferences to which the UK Government sends a representative, public inquiries, bodies formed in the UK to promote the arts, science, religion, learning, trade, business and industry; associations for promoting sports and pastimes to which the public are invited, public meetings held for a lawful purpose, meetings of local authorities, committees or tribunals appointed by Act of Parliament, and reports of notices or information issued to the public by the Government, local authority or police.

Schedules listing these and other occasions of qualified privilege, and also spelling out some important exceptions, are published as part of the 1952 Defamation Act and its successors.

For the subeditor, danger can crop up with statements made by some public bodies covered by qualified privilege in which the background material to which the newspaper might have access is not so covered. The advice of the office lawyer or legal reader is the only course in some cases.

The publication of material not covered by qualified privilege does not mean that the newspaper is automatically in trouble – only that if a court action follows, qualified privilege cannot be used as a defence.

When to rewrite

Subs are generally thought by reporters to be too keen to rewrite copy. It can be galling for a reporter who has taken care over writing up a difficult assignment to find that half the words in the published version, perhaps under the reporter's name, are unrecognizable.

> Do not alter or rewrite copy just for the sake of it. On a well-run subs' table this does not happen. For one thing, subs should be too busy editing to page deadlines to devote time unnecessarily to a story. For another, the chief sub would not stand for a well-turned story which earned its space being pulled apart.

Yet rewriting can be necessary just as heavy editing is necessary for reasons that have nothing to with the way the reporter has written a story. The treatment of copy, as we have seen, is influenced by the volume and changing pattern of news on the day, and the availability of space on the page, which might change after the story has been completed and the reporter gone home. It may also be governed by new developments that put a story in a different light, the inclusion of other copy sources, a change of emphasis to suit a night editor's or chief subeditor's judgement, a clash with editorial policy, or simply changes for editions. It can happen that the work that needs to be done on a story for these reasons is so complex that rewriting is the quickest solution.

The following examples show where rewriting or partial rewriting would be the best means of editing.

Angling

There is nothing sinister about angling a story. It simply means deciding the viewpoint from which to tell it. The intro of any story in effect defines the angle. The fact sequence that follows supports and justifies what the first paragraph has to say.

It can happen that the night editor or chief-sub, with more mature judgement, sees a story differently from the reporter, and the sub is instructed to *re-nose* it for the page from a new angle. Here are some examples of what might result:

1 A simple local paper account of a street accident becomes a 'death trap claims new victim' story because the sub remembers cuttings of previous stories of accidents at the same spot and draws the chief sub's attention to them.
2 Bequests in a will are brought alive through the eagle eye of the night editor who called for cuttings of some interesting beneficiaries. An unexpected human interest angle emerges.
3 A decision of the local planning committee is found through copy from another reporter to have vital implications for the community that were not immediately apparent in the report of a council meeting.
4 A story about an old lady found dead in a flat in which she lived alone is combined with other material into a story to exemplify a campaign the newspaper is running about urban loneliness.

Angling as demonstrated shows how the creative assessment of a story after it has left the reporter's hands can result in recasting of the material by the subeditor even if it is not totally rewritten.

There is also the more general angling of stories to suit the readership. Political stories, we have seen, are sometimes presented in regional and town papers in terms of local connections of the politician or of proposed legislation. A paper's political writers are aware of this and it does not often fall to subs to re-nose their copy. Other jobs can entail a considerable amount of work by the sub to bring out the local angle, often for different editions. The casualty figure in a crash or disaster story might include local people and the story, especially from the more general agency copy, will be edited from this viewpoint. Likewise, trade and industry stories are angled on local connections.

Multiple copy sources

Sometimes you will be given a story which has copy from more than one source. It might be story with several *ends* in which a main section is perhaps by a staff reporter with *legwork* provided by area correspondents. For instance an air crash might have local interviews, or a rescue story material from several areas. Sometimes agency copy, either from home agency such as Press Association (PA) or an international agency, has coverage which is relevant. Some stories have foreign ends which have important links with the main story. File background has to be worked in and perhaps a financial angle from the City correspondent, or other specialist contribution.

Keeping up with this amount of copy in a complicated many-sided story requires an eye for vital detail, especially when extra copy arrives during the subbing of the story or even while it is being fitted into the page. You cannot afford to leave out anything of importance, and you must see that new facts, however late in arriving, are placed in correct sequence. Rewriting is often the answer. Most newspapers require staff reporters' copy to be used where possible in such stories, with agency copy filling the gaps, but the agency version might provide an important element. Such stories should carry a combined staff and agency *credit.*

Bad copy

A more obvious candidate for rewriting is the story that is badly written, either for lack of time by the reporter or through a wrongly judged style or approach. Such copy might be sent back for the reporter to try again, but if time is short or the reporter is out on another job the sub is instructed to 'knock it into shape.' This could include 'cleaning it up', which means taking out explicit sex, obscenities, excessive violence or things likely to offend the readers; 'sharpening it up', getting rid of dull writing, tedious phrasing and wordiness; or 'toning it down,' ridding it of extravagant or emotive language, excessive use of adjectives, or gush.

> Some reporters who are employed because they are brilliant news gatherers, maybe with important contacts, are indifferent with the pen and rely upon the subeditor for the final polish. In American practice this need is recognized by the use of rewrite people separate from the subs. In most British papers it is found useful, for page making purposes, to keep rewriting within the subbing orbit, although more use is made these days of newsroom rewrite staff.

The precise boundary in rewriting between what should be done in the newsroom before submitting copy and what should be left to the subs is a matter for house practice. There is no doubt that basic newsroom collating of source material simplifies the sub's job, yet with imminent page and edition deadlines the arrival of late or additional material is best dealt with by the subeditor, who is closer to the space requirements and may be already well into editing the story. Daily newspapers, especially town evenings, are much more subs' papers than they are writers'.

Electronic tools

Electronic editing offers no handicap to jobs that entail collating and rewriting. Computers have a prodigious capacity for storage and retrieval of material and, although split screen allows only two stories to be displayed comfortably at a time, you can display the main edited text on one side and work in material from other stories successively from the other side on those systems that offer the facility.

In most cases where there are multiple sources, copy feeds into the main story file to which it relates – the running story in Chapter 10 is an example – and the computer makes easy the task of inserting, adding, rearranging and rewriting the material. Original text can be left in the computer in the form of notes to get back to if needed.

By the same coin, where separate story files are merged it is not difficult to copy required material from one file to another as part of the editing job.

Rewrite subbing from complex sources is a job for an experienced sub. Such a person can sift through a varied input of copy, do the necessary checking by reference book or cuttings, and within minutes begin writing the story from intro onwards, or with intro to follow.

The following points should be watched with rewrites, particularly by subs new to the table:

1 Is the rewrite necessary? Is using part of the reporter's copy, with subbing adjustments, just as quick, or quicker?
2 Have you checked quotes, names, ages, addresses etc. against the original copy?
3 Have you transcribed all quotes accurately or paraphrased them fairly?
4 Have you followed house style in spellings, abbreviations, use of colloquial-isms etc?

Revising and editionizing

National dailies in Britain publish four or five main editions during a production cycle lasting from midday to about 2.30 a.m. the following morning. At one time most nationals printed in London and Manchester, and sometimes Glasgow, from where the various edition areas were served Those editions furthest away – Ulster or Northern Scotland, say – went to press earliest. The main pages were transmitted from London by page facsimile, with late or edition area pages being inserted at the regional printing centres to make up a paper which looked the same wherever it was bought.

Today, the computer and the electronic systems available have enabled national papers to decentralize their printing to any number of sites around the country to facilitate faster distribution. Some of these printing plants are directly owned and managed; others are provincially-owned centres that print a variety of national and local papers by contract. Thus a paper can be printed at the same time wherever a company chooses for whatever edition areas it wishes to cover. This has resulted in editorial control becoming concentrated in London where all the changes are originated, with the pages being transmitted instantly to whichever presses need them. It is not even necessary to print papers on the same site where they are edited.

Area changes in national paper editions are mainly concerned with sport, with full-length match reports in football and cricket being substituted on the sports pages for each readership area. One or two pages might be kept open for big regional stories but the bulk of the news changes concern the updating of national stories or the introducing of later news and pictures in place of earlier items. Stories that are likely to need updating are carried on page one, the back page and dedicated inside pages; including TV and radio programme pages, with the greater number of pages – including the features – staying the same through all editions.

Provincial papers – town evening papers and local weeklies, printing mostly on one site, update general news and sport in their main editions, but also change special area pages of community news, sometimes to the extent of varying the title of the paper to emphasize its local identity. Thus the *Hoylake News and Advertiser* becomes the *Heswall and Neston News and Advertiser,* and the *Malton Gazette and Herald* becomes the *Pickering Gazette and Herald.* Big town evenings run as many as six or seven editions in a production cycle lasting from about 11.00 a.m. to 5.30 p.m. In evenings and weeklies the pagination is arranged (depending on whether the paper is tabloid or broadsheet) so that pages devoted to area news can be replaced at each edition change. The front and back pages usually change with every edition and contain the general stories that most likely need updating or replacing. With tabloid size, remember that pages go on the press in pairs.

If the need is urgent it is possible to 'slip' a page (or pair of pages) on its own between editions in order to change or update a story, thus creating a special or 'slip' edition. This is done if new facts or news have to be carried and the editor does not wish to wait until the next edition to get at the page.

In the case of edition coverage the stories are catch-lined with their edition when subbed and are stored type-set to length in the computer to be called into pages as changes become due. You might find yourself subbing a story in different versions to different deadlines to bring out edition angles. A story in one edition of a Yorkshire evening paper about a robbery in Bradford might be angled in another as 'Huddersfield man accused.' A story in a West Country paper about a Bristol bride can turn up in another edition as a story about a Swindon bridegroom

It is usual on evening papers to list editions and page press times on an information sheet so that subs, especially new ones, can refer quickly to the deadlines for whatever story or edition they working on.

Rejigs

The revised form of a story is called a *rejig* or *redress.* Your job as a sub is to work in later material from the reporter or agency or whatever other source to update the text for each edition. *Add matter* is intended to go conveniently at the end (it is not often as simple as that). If the story length in the page is the same, a cut has to be made to accommodate it. This is the simplest form of rejig with the headline and body of the story staying the same.

Where the later material is more important or complex it can involve *re-nosing* and re-headlining the story for the next edition. This might entail reworking the whole story although it is likely you can pick up some of the old material, provided it is not outdated by the new. In such a case you should give the story a new catchline, or add an *x* or a *z* to the present one to differentiate it from the old one that might still be in the computer. Alternatively you can erase the old story if you are certain parts of it are not going to be needed. Unless more space has been allowed for the rejigged story – maybe a page lead instead of a single-column top – you cast it off to the same length as the version it replaces.

Later material can also arrive on screen as *inserts* – perhaps A and B – marked by the writer to particular parts of the story. Here again, cuts need to be made so that the length in the page is preserved.

For the more complex problems of revision and edition changes, see Chapter 10.

Caption writing

Writing picture captions, a job that usually falls to the page editor or sub, is a world on its own. While a picture cannot stand without them, the wording should not stress the obvious but should try to extend what the picture is saying by offering explanation and context. For instance, a caption to a picture of a man playing golf would be banal if it said:

Faldo playing a long shot

It would be better if it told the reader:

Faldo: a record round

or

The Faldo style: today's picture

Which at least makes the point that the picture is hot from the camera (if it is). Likewise, a rail crash picture would have to say something more creative than:

The crash scene at Extown junction

For instance it could tell the reader:

The upended coach in which ten survived

Even stock pictures used on TV programme pages can be brought to life and not just give names. For example:

WOGAN: A sit-com debut

at least gives readers a piece of information that sends them looking into the programme details. And note the use of the name in caps. This is a good ploy with 'mug shot' captions.

These examples aim to extend readers' awareness of the accompanying text as well as explaining the picture. By giving titbits of information they persuade the reader to read on. Note that identification is paramount in a caption, whereas time and location are not always necessary.

Do's and don'ts about caption writing

★ Try to use the present tense. It can give even a stock head shot immediacy.
★ Try to place the caption adjacent to the picture, preferably under it. A caption that has to be looked for has failed.
★ Try to avoid having composite captions that cover a number of pictures. Directions such as below left, bottom right, above centre, etc. can exasperate readers – especially if one of the references proves to be wrong.
★ Do not repeat the wording of the headline or intro. The reader needs to be told something new

---

Most captions appear alongside the story which the picture illustrates and therefore do not have to say more than will justify the picture, but some display pictures do not tie in with stories and depend on their own self-contained caption. The material usually still has a news point, even if it is just a new portrait of one of the Royal Family, or of the new mayoress trying on her chain of office.

A difficulty arises in the popular tabloids, however, where a girlie picture appears in a regular slot because this is where the reader expects to find it rather than for any other justification. It is here, in providing self-contained captions to primarily display pictures that the caption writer's art is most clearly demonstrated. Absolved almost from dealing in facts – or restricted to the very barest – the writer has to use comment, whimsy and clever writing to bring the words alive. Even so, the conventions of identification, justification and the use of the present tense have to be applied. The reader has to be guided.

Caption typography

This is best kept simple. It should be different from the adjacent reading text, usually in bolder type and a size bigger. In captions of more than one line the writer should aim at even lines. The use of stars, blobs, squares and other graphic decoration to draw attention to captions is unnecessary.

Some captions where the material is self-contained, and even those where the picture is exceptional, can be usefully given a headline. Here, a label heading, usually banished from news stories, can effectively draw the readers' attention to the message in the picture, especially if there is already a main headline on the story. For example, a sports picture headline might say:

HOWZAT!

or:

CAUGHT NAPPING!

or:

ENGLAND'S GLORY

On a human interest picture a headline might say:

THE LOVE CHILD SHE NEVER FORGOT

or on a train crash rescue:

THE MOMENT OF FREEDOM

Picture headlines which sometimes consist of clusters of words, perhaps in the form of a quotation, such as:

Dawn breaks over the base camp on the mountain that nearly cost them their lives

are not trying to tell you the essentials of the story. These are given in the news headline close by. They are trying to connect you with a fleeting moment in time caught by the camera. They are a rare example, as captions themselves sometimes are, of comment being allowed to intrude into a news page, though intrude is not the right word. What comment is doing in this case is to orchestrate and heighten what the picture is saying so that you are drawn to read the facts of the story.

Writing contents bills

One of the lesser known jobs associated with subbing is the writing of news bills, usually called *contents bills* (*posters* in the US). Part of a newspaper's self-publicity is to display these bills outside news-stands at strategic points in the circulation area.

There are various types. *Stock bills* are those that remind readers that racing form cards or TV programmes or 'latest sports news' can be found in the paper that night or morning. These are pre-printed with stock wording such as 'Today's race cards' or 'All tomorrow's TV programmes.' *General bills* are those that advertise an important story or new serial, and are placed at all display points in the circulation area. Third are *local bills*, which emphasize the local connection of stories and are placed in their own area.

On some papers a senior sub writes all the bills, taking the material off-screen as each page is made ready. In others, subs and page editors are asked to write off bills on any stories they are handling that they consider 'billable.'

The technique of writing contents bills is to disclose enough information to arouse the readers' interest without saying so much that the reader has no need to buy the paper – a legitimate advertising and publicity ruse. In this sense they are not explicit in the way headlines are, which are intended for the reader who has already bought the paper. For instance:

FLEET IN
STAND-BY
SENSATION

has urgency yet suggests an intriguing range of possibilities, and is typical wording for a general bill.

POP STAR IN
MARRIAGE
RIDDLE

likewise gives in general terms a story of wide-ranging possibilities, as does:

SEAMEN'S
STRIKE
DECISION

It would be self-defeating (and bad practice) if the wording deliberately misled the reader – for example, if the fleet turned out to be the Italian fleet or the pop star an obscure American West coast singer, or the seamen were from Danish ships. A good general bill should honestly justify the 'bait' placed before the passing reader.

With local bills the place name is all-important. A national paper which avoided the town's name in a headline would bill a story to its area as BRISTOL WIFE IN POISON RIDDLE if it felt the story were good enough to garner a few extra local sales. A town evening paper might exploit suburban references to bump up sales. The *Birmingham Mail* might bill the same story as HANDSWORTH WIFE IN COURT RUMPUS and WIFE IN SOLIHULL COURT RUMPUS. In cases of casualty figures or local election results, one story might yield a handful of local bills, each containing a different area name.

Bills can be 'local' in a different sense than in place names. A national story about universities might suggest 'local' bills for all university towns, or a council decision about housing be billed to all housing estates in an area. A story about theatres in general could be billed outside all London West End theatres.

Bills are unashamedly labels. While the active verb is not excluded it is not often there. The wording thrives on evocative but very general terms such as *rumpus, riddle, sensation, row* and *drama,* which would be frowned upon in headlines by most chief subs, but whose lack of precision is a virtue for the purpose of a bill. Long words should be avoided so that the words can be given maximum size for instant reading, with four or five words the maximum. The message should be simple, consisting of one thought. Bills that try to say too much do not get read.

The usual system is that bills are sent, hand-written, to the circulation department who produce them by stencil or heavy hand lettering on standard headed sheets for delivery by newspaper vans to distribution sites.

10

CHAPTER TEN

HANDLING A RUNNING STORY

A running story is one that continues to yield copy edition by edition throughout the day, and sometimes through several days. Handling it is the supreme test of a cool sub. It is so-called because it involves a continuous process of editing, revising and re-headlining the material, and often revising the layout, right up to the last press time of the last edition. It is a job for an experienced subeditor because of its speed and complexity, although a modest three- or four-paragraph story given to the newest sub on the table can turn into a running story and unexpectedly provide a career baptism of fire.

A wide variety of news events can become running stories, some of them foreseen, others totally unpredictable. The more obvious – and unpredictable – are disasters and rescue stories with the long-running drama of casualties and the hunt for survivors. Those that can be planned ahead include elections, with the cliff-hanger of the shifting balance of power as results are announced, and important trials taking several days in which evidence is covered by relays of reporters. Public inquiries, tennis tournaments, Test matches and political crises are other stories of this sort.

To edit a running story, sometimes in the intervals of handling other stories, you need a clear head, an acute news sense and speed. You give the story its required shape for the first edition using the copy available, if need be inserting the intro and leading paragraphs last so as to start with the most up-to-date situation. Yet no sooner is the story complete and the page sent than you begin reshaping it for the next edition, again with the intro being the last part to be written.

> The easy revision now possible in screen editing and make-up can allow for quick changes in all but the most complex of running stories. Here, a newsroom-collated new lead (if there is time to wait for it) can help where there is a rapidly changing situation or a variety of copy sources. More generally, the responsibility for the text falls on the sub, with newsroom and agency inputs arriving on screen thick and fast right up to the page deadline.

You can rejig and update a story as many times as there are editions if an ongoing situation demands it and the input of copy warrants it. In doing so, watch any figures and amounts carefully so that the middle of the story and the headline are updated along with the intro and there is no discrepancy. Later information can change the picture entirely and the whole sequence of paragraphs has to be kept under review. For instance, in a train crash story you must ensure you do not report in paragraph ten that rescuers are searching for someone who in paragraph two has been found.

More precise information later can alter impressions drawn from first eyewitness accounts. Keep in only those aspects of the earlier version that are still relevant to the narrative and not in contradiction to the fuller picture that is emerging. Sometimes the story as finally revised contains almost nothing of the first version. During revisions check that any material you keep in from an earlier version to fill the allotted space is not contradictory.

Dealing with the text

Here is how a broadsheet evening paper using screen make-up might handle a running story. This one is based on real-life actualities in order to show the problems involved:

10.00 a.m. Reuters news flash reports: SCHEDULED FLIGHT FROM LONDON HEATHROW TO CHILE TWO HOURS OVERDUE AT SANTIAGO. The newsroom checks flights to Santiago and identifies the aircraft as almost certainly British Airways Flight 004 from London but can get no confirmation from the airport.

11.00 a.m. The editor at his main production conference decides to get a story into page one of the first edition, due to press at 12.30 hours, and gives it the right-hand end column, the usual late news spot, on the assumption that more copy will arrive.

11.15 a.m. A second Reuters news flash reports: WRECKAGE OF AIRLINER SIGHTED BY MILITARY AIRCRAFT ON MOUNTAIN TOP NEAR CUZCO, PERU. It is 6 o'clock in the morning in Peru.

11.30 a.m. The two Reuters flashes and a background piece from the newsroom, who have identified Flight 004 as being a Boeing 747, are given to the page one sub to prepare a quick story. The empty page slot with headline and body setting marked in is the only hole remaining on screen in an otherwise made-up page one. The page-to-plate deadline is 11.45 a.m.

11.35 a.m. The editor switches the story from single column to a double-column shape alongside an 'own correspondent' political splash (Figure 44) and gives it his own headline in three lines of 60pt capitals:

BRITONS FEARED LOST IN ANDES AIR DISASTER

There is some discussion over the words 'Britons' and 'disaster' but the editor takes the view that the flight, since it is a British Airways flight from London, must be carrying some Britons and that a passenger airliner coming down on a mountain top is the

Figure 44 First inkling of a disaster story – layout 1

disaster category. The airline has still not confirmed that it is Boeing 747 Flight 004, though they have not denied it. The picture library offers stock pictures of Boeing 747s in British Airways livery.

11.45 a.m. The sub has managed to put together seven paragraphs based on the Reuters flashes, the news room inquiries, information on the aircraft's known stops and help from an atlas, and it spills neatly, all in double column, down the shape in the page (Figure 45). It is a line short but the sub presses the vertical justification key and seven left-over points of space is leaded evenly through the text so that it fills. A third Reuters flash, HELICOPTER REPORTS NO SIGN OF LIFE IN AIRLINER WRECKAGE IN ANDES, arrives just in time for the intro paragraphs, which the sub is able to reword as:

A number of Britons were believed to be on board a British Airways Boeing 747 jet which crashed in the high Andes in Peru early today with a feared big loss of life.

11.49 a.m. The re-worded version is dropped into the page by the sub a tolerable four minutes late. The earlier pages have gone well and the plate room is happy. The editor hopes still to have the edition out on time.

12.15 p.m. A *lead* story now comes from the agency, building on the earlier flashes and a *rush* message about the flight being off course, together with the agency's own background sources, into a twelve-paragraph story but it goes no further than the sub's own effort. There have been no further rushes and the editor is pleased there is a useful story in the first edition.

12.30 p.m. A news agency rush, followed by *snaps* giving details, announces that 27 Britons joined Flight 004 at Heathrow. British Airways, who have made a statement to the press, say that first indications suggest there may not be many survivors. Peruvian Army helicopter units are trying to reach the crashed aircraft which is on the edge of a small plateau.

12.40 p.m. The editor consults the managing editor and the chief-sub and decides to make the story the page one *splash* now that 27 Britons are known to be involved. The managing editor orders a location map from the art desk and gives the graphics assistant the atlas reference and geographical details. The chief-sub is told to get the old political splash reduced to a double in the vacant end two columns.

12.45 p.m. Further agency snaps arrive. The Peruvian Army is being helpful. It is airlifting a rescue team with radio by helicopter to the crash scene. The team is in contact with the army base near Cuzco.

Figure 45 The story develops – layout 2

12.50 p.m.   The Press Association (national) agency puts out an ADD ANDES AIR CRASH STORY saying that the 27 Britons on board are believed to include a national team of 12 women gymnasts bound for a pre-Olympic work-out at Valparaiso. The story gives no names. With this information the news desk checks out the likely members of the team who would have taken Flight 004. As is usual, British Airways do not name crash victims until names are confirmed and next-of-kin have been informed.

12.55 p.m. The page one sub, armed with the first edition just off the press, the Reuters lead, the PA *add* story, the latest snaps and a piece from the news room on the women gymnasts, starts updating the story for the second edition splash. It has a 1.15 p.m. page deadline. The editor soothes the political correspondent for downgrading his important story, which is to do with the effect of new housing legislation on the town, and suggests a follow-up feature on it for next day's paper in addition to the half-lead still on page one.

There are 20 minutes in which to prepare the splash. Twelve column inches (300 mm) plus an intro across three columns are being kept for it. The centre and top of the page are reshaped to allow for the display the editor wants. A column one story about a local councillor finishes down column six. The political lead and the tie-in material above it are combined and cut by another sub to fit the space in columns seven and eight. Some cuts offered by the political correspondent are gratefully accepted; even with screen make-up it is all hands to the pumps when there is a lot of work on a text-size page and not much time.

Pictures are the real problem, the stock jumbo jet being a bit static (Figure 45), although the map is now on screen and waiting. The first edition air crash story was short and set in 10pt across two columns, but the new story is mostly in single column and a good deal longer. It is almost a complete re-write to take in new facts.

The sub drops the main part of the story into the page, leaving the first two paragraphs until last. The chief-sub writes the new headline which says in 120pt 'disaster caps':

FEARS FOR 27 BRITONS IN JET DISASTER

It carries the strapline:

Big death roll as London airliner hits mountain top

The story is wrapped round a three-column picture of the Boeing 747 from stock, carefully captioned. To the left of the intro

with the stringer there and has found the Army authorities helpful. The Army has even agreed to airlift both of them to the forward base from which the search is being directed.

Meanwhile the newsroom has produced a background story about the gymnasts with a recent picture of the team, two of whom come from the circulation area. It is not known for certain if all of them boarded the flight. There is some discussion between the editor and the news editor. The picture would be useful on page one but with the passenger list still not released it poses a delicate problem. The editor decides, on the grounds of taste, not to use it for the present but to have it scanned and prepared.

2.00 p.m.   The editor changes his mind about the gymnasts picture and decides it will be reasonable to use it provided it has a non-committal caption and goes with a separate story and headline. It must in no way be interpreted as being part of a list of casualties.

The managing editor, who has more or less taken control of the crash situation, asks the chief sub to find a home for the projected dog rescue story and picture on page two in order to clear the way for the gymnasts. The new picture is schemed across four columns below the fold, almost the same shape as the dog picture but slightly shallower. The sub who did the jumbo jet tie-in story is given the job of preparing careful copy to go with the gymnast's picture. This is slotted into columns one and two in place of the tie-in story. The newsroom has supplied only identification material, not being certain how the picture would be used with the main crash story.

2.05 p.m.   The splash sub begins revising for the 2.40 p.m. page deadline for the 3 o'clock edition. Leaving the intro again till last, the sub works in the new details, picking up the earlier text where it still applies and restoring the material on previous jumbo crashes, which is run on at the end. This will make a useful late cut if the story gets too long since it is the least important part of it.

2.22 p.m.   The Reuters pair, who have managed to get their first message to London from the forward base using Army facilities, send a description of the scene on the plateau, where it is now 9 a.m. local time. Cloud has lifted and 12 rescuers are combing the wreckage, though hampered by the high altitude. The sub decides to work this material into the intro.

2.30 p.m.   A Reuters rush says: THREE CRASH SURVIVORS FOUND. ENGLISH STEWARDESS SLIGHTLY HURT. TWO PASSEN-GERS IN SERIOUS CONDITION. NO SIGN FURTHER SUR-VIVORS. The information is just in time to be included in the intro which now reads:

An English stewardess and two passengers are thought to be the only survivors of a British Airways Boeing 747 jumbo jet which crashed in the high Andes in Peru early today.

The stewardess, who is only slightly hurt, was being airlifted by helicopter along with the two injured passengers, to a hospital in Cuzco, 200 miles away from the cash scene.

Peruvian Army mountain rescue troops are still searching the wreckage of the airliner whose 220 passengers and crew includes 47 Britons. Among them are members of a team of women gymnasts who boarded the aircraft in London. Two of the team are believed to come from Lancashire (*i.e. in the circulation area*).

This means reducing part of the rescue description for the present, but the sub knows it is important to *nose* the story on the latest information since the fact of the crash will already be known to readers through radio and television newscasts. The thrust of the story must now centre on the rescue operation and the survivors, in which the journalists on the spot have an unbeatable advantage. The one snag is that, being agency reporters, there will be no exclusive angles available to any paper.

The final step for the 3 o'clock edition is to update the splash headlines (Figure 46), which are changed to read:

Air hostess and couple survive
out of 220 in air crash

THREE ALIVE
IN BRITISH JUMBO
JET WRECKAGE

The splash story now spills round the headline and picture of the gymnasts, and runs down almost to the foot of column six.

2.50 p.m. A Press Association 'with air crash' story begins running, giving the names of the crew of the jumbo, which have been released by

185

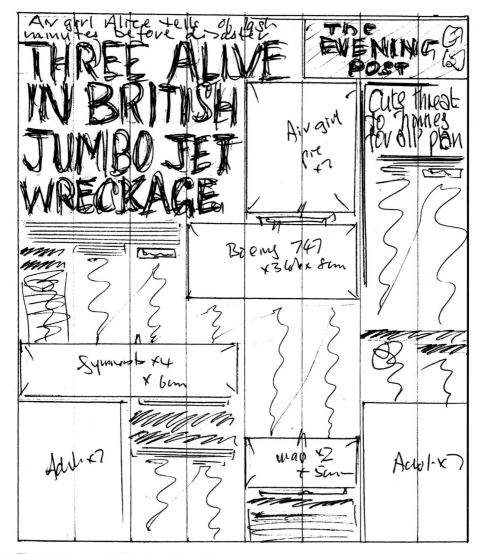

Figure 47 . . . and still more – layout 4

British Airways. Four stewardesses are included but the one that has been found alive has not been identified. PA promises pictures to follow.

3.00 p.m. The editor holds a last page one conference with senior colleagues before going off duty at 4 o'clock and handing over to the managing editor. They decide to build up the local end – the two Lancashire women in the gymnasts team – but to keep the splash in its present space. In the absence of pictures from the scene, the one of the gymnasts, which has been provided by a reader, becomes a key element on page one. Also, it is exclusive.

The news editor suggests sending a reporter to see the families of the two women but the editor rules against this on the ground of taste since it has not been confirmed that they actually caught the flight. Also, the official casualty figures have still not been released, nor are they likely to be before the last press time of 4.45p.m. For the present, the local end would have to rest on the team picture and the background material which the newsroom has culled from cuttings. The editor says that the local end should be included in the strapline.

3.10 p.m.   The sub meanwhile begins revising for the 3.40 deadline for the 4 o'clock edition, lifting the reference to the two Lancashire gymnasts, on instructions, into the second paragraph. He covers this by saying that although the names of the crash dead have yet to be released, the two were members of the team of gymnasts who were known to have boarded the flight at Heathrow.

3.25 p.m.   A Reuters rush message gives the names of the survivors which have been announced by the hospital in Cuzco. The stewardess is Alice Merrin, aged 26, of Hampstead, London, and the other two a husband and wife named Williams from Cardiff. The sub quickly re-noses the splash to bring in this information, dropping down the local reference to paragraph four.

By this time the promised Press Association photographs of crew members have arrived and a stand-by picture of Alice Merrin is scanned and imaged into a two-column slot the managing editor has prepared for it in the page. This is done rather neatly. The pictures of the aircraft, the gymnasts and the map are moved round, the map finishing up down columns five and six, so that most of the elements, including the rejigged splash, can still be used (Figure 47). The main heading is the same but is broken into four lines so that the two-column picture of the stewardess can go at the top of columns five and six. The gymnasts copy is cut and reset into a short single-column piece in column one, a story is lost down column three and the rest of the page is left as it is.

3.37 p.m.   An agency second new lead noses on the survivors' names and gives an account of the crash scene by their correspondents seen from their helicopter. This enterprising piece of reportage comes too late for the revised story, which is past its press time for the 4 o'clock edition. The managing editor decides to get back at the text in the 4.45 p.m. *slip* edition. This is a permitted quick plate change used for mopping up late stories on page one and late racing and sports fixtures on the back. The page plan is not altered and the changes have to be in-and-out text or headline segments. The deadline for this is 4.20 p.m.

3.50 p.m. Reuters snaps report the air stewardess as saying: AIRCRAFT RAN INTO VIOLENT THUNDER, LIGHTNING BEFORE CRASH. PILOT UNABLE TO REACH AIR CONTROL AT LIMA.

The first inkling of the crash cause from a survivor is worth a new intro, and also a new strapline, which is changed to read:

Air girl Alice tells of
last minutes before disaster

The sub reworks the first eight paragraphs of the story with the first local reference dropping further to paragraph six. Some of the description has to be left out so that the reworked paragraphs fit the space. The local end is still covered in the separate background piece now above the picture of the gymnasts, but there have been no further developments to this part of the story and nosing on the dramatic details about the survivors is inevitable. Also, the stewardess's story bears out the perceptive item from the group's air correspondent about local weather conditions.

4.15 p.m. A Reuters message says, PILOT'S BLACK BOX RECORDER FOUND BY ARMY RESCUE TEAM. Since this will hold the secrets of the aircraft's last minutes, the chief sub prepares this news, despite its lateness, as a self-contained *cut-off* item to drop into the middle of the story under the simple heading of LATE NEWS FLASH. The managing editor agrees this is the best way to handle it and a cut is made in the text to accommodate the cut-off. It will stand out in the page and achieve its purpose.

This last dramatic development marks the end of the evening paper's coverage of the air crash. With local time five hours behind Britain there should be plenty of material for morning paper follow-ups, with an interview with the stewardess being the prize to aim for, and with probably crash pictures and more technical data about the causes. By the end of the morning paper editions there is every likelihood, too, that an official casualty list will be available. It could be as busy a night on the morning paper as it has been a busy day on the evening.

FEATURES: PLANNING AND DESIGN

Features is broadly the part of the newspaper that contains opinion, assessment and advice – the subjective rather than the objective material of the news pages. In practice the features department (even the smallest of newspapers usually has one) deals with all manner of non-news content ranging from crossword puzzles to serials and articles by the famous, taking in along the way such things as women's pages, showbusiness gossip, TV programme notes and agony columns.

In production terms, the subbing calls for differences in routine and approach from the news pages. There are a number of reasons for this. While the features department might seem the counterpart of the newsroom, with the features editor in charge of writers and copy inputs, the work is more programmatic, with some autonomy being allowed to specialist writers who provide features on their topics. This material tends to be placed regularly in pre-selected part of the paper such as the political or leader pages, the women's page or the showbusiness or arts section. The quality Sundays – and dailies both national and regional on Saturdays – have separate sections given over to a variety of features.

There is more forward planning in this part of the paper and more time spent on copy preparation. When important books are serialized there can be weeks of negotiation and discussion followed by a careful 'gutting' of the text to provide a series of instalments. Some features require in-depth investigation over a period. The arts, showbusiness, fashion, holiday supplements and a good deal of sport are other areas where the writing, being tied to events, can be planned in advance.

Background articles to news events have to be written, it is true, but on the whole the features editor is able to operate a much longer term work schedule than his or her colleague in the news room, and the department's workload, down to the making up of the pages, can be programmed without the hazards of copy flow suffered on the news pages.

Copy sources

The longer time scale, guaranteed columnage and need for persuasive. opinion-forming writing means there is more scope for creative prose, or writing on which writers can impress their own personal style. There are usually a few gifted stylists who can turn their hand to a variety of contemporary topics under by-lines which become the paper's brand names. Many writers, however, specialize tightly, using their own particular knowledge, experience or training to write on subjects such as politics, education, economics, technology, finance, fashion, motoring, travel and even hobbies.

Some of these are staff writers where the demand for their subject is regular. Others are outside contributors who are paid a retainer or fee per article and who might also write for other publications on their speciality, not necessarily under the same name. Some newspapers share the work of group feature writers working for the same company.

Material such as crossword puzzles, comic strips, cartoons and horoscopes is supplied by syndication agencies operating nationally or even internationally. Some agencies also provide topical features with photographs and worldwide background situationers.

Special articles might be ordered from non-journalist experts such as ex-Cabinet Ministers, sports stars, trade unions leaders, or leading local politicians

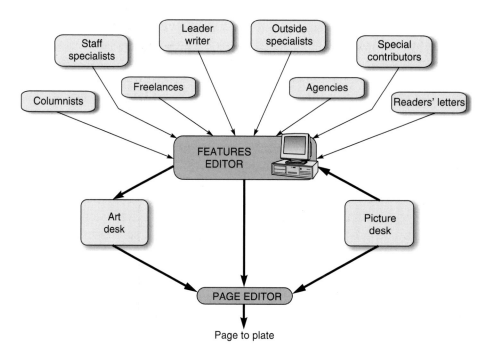

Figure 48 The features department: copy flow from writers to features editors and thence to page make-up

who happen to be in the news or whose views are though to be good for circulation. Freelance writers who submit material 'on spec' might find their work chosen if it fits the newspaper's plans.

Readers' letters form a significant part of features pages, not only in general columns but as the basis of advice or service columns written by experts ranging from travel writers and financial and legal experts to the 'agony aunts' who deal with readers' emotional and personal problems (Figure 49). Some staff experts give advice by letter as well as basing their column on letters. Letters might also be solicited on specific subjects where reader-participation features are planned. (See F. W. Hodgson, *Modern Newspaper Practice*, Focal Press, 4th edition, 1996, Chapter 4.)

Copy sources are thus more diverse than with news, but also more pre-planned and subject to precise arrangements (Figure 48).

Planning

Filling the features pages forms part of the same planning process, by discussion and conference, as the news pages. Some of the material is tied to the news. At executive level ideas are discussed and exchanged, the features editor reports on the day's proposed input, and spin-off articles arising from the news are set in motion for the day or for subsequent days.

There is a greater participation by the editor in the features to be run since many express the opinions and policy of the paper, although some writers have a free hand, within limits, to express their own. There is a close relationship between the editor and industrial and political writers in the planning of the editorial opinion, or leader, which is the mouthpiece of the paper. This can be written by the editor (although national papers have specialist leader writers) and it is an important subject for conference discussion.

Where there is particular topicality to a specialist subject, such as a controversial television programme, the launching of a new range of cars, or a worrying phase of industrial trouble, special space might be allocated. Sometimes, feature writers are asked to provide a comment piece to add to a news story. Running a one-off piece by a big-name contributor might mean having a page one *blurb* on the day, or the day before, so the readers know about it. Contents bills might need to be ordered to publicize an important feature, at points of sale or a special placing given to news stories connected with it. All these features matters are brought up at the planning conference.

Inevitably there is overlap with news. By-line experts might be called in to report on stories relevant to their field as well as provide features. Reporters might be asked to help out with investigative features where *legwork* is needed.

Figure 49 The agony aunts – mainstay at the popular end of the market in the national tabloids and in many provincial papers. These examples are from the *Birmingham Evening Mail* and *The Sun*

In some newspapers, where by-line writers are allowed to inject comment into news they are covering, it can be hard to tell whether a piece is a news item or a feature. This is a controversial area where editors who allow this sort of overlap might encounter complaints about bias in news coverage.

Topicality remains a strong element with features as it does with news. Subjects might still be pegged to seasonal or contemporary events, as with show business and fashion writing, travel, holidays, the arts and family features. Even writing on food and recipes tends to have a seasonal basis. Feedback and criticism from readers are also taken into account in establishing a content in which the news and features are complementary and jointly targeted on the readership.

Features production

The difference in production terms between features and news is that, with the exception of one or two 'live' pages, features pages are planned and made up in advance of news pages, some on morning and evening papers being prepared the day before. The reasons for this are twofold:

1 Except for spin-offs from news of the day, the longer-term ordering and planning in features departments enables copy and pictures to be made available earlier, often with the advantage of pre-determined copy length.
2 Features are prepared mostly for fixed slots or for display on pages where space is planned and the advertisements sold early, so the pages can be made up without hindrance or delay.

The consequence of this is that editorial production is planned so that the subbing and making up of news pages does not find itself clashing with the TV programme pages or last night's theatre reviews. Features pages, whether made up on screen or still by paste-up, are the first to be completed and consigned to the plateroom.

On morning and evening papers, where editorial production usually splits into shifts, the early subs or page editors deal first with the features pages, then move on to the news pages. On some papers, production is separate from news and there is a features chief subeditor responsible to the features editor or assistant editor (features), with separate subeditors. A big national paper might have a separate art desk for page design.

The features page that is left until last is the one containing the editorial opinion, which needs to be up to the minute, the main feature article of the day, and perhaps the political column. This page is 'sent' just before page one and the back page.

The main difference on smaller papers is that the chief sub usually supervises the subbing and making up of both news and features pages, with the features editor supplying the more important page plans and having the final authority over the pages.

While there is a good deal of common ground in the subbing and making up of news and features pages there are also some important differences. These concern particularly the handling of text and page design. These differences will be dealt with in the rest of this chapter and in the following chapter.

Page design

News pages have a balanced arrangement of stories with a lead, half lead and maybe six to ten other stories (including briefs) forming a pattern based on headlines, pictures and text. Features pages have maybe just two or three items and sometimes only one. As a result, the projection is more contrived and thematic than with news (Figures 52 and 53), with emotive or eye-catching headlines and a more deliberate visual pattern. Type and pictures are used with greater freedom.

Typography

To offset the longer features texts, the typography is generally bolder and more varied, with quotes and subsidiary headlines used as breakers. Panel rules often divide a feature from the remainder of the page. Stars, blobs and reverse type (white on black or colour, or black on tint) might be used to highlight parts of the text.

The type chosen for the main feature headlines is likely (though not always) to be different from the rest of the paper, and the choice of type can be influenced by the theme of the text. Thus, depending on the type character of the paper, lighter faced types such as Helvetica light, Record Gothic, Futura, Century light and old seriffed faces such as Garamond might be used for softer features, while bold expanded faces are brought in for headlines that demand impact.

Type decoration can range from holly borders for Christmas to crowns and architectural rules for royal features, and drawn diagrams, motifs and bleachouts of all kinds to set moods and supplement half-tone illustrations. Computer graphics have greatly increased the choice of such material in screen make-up. Artistically placed white space remains an important element.

Pictures

Pictures on features pages are often bigger, or used in series or as part of a compo or montage (see Figure 50), and are generally more integral to the display. Where a picture is chosen for a news page usually for its news value, on a features page it can be used to establish mood or atmosphere, or be given a deliberate display function.

The text

The text generally has the same body type as the news pages but the measure, or setting width, often varies from the set columns. Drop capital letters on intros, little used in modern news pages, have made a comeback and are sometimes house style, turning up as eye breakers in place of cross-heads. Indented setting is commonly used to show greater white space; column rules, which are used to separate stories on news pages, are dispensed with and columnar white space used for separation instead.

Crossheads – often some formal 12-point line on news stories – are chosen from display faces to match the headline type rather than conforming to a general style, and can be of two lines instead of one, sometimes with underscores. Italic or bold paragraphs to give emphasis, or as eye breaks, are more likely to be found on features pages because of their usefulness in breaking up long texts.

Other devices used in the cause of display are *stand-firsts,* which are short blurbs in different type placed above the intro (thus standing first) to introduce the feature; and *by-lines* or *sign-offs* giving the writer's name, often in display type and maybe set in a panel (see Figure 50). A stand-first might include the credentials of the writer. If the name is well known it will be given special prominence; in the case of exclusive stories by the famous it can be the biggest type on the page.

It would be wrong to use all the typographical devices mentioned above on features pages, or in one newspaper. Even though there is a freer approach to display, newspapers retain a typographical style that encompasses the sort of type and devices that may be used with features text so that the paper does not become a typographical mish-mash, and so that its type character is preserved.

Guiding the reader

Stock logos, or identification devices, are commonly used to flag regular features such as television programmes, cartoons, horoscopes and the editorial opinion column (Figure 50). Where possible these features appear in a fixed spot in each issue of the paper to facilitate easy finding. The logo message is simple: *Opinion, Your Stars, Sunday Fun,* or simply the writer's name in biggish type in the case of a regular commentator on current events or a challenging personal column. Here the name, with picture, gets the display, the headline being of lesser importance.

Figure 50 The furniture of the features pages: a selection of columnist by-lines and logos for a variety of service columns and special features

The 'selling' of regular columnists tends to be low-key. They might be allowed regular slots on pages which are otherwise given over to news, but they are differentiated by their logo and static familiar display, and perhaps the use of *drop letters,* so there is no danger of mistaking them for news.

> The typesetting and flagging of TV and radio programmes is an important area for the familiarity technique. Newspapers take a good deal of trouble to give programmes a format which makes the details readable and instantly findable as well as accurate. Bold type is used to highlight the names and times of programme and 'still' shots from the day's offerings included to catch the eye (see page 46).

The contrasting elements of bold display and familiarity can be seen in the Birmingham *Evening Mail* features spread reproduced in this chapter (Figure 51). The imaginative page design, built around pictures, is flagged at the top with a white-on-tint stencil logo, and lower down a white-on-black 'Factfile', telling the readers that it is one the paper's 'Talking Point' investigations. In this example there is another familiarity touch – the paper's Comment column in its regular deep panel on the left. It is a technique much used in the national Sunday papers, where episodes of series are presented with a well pictured display to carry the 'big read' and a familiar logo to remind the reader about it.

It will be seen from the page examples analysed below that headlines can be subservient to pictures in drawing the eye to features material. In some cases the headline might be relegated to a decorative breaker in the text. It will also be seen that there is a good deal of variation in the way type and pictures are used, depending upon the readership market of the paper.

Features workshop

The pages reproduced in this chapter are intended to show the freer approach to features page design whatever the type of newspaper, and to demonstrate the ideas that have been discussed above. They should be compared with the more static design effects in the news pages shown in the earlier chapters.

The two-page spread from the tabloid-sized Birmingham *Evening Mail* (Figure 51) is an example of the imaginative use of type, half-tone and display devices in tackling a serious subject – in this case 'stalking' – across the paper's 14-column double width. The layout takes advantage of the absence of advertisements to run a daringly cut page-deep picture of a look-alike model, balanced visually by the bold deep Comment panel on the left.

As the reading eye traverses from right to left, it encounters the other main focal point – the big headline:

Looking
into the
eyes of
TERROR

In a heavy condensed sans type of a 'bastard' 114-point depth. Between the two are the 'eyes' of the headline peering through a partly open door. Only then, after the impact has been achieved, does the reader's attention switch to the strap-line, the logo, and thence to the stand-first and the start of the story.

It is a model of visual persuasion. It is also an example of the sort of subject that gains in drama from black and white illustration rather than colour. A degree of mono 'colour' is obtained down the page by running the subsidiary text and its headline in type-on-dark tint fading to light. Other than that there is a simple 4-point black rule tying in the top of the spread, and a standfirst is of correct weight against the intro type. The lighter sans headings in the Comment panel and its Helvetica body setting are useful foils against the feature types.

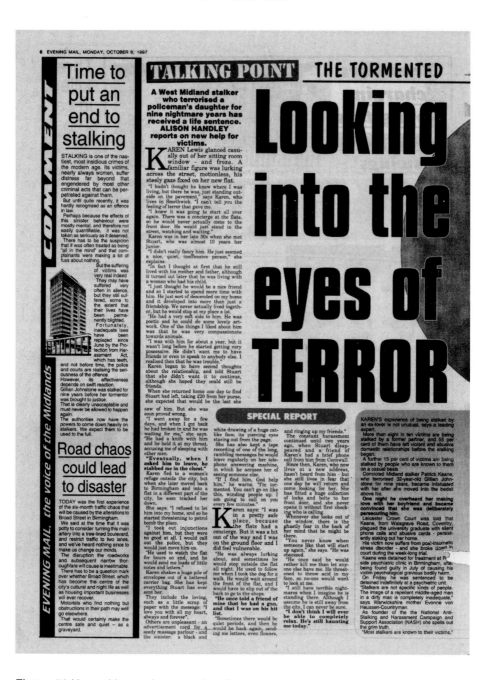

Figure 51 How a big evening paper handles a double-page features spread: a *Birmingham Evening Mail* special report on women plagued by stalkers

EVENING MAIL, MONDAY, OCTOBER 6, 1997 7

WOMEN WHO ARE PLAGUED BY STALKERS

FACTFILE

● More than 8,000 victims of stalking contacted NASH for advice, counselling or support, between January 1994 and January 1997. Only 210 of them were men.
● 95 per cent of victims said they had received inadequate help from the police.
● A third of victims had suffered rape or sexual abuse at the hands of their stalker.
● There were 17 stalking-related deaths of victims nationwide between spring 1994 and 1996.
● Stalking basically falls into three categories: post domestic stalking following the break-up of a relationship; casual contact stalking in which the stalker and victim are merely acquaintances; and cases where the stalker is a total stranger to the victim.
● Many victims of stalking suffer depression, panic attacks, agoraphobia and acute or chronic post traumatic stress disorder.
● NASH can be contacted on 01926 850089.

Trapped in a deadly game of obsession

she warns. "Only five per cent of stalking victims claim that their stalker is a complete stranger.

"However, you can be stalked for a long time before you actually find out WHO your stalker is.

"A lot of stalkers will sit in front of their victim on the train, or opposite them in a restaurant, or beside them on the bus.

"Because they look like an ordinary commuter or diner, the victim isn't aware of their identity, until they are eventually confronted. It's at that point they will think 'I have seen that face'.

"That's where the power and control comes in. The stalker is near enough to kill you, but you don't know who they are."

It was her own teenage daughter's ordeal at the hands of a stalker which prompted Evonne to set up NASH in 1993. At the time, the word 'stalking' wasn't even part of the British vocabulary.

"I introduced the term into British usage when my daughter, my husband and I visited our MP," explains Evonne. "We wanted him to intervene with the Chief Constable on my daughter's behalf.

"She was an A-level student and she was being pursued by a deranged and dangerous man.

"The MP's response was simple - the law cannot be changed just because a young man finds your daughter attractive.

"It was a great pleasure three and a half years later to see him in the Commons, about to vote for a law that he said could never be enacted."

Evonne worked closely with the Home Office on tough new anti-stalking legislation which finally came into power earlier this year.

The Protection from Harassment Act, which covers a wide range of behaviour, including conduct causing alarm or distress, carries a maximum penalty of five years imprisonment or a substantial fine.

Although the legislation marked a successful end to the NASH campaign, Evonne has been busy helping to make the police and legal profession aware of how it will work in practice.

She is also working on plans for a network of support groups, beginning with one in Birmingham, to offer advice and support to the victims of stalking.

The groups will be run by people who have experienced stalking themselves, or within their families.

Says Evonne: "To keep this issue in the hands of the professionals is never going to empower victims. People can only truly empathise if it has happened to them.

"When you are being stalked your life is taken over. We are trying to give victims back their self-confidence and self-respect and help them restore their control over their lives."

TERRORISED: Gillian Johnstone was haunted by a stalker for nine years. Stalker picture posed by a model

If one had any carping criticism to make it would be that the Factfile WOB intrudes too much into the circular half-tone, and that an extra drop letter as an eye-break would have helped in the first column of the spread – preferably not another K.

Avant garde by the standards of its quality colleagues, *The Guardian* continues to plough its own furrow in page design. The arts page in Figure 52 groups photographs in a solid slab down the focal centre to illustrate a feature on television drama, balancing them against a 60-point Univers bold main heading:

Prison's too good for us

And some tantalizing white under an upended arts logo. Up-ended logos are de rigeur these days in the glossies and even in the artier features pages of some regional dailies, but never was 120-point Univers deployed to such striking effect as in this *Guardian* design. Nor would it normally be atop such an interesting slab of white, but then the creative use of white is *The Guardian's* own special contribution to the pages we read.

The *Guardian* style is no longer regarded as a designer's gimmick. Witness the traverse of the eye in this case: first, the immaculately cropped study from *Cathy Come Home*, then the bold headline, through the enticing stand-first and – taking a deep breath – into the intro. After a few paragraphs, curiosity strikes: the eye feels it must still leap away to explore down the white hole to the 'Shooting Stars' items. This done, it settles back into the meat of Peter Ansorge's thesis despite it being aggressively lacking in crossheads or eye-breaks, as is *The Guardian's* style. As this unfolds, the relevance of the remaining small pictures in the 'slab' becomes clear.

The reader is captured, and there is still the bonus of the Laurence Donegan piece on the Burrell Collection neatly tucked away underneath to move to next with its characteristic *Guardian*-style thumbnail cartoon. It is perhaps a tribute to the copywriter's art that the advert on the bottom left seems a natural extension of this page design and raises a momentary query in the reader's mind.

Perhaps because it is a book review (Figure 53), the *Daily Mail* arts page takes a very different approach. The design here shows how simple type balance and well cut, if static, pictures can give a touch of traditional elegance. The Century bold condensed type, which the *Mail* retains for its features pages, allows a good character count, enabling a meaningful headline to be achieved in 84-point. The 'Books' label and the by-line are admirably discreet, and the *stand-up* drop letters in the *Mail's* features style make useful text breaks. The bold adverts on

Figure 52 Features display *Guardian* style: daring white spaces and eye-grabbing big picture

Figure 53 The elegance of a *Daily Mail* books page: stand-up drop letters, neat picture balance and clean uncluttered setting are the ideal foil against cluttered advertising

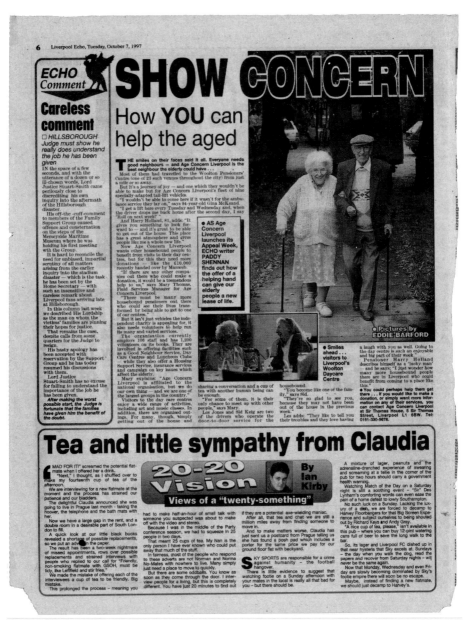

Figure 54 A leader page for all tastes: a strongly pictured main feature, a perceptive leading article and a light-hearted columnist go together well in this *Liverpool Echo* design

the right are left to their own space without clash of type or half-tone from the editorial content.

The picture crops are subtle, the space on either side of the head in the main portrait giving a feeling of depth, the oval looking nicely in period for the flashback picture of the subject. Add to this the fine rule round the type-on-light-tint headline and the one enclosing the oval picture, and we have another example of how mono still can score in the right page environment.

Our final sample in this features workshop is a very professional leader page from the *Liverpool Echo* (Figure 54). Here, you have eye appeal based on good type and picture balance, and yet the page has a feeling of busyness which a big city evening paper should have.

The main feature publicizing the paper's campaign to help the city's aged gains in impact through the cropping of the picture of the elderly couple, who are highlighted against the retained background. They seem to be walking out of the trees and into the page. The overprinting of the headline SHOW CONCERN on to the top of picture accentuates its significance rather than detracts from it. The smaller picture adds a cheerful extra dimension and usefully holds up the shadow box *stand-first* (though here not really standing first), thus providing two focal points centre-page.

The *Echo* Comment, with its rounded-corners box and liver bird motif, provides visual balance to the left of the page. The Ian Kirby column with its flip headline 'Tea and a little sympathy from Claudia' and type-and-picture *compo* nicely holds up the bottom. It also gives subject balance to the whole by providing lighter reading as a foil to the more serious items – a useful function on a leader page.

12 FEATURES: EDITING AND PROJECTION

The essentials of subediting are the same for features as for news. You check copy for factual and grammatical accuracy and for legality, you edit it to the required length, and eliminate ambiguity, sloppy writing and errors of house style. You write headlines and captions in the type and setting required and – these days – fit the text and the pictures together on to a layout blocked out on screen until the page corresponds with the ideas of the page executive who originated it.

So far so good, but the features sub needs to be aware of some important differences from news in the handling of text and the projecting of material. Headline writing, for instance, can be very different.

Accuracy

First a warning: do not assume experts always to get their facts right. Some who are close to their subject rely too much on their knowledge and memory and let through basic mistakes where the less informed would have checked. Memory can play false with names, titles and functions and with dates – for instance, of Acts of Parliament. Politicians as contributors are notorious for factual blind spots when not being briefed by their researchers. Always add up figures and check statistics and tables in stories, where possible, to see that they work out.

It is with non-journalist and some freelance contributors, unused to newspaper discipline, where the greatest chance of error lies. Since such contributions are often specially ordered and well displayed they throw a greater burden of checking on the subeditor. It will be no use you blaming the writer when you have been put there to spot any errors.

With regular staff writers the danger is less but the responsibility remains. Advice columns, upon which readers will rely, cannot afford to make mistakes. Merchandizing information in fashion pages has to be right. Crossword puzzles have to be checked to see that the clues work out. Television and radio programme details, a tedious editing chore that can fall to new subs, are a minefield for the unwary. Readers are quick to complain if anything is wrong.

Mistakes in figures in newspaper competitions, usually looked after by the features department, can result in bad publicity and cost newspapers money. A greater danger arises from the failure to spot factual errors or unjustified statements that might get the paper into legal trouble (see Chapter 9). Features material is not only more deliberately displayed than news; it can also be controversial and provocative, and this makes checking for accuracy a high priority in features subbing.

Language

Because features are mostly written to length and are often important for the way they say things rather than what they say, they are not normally given 'heavy' editing. The sort of rewriting carried out on news stories, because of bad copy, complex copy sources or shifts in emphasis, should not be needed.

There is a freer approach to intro, structure and sequence. These, however, are normally imposed by the writer. A feature that needs re-nosing and re-structuring by the subeditor is an exception, although it can happen.

Freed from the pressure on space and relentless word economy of the news pages, feature writers writing under their own by-lines adopt a wider range of vocabulary and idiosyncrasy of phrase. In some specialist areas the vocabulary might seem outside an ordinary reader's, as for example in articles on science, finance and some areas of sport.

Another reason why 'heavy' editing should not normally be needed is that the pages are free of the changes of space arising from the arrival of late news pictures, the revising for later editions or the organizing of running stories. In this sense the features subs' work lacks the excitement and 'dicing with the clock' of the news pages.

Style

What has to be allowed for is a greater regard for *style*. Copy can contain persuasive argument and description by which specialist writers communicate more directly and more personally with their readers. This can involve longer sentences and longer paragraphs. 'Repair' and improvements may still be necessary but in correcting weaknesses of grammar or word sequence you must be careful to preserve the writer's way with words. Style is a fugitive thing that can be damaged by insensitive or unnecessary editing. You should be seeking to keep in the colour, feel and pace of a well written feature, to use editing as a means of preserving and enhancing these qualities in addition to checking that the facts are right.

Here, from *The Times,* is an example of style in a feature from columnist Nigella Lawson:

> Seriously: how can anyone be shocked by the idea of an Oxford undergraduate earning money as a stripper? Modesty is a defunct virtue, informing most people's lives as little as that other super-annuated accomplishment, watercolouring. We retain enough of a memory of decorum to enjoy the frisson of surprise. But it's just a mime, not rooted in any moral dismay.
>
> Far from it: those under a certain age would rather admire Melissa Butler for strutting her stuff at the Sunset Strip in Soho. For them, the stripper is not some sleazy figure, but a strong woman who owns her body and is happy with it; a woman who gets what she wants – money and applause – for revealing what she is.

The first sentence establishes the tone of gentle mockery. And from the same edition of the same paper, Alan Coren pursues an almost equally idiosyncratic vein on the subject of telly watching in Bosnia:

> For what has stricken the Bosnian Serbs is the lack of decent telly. Confronted with an unremitting barrage of regional cultural pro-grammes, many of them repeats, those previously loyal to Nanja Luka's SRT TV have fled in their pitiable hordes. Unable to take any more wobbly documentaries about well-dressing or donkey enemas or jamjar museums, or rural hats, they have taken instead to the street. They have become box refugees. They do not know which way to turn.

Even seasonal fare can take on a certain quality in the hands of a stylist (this from the *Daily Telegraph*):

> Our Christmas feastings are nothing to those of our ancestors. From medieval times until Cromwell's Commonwealth the Twelve Days of Christmas were celebrated with feasting that could reach wild excess. Then the Puritans abolished Christmas festivities. A popular song of the time ran:
>
> > Plum broth was Popish, and mince-pies,
> > Oh, that was for idolatry
>
> With the restoration of the monarchy under Charles II, feasting returned, though never to the same extent, and favourite Christmas foods could be safely enjoyed once more.

> Plum broth, or Christmas Porridge or pottage, was the forerunner to the Christmas Pudding. A rich soup stuffed with dried fruit, thickened with breadcrumbs and enlivened with alcohol, it is quite delicious. Pepys noted on Christmas Day, 1662, that he enjoyed 'a mess of brave plum pottage' before his roast beef.

Not just a recipe, but titbits of information enlivened by a snatch of song and a cascade of mouth-watering verbs.

Some by-line contributors whose style is their brand image have contracts that specify that their copy should not be altered without their agreement. Editors try to limit the number of these arrangements since they can constrict production. Also, however good the writer there can still be space problems due to changes in advertising, or writers exceeding the ordered length, or where parts of a feature are not liked for legal reasons or on grounds of taste. The task of amendment remains with the subeditor. It is just that tact and discretion have to be added on to the attributes a news sub would be expected to have.

If one is looking for sacred cows then the one piece of copy you should not cut or alter is the paper's editorial opinion, although the facts, dates, quotations etc. still have to be checked. An error allowed through here would be akin to an act of sabotage. Ask the editor or leader writer for any cuts needed.

Ghost writing

In some newspapers, notably the national Sundays, the practice of ghost writing might be found. This is where a feature or even a book, is written by a professional writer for the person under whose name it appears.

Ghosting might at first sight seem an indefensible practice. It is certainly not one that newspaper journalists want to see encouraged, yet it may be the only means by which important one-off pieces of writing can reach the reader. It is used where a newspaper wants to carry a personal story by someone in the news, or whose experiences and opinions are of interest to the readers, but who might be too busy or have insufficient skill with words to provide copy in an acceptable form.

A feature writer who is an experienced 'ghost' is put in with the person by agreement, often with a tape recorder, but sometimes with a notebook, to 'talk out' the material. Ghosting can be done even over the telephone. The feature is then written, keeping intact the opinions and verbal style of the person – who might perhaps be a trade union leader, a sports personality or even a politician.

When complete, the text is shown for approval to the celebrity whose name it will carry. Any adjustments to wording or content are made and the finished article is signed as being agreed by the 'author'. It is then printed as an authentic piece of writing.

Writers employed on ghosting have to be adept at picking up nuances and shades of expression in conversation which they use in the writing, and they are expected to carry out their role sympathetically. The best are often professional freelances whose skill brings them a regular living from this sort of work.

If given ghosted work as the page sub you should handle the copy with the same care as the written work of any big-name outside contributor, checking back for approval any proposed changes in text or cutting to length, but checking above all for its accuracy and legality.

Reader participation

Reader participation is the stuff of features pages. Not only are readers' views aired regularly in letters columns but their opinions are solicited on subjects on which it is intended to run 'viewpoint' features – the Government's standing, favourite holiday stories, the popularity of TV programmes, the state of the roads, and so on. Advice and service columns also live off letters, while competitions of many sorts could not survive without willing and hopeful participants.

This promotional side of the paper is, in fact, carried out largely by the features department, helped by the promotions department where there is one. It serves the triple purpose of providing the readers with a platform, and often a service, and also getting the paper publicized and talked about.

Yet publishing letters can be fraught with danger. Readers write in hundreds and thousands each week with no idea of the limitations of space into which they have to fit if used (fewer than one in twenty letters to *The Times*, for instance, get published). Choosing them is the easy part – topicality and originality are looked for – but editing them to fit can court complaints of misrepresentation when perhaps fourteen to twenty paragraphs are reduced to three or four to give the point of a letter along with nine or ten others.

The total area available for them in a national paper might come to no more than a column and a half, including the space for the main headline and a number of smaller ones. There is usually more room set aside for them in regional and local papers. Some evening papers (see Figure 55) run a double page spread of letters to foster feedback to the editor of topics occupying readers' minds.

You need to be a sympathetic subeditor to edit letters in a succinct fashion without upsetting the writers. The practice with most papers is to check with the writer if the subject is controversial or personal. At *The Times*, the letters used are cut only by permission of the writers and the cut version read back to them, or faxed, over the telephone. A check with the writer is made by most papers if

Figure 55 Reader participation: letters are rated highly in all manner of newspapers, but there can be traps in running a Letters to the Editor column. These busy, well-filled examples are from the *Nottingham Evening Post* and the *Hull Daily Mail*

there is a fear that a seemingly newsworthy letter might not be genuine, or be part of a publicity stunt – a practice not unknown to editors.

> In cutting letters, try to keep in the essential point the reader is making by using their own words with the minimum of alteration even if a good deal of the letter cannot be used for space reasons. Well known in newspaper offices is the dictum of the old Press Council (now the Press Complaints Commission) that in a letters column 'editing should be done solely to qualify a letter for publication, and it should never be allowed to defeat or obscure the points or points the correspondent wanted to make.'

In other words, beware of taking phrases away from their context. In more general letters-based features, readers' views are quoted as part of a pattern of opinion supporting the aim of the article. When they are quoted in advice columns, usually only the relevant part of the reader's question is used.

Features and the law

Features pages give the office lawyer a lot more trouble than the news pages. The opinion and criticism they contain are more likely to wound than the objective reporting of fact. Some of the more sensational 'confessions' and 'lid off it all' series that appear in the national Sunday papers can suffer legal revision – and applications to the court for injunctions – right up to press time and have been known to die to the death as a result of the court's intervention after the page has been made up.

In buying such series, newspapers are aware that they are dependent on what the lawyer will allow because of the danger that lurks in the law of libel and contempt of court. Editors' belief that the public has a right to know what they have uncovered has to be tempered by their preference not to have to go to jail.

Investigative journalism in which matters of public concern, often concerning crime, are examined by skilled reporters who might get evidence from unorthodox sources, are a particular headache to lawyers.

You are likely to be given tricky jobs like these to edit only after the legal vetting process is complete, but the need for vigilance remains. A shift in a delicate situation or legal second thoughts – or even the wording of a headline – can result in a page being ripped apart at an inconveniently late hour and in changes in editing being carried out, and even pictures having to be replaced.

Projection

You are more involved with the projection of the edited material on features pages than is the case with news. A main feature is 'sold' visually to the reader by a complex of headlines, pictures, blurb, stand-firsts and quotations in which the sub has the vital promotional role. Not only are you editing the copy; you are persuading the reader of its importance and drawing attention to special aspects.

Thus editing ideas go beyond headline and intro. They require a degree of identity with the aims of the writer and an ability to exploit display techniques. You are drawing out the mood and underlying substance of the material and transmuting these in terms of picture, caption and significant quotation as well as headline. The editing, in short, is more visual and the subeditor is integrally involved in the design of the page.

Even in stock features occupying regular slots, such as a nature column or the arts reviews, mood is an important ingredient of the headline and you have to be responsive to this.

A *blurb,* which a feature might require (see Figure 56), is best described as a piece of self-advertisement carried by the newspaper, not necessarily on the same page as the feature, inviting readers to turn to it. Sometimes it consists only of one selling line that identifies the story (for example, 'confessions of a wayward star' or 'your verdict on the great drugs debate') accompanied by a page reference; or it might have several sentences of description. You aim to present a compelling reason, or reasons, why the reader should read the feature. Blurbs are mostly given a bold display that will stand out from the page. They

Figure 56 The front page blurb – and sometimes the back page – is the shop window for the day's big feature offering

might include a picture as well as type, with maybe the use of type reversed as a *WOB* or *BOT*. They combine the visual role of a display advertisement with that of a news bill or poster.

A *stand-first* (see examples on pages 198, 201 and 203) is likely to be used on a feature, especially a series which arises from special circumstances, to explain how or why the article came to be written. The aim is to justify or qualify what follows so as to enhance the readers' understanding or acceptance of it.

Blurbs and stand-firsts, the writing of which falls to the sub, are fundamental to the projection and call for imaginative and yet concise use of words so that within a small compass the reader can be given a compelling reason for reading on.

● Here, for students, is a useful exercise in features projection. An investigation has been made by a small team into the effects of loneliness on the aged in a big city. Three separate reports have been filed plus an exceptionally good mood picture worth running as a deep horizontal six-column illustration. There are two other smaller pictures of interior shots and some statistics from the local council. From these, devise a page one blurb, one main headline and two subsidiary ones, a stand-first and a panel of statistics, and project the material:

1 As a broadsheet display on a page with modest advertising.
2 As a double-page spread in a tabloid paper with no advertising.

A separate static feature, perhaps the Opinion column, could be used in each case as a foil to the main projection.

A number of scenarios like this could set a pattern for workshop projects. They could also include devising a static layout for television and radio programmes, and one for a weekly 'name' columnist writing pithy comments on current news, in which witty one-liners in, say, 14-point, might be used.

Features headlines

Headline writing, as with page design, has a freer approach than with news. The headline must still draw attention to the text and form a focal point in the display but these aims are merged in a big feature into a general projection in which pictures play a bigger part (most news stories are fairly short and do not have pictures) and in which blurb, stand-first, display quotations and even cross-heads and by-line all have a role.

While a headline might sum up the vital facts it need not necessarily do so. For a start, many features are built around comment or opinion or deduction arising out of facts that are already known. The headline is more likely to hinge on what the writer is trying to say or what the pictures on the page symbolize.

Take, for example, the features spread from the *Birmingham Evening Mail* (Figure 51, page 198). The headline LOOKING INTO THE EYES OF TERROR owes its existence to the boldly cut pictures of the frightened girl and the one of the eyes through the partly opened door. On its own it would be a meaningless label. But having been caught by the main display, the reader wants to know more. The 'Talking Point' logo and the strap heading, THE TORMENTED WOMEN WHO ARE PLAGUED BY STALKERS supply the necessary information. The stand-first and by-line pull the reader's eye down into the text. The Factfile WOB is there to give back-up. The combined assault upon the reader by the page designer and subeditor has worked.

The main picture also dominates *The Guardian* feature on TV drama (Figure 52 on page 201). The young mother holding the feeding bottle and looking bleakly across the page symbolizes the poignancy of *Cathy Come Home*. It is a striking picture cut to accentuate the look in the woman's eyes and it says more about a landmark TV drama than any words could have done. It is the woman and the feeding bottle that captures the eye and the imagination, compared to which the headline PRISON'S TOO GOOD FOR US remains an enigma and has to await explanation from the text. The stand-first does, however, give an inkling. The smaller pictures are there to support the thesis, and to invite the reader to play a who-was-who game with clips from yesteryear's dramas – no bad thing in a show-business feature.

The main headline and picture occupy about equal billing visually in the *Daily Mail* books page (Figure 53 on page 202). Actor-novelist Stephen Fry (also in cameo flashback) is a good picture subject, but the headline LOVE, SELF-LOATHING AND THE LIFE OF FRY is an inspired 'comment' headline that a reader with any interest in the subject would find it hard to resist, and it has to take precedence. The intro supports the headline immediately.

One summer afternoon at prep school, when he was about 11, Stephen Fry was off games and sloping around one of the dormitories when he came upon a joke shop catalogue.

Discovering that a half-crown postal order would acquire him, among other delights, chattering false teeth, a bar of soap that turned the user black, and a sugar cube that melted leaving a realistic-looking spider floating in the victim's teacup, etc.

Quiet elegance is the only additive such readable text requires. This is provided by clean 11-em setting, drop-letter eye-breaks and the discreet use of white space. It is a path that has been well trodden by the *Mail*.

The *Liverpool Echo's* main feature (Figure 54 on page 203) invites the readers' participation by yoking headline and main picture together in a successful read-me compo. SHOW CONCERN is the message for the day. Printing it across the top of the picture in this case highlights both headline and illustration, but it is the quality of the picture – in this case the old couple – that again dominates. The stand-first and the smaller picture are used to turn the text neatly round and under, leaving a useful amount of space on which to display the rest of the leader page contents. The result is a busy and attractive features page.

Here are examples of particular styles of features page headlines:

The emotive phrase

The Sun is rather good at this sort of headline, as in I JUST WANT TO DIE WITH DIGNITY IN THE ARMS OF PEOPLE I LOVE, and the terser MY EX IS SLEEPING WITH MY MOTHER.

The whimsical phrase

This goes well with the less serious sort of feature, as with the *Daily Telegraph's* GREAT COATS for a fashion feature on women's coats. Whimsy, however, can be serious, as in *The Times's* THE UNDERWRITING ON THE WALL.

The informative phrase

A headline that is better with a verb, even though it can still manage without the active voice, as in, HOLY GHOSTS: HOW A VICAR CAME TO BELIEVE SPIRITS ARE EVERYWHERE, in the *Daily Mail,* about a vicar with psychic powers. An enigmatic example from *The Independent*: HOW TO LEARN TO LOVE STOCK MARKETS EVEN WHEN THEY CRASH. And another how-it's-done one in the *Daily Mail*, on a Lynda Lee-Potter interview: HOW JOHN CLEESE BECAME AN EX-NEUROTIC.

The decorative phrase

Harnessing a pun or an old song title is the resort of the subeditor when confronted by an awkward review, a feature full of useful titbits for readers – or a bland holiday article. The *Daily Mail* offers, OH, ISLANDS IN THE SUN on its travel page; the *Liverpool Echo* counters with WE DO LIKE TO BE BESIDE THE SEASIDE. A review in *The Times* (they're good at word play) of a play once attributed to the Bard, has the neat HAM WROTE SHAKESPEARE, NOT BACON.

The confessional

My fifth category remains the tour de force of headline approaches and one that Fleet Street believes sells papers. The *News of the World* has unrivalled experience in this field with such blockbusters as MY ELECTRIC NIGHT SHIFTS WITH SORAYA and AGONY OF LOVING MY EAST-EASTENDERS CO-STAR. Then there is *The Express's* more sedate,

CHILDHOOD TRAUMA HAS LEFT ME HAUNTED BY FEAR, and *The Guardian's* avante garde version of the genre, I'M ALWAYS HOPING THAT I WILL WEAR OUT BEFORE MY CLOTHES DO.

You will see from these examples that space and word count are not usually the problem with features headlines since the page pattern is less formularized and the items fewer. Even with the constraints of narrow measure which can apply with static features in regular single- and double-column slots you have greater freedom of wording, and a good deal more professional pleasure, because of the variety of headline approaches possible with features material.

Moreover, you will find that the use of mood and colour in headlines and the freedom from hard news concepts removes dependence on headlinese even in tight headlines. Such tired cliché words as probe, shock, horror, quiz, rap and drama, which mar news page headlines, should not have to be resorted to.

PRESS COMPLAINTS COMMISSION CODE OF PRACTICE

The Press Complaints Commission is charged with enforcing the following Code of Practice which was framed by the newspaper and periodical industry and ratified by the Press Complaints Commission on 26 November 1997.

All members of the press have a duty to maintain the highest professional and ethical standards. This Code sets the benchmarks for those standards. It both protects the rights of the individual and upholds the public's right to know.

The Code is the cornerstone of the system of self-regulation to which the industry has made a binding commitment. Editors and publishers must ensure that the Code is observed rigorously not only by their staff but also by anyone who contributes to their publications.

It is essential to the workings of an agreed code that it be honoured not only to the letter but in the full spirit. The Code should not be interpreted so narrowly as to compromise its commitment to respect the rights of the individual, nor so broadly that it prevents publication in the public interest.

It is the responsibility of editors to co-operate with the PCC as swiftly as possible in the resolution of complaints.

Any publication which is criticized by the PCC under one of the following clauses must print the adjudication which follows in full and with due prominence.

1 Accuracy

(i)   Newspapers and periodicals must take care not to publish inaccurate, misleading or distorted material including pictures.

(ii) Whenever it is recognized that a significant inaccuracy, misleading statement or distorted report has been published, it must be corrected promptly and with due prominence.

(iii) An apology must be published whenever appropriate.

(iv) Newspapers, whilst free to be partisan, must distinguish clearly between comment, conjecture and fact.

(v) A newspaper or periodical must report fairly and accurately the outcome of an action for defamation to which it has been a party.

2 Opportunity to reply

A fair opportunity to reply to inaccuracies must be given to individuals or organizations when reasonably called for.

3 Privacy *

(i) Everyone is entitled to respect for his or her private and family life, home, health and correspondence. A publication will be expected to justify intrusions into any individual's private life without consent.

(ii) The use of long lens photography to take pictures of people in private places without their consent is unacceptable.

    Note – Private places are public or private property where there is a reasonable expectation of privacy.

4 Harassment *

(i) Journalists and photographers must neither obtain, nor seek to obtain, information or pictures through intimidation, harassment or persistent pursuit.

(ii) They must not photograph individuals in private places (as defined in the note to Clause 3) without their consent; must not persist in telephoning, questioning, pursuing or photographing individuals after having been asked to leave and must not follow them.

(iii) Editors must ensure that those working for them comply with these requirements and must not publish material from other sources which does not meet these requirements.

5 Intrusion into grief or shock

In cases involving grief or shock, enquiries must be carried out and approaches made with sympathy and discretion. Publication must be handled sensitively at such times, but this should not be interpreted as restricting the right to report judicial proceedings.

6 Children *

(i) Young people should be free to complete their time at school without unnecessary intrusion.

(ii) Journalists must not interview or photograph children under the age of 16 on subjects involving the welfare of the child or of any other child, in the absence of or without the consent of a parent or other adult who is responsible for the children.

(iii) Pupils must not be approached or photographed while at school without the permission of the school authorities.

(iv) There must be no payment to minors for material involving the welfare of children nor payment to parents or guardians for material about their children or wards unless it is demonstrably in the child's interest.

(v) Where material about the private life of a child is published there must be justification for publication other than the fame, notoriety of his or her parents or guardian.

7 Children in sex cases

1 The press must not, even where the law does not prohibit it, identify children under the age of 16 who are involved in cases concerning sexual offences, whether as victims or as witnesses.

2 In any press report of a case involving a sexual offence against a child –

(i) The child must not be identified.

(ii) The adult may be identified.

(iii) The word 'incest' must not be used where a child victim might be identified.

(iv) Care must be taken that nothing in the report implies the relationship between the accused and the child.

8 Listening devices *

Journalists must not obtain or publish material obtained by using clandestine listening devices or by intercepting private telephone conversations.

9 Hospitals *

(i) Journalists or photographers making enquiries at hospitals or similar institutions must identify themselves to a responsible executive and obtain permission before entering non-public areas.

(ii) The restrictions on intruding into privacy are particularly relevant to enquiries about individuals in hospitals or similar institutions.

10 Innocent relatives and friends *

The press must avoid identifying relatives or friends of persons convicted or accused of crime without their consent.

11 Misrepresentation *

(i) Journalists must not generally obtain or seek to obtain information or pictures through misrepresentation or subterfuge.
(ii) Documents or photographs should be removed only with the consent of the owner.
(iii) Subterfuge can be justified only in the public interest and only when material cannot be obtained by any other means.

12 Victims of sexual assault

The press must not identify victims of sexual assault or publish material likely to contribute to such identification unless there is adequate justification and, by law, they are free to do so.

13 Discrimination

(i) The press must avoid prejudicial or pejorative reference to a person's race, colour, religion, sex or sexual orientation or to any physical or mental illness or disability.
(ii) It must avoid publishing details of a person's race, colour, religion, sexual orientation, physical or mental illness or disability unless these are directly relevant to the story.

14 Financial journalism

(i) Even where the law does not prohibit it, journalists must not use for their own profit financial information they receive in advance of its general publication, nor should they pass such information to others.

(ii) They must not write about shares or securities in whose performance they know that they or their close families have a significant financial interest, without disclosing the interest to the editor or financial editor.

(iii) They must not buy or sell, either directly or through nominees or agents, shares or securities about which they have written recently or about which they intend to write in the near future.

15 Confidential sources

Journalists have a moral obligation to protect confidential sources of information.

16 Payment for articles *

(i) Payment or offers of payment for stories or information must not be made or through agents to witnesses or potential witnesses in current criminal proceedings except where the material concerned ought to be published in the public interest and there is an overriding need to make or promise to make a payment for this to be done.

   Journalists must take every possible step to ensure that no financial dealings have influence on the evidence that those witnesses may give. (An editor authorizing such a payment must be prepared to demonstrate that there is a legitimate public interest at stake involving matters that the public has a right to know. The payment or, where accepted, the offer of payment to any witness who is actually cited to give evidence must be disclosed to the prosecution and the defence and the witness should be advised of this.)

(ii) Payment or offers of payment for stories, pictures or information, must not be made directly or through agents to convicted or self-confessed criminals or their associates – who may include family, friends and colleagues – except where the material concerned ought to be published in the public interest and payment is necessary for this to be done.

The public interest

There may be exceptions to the clauses marked ★ where they can be demonstrated to be in the public interest.

1 The public interest includes:
  (i)   Detecting or exposing crime or a serious misdemeanour.
  (ii) Protecting public health and safety.
  (iii) Preventing the public from being misled by some statement or action of an individual or organization.
2 In any case where the public interest is invoked, the Press Complaints Commission will require a full explanation by the editor demonstrating how the public interest was served.
3 In cases involving children editors must demonstrate an exceptional public interest to override the normally paramount interests of the child.

GLOSSARY

ABC   Audit Bureau of Circulations, the body that authenticates and publishes newspaper circulation figures.

Ad   Advertisement

Ad dummy   The blank sets of pages of an edition with the shapes and positions of advertisements marked in; also on screen.

Ad rule   The rule or border separating editorial matter from advertisements on a page.

Add   Copy added to a story already written or subedited.

Advance   Printed hand-out of a speech or statement issued in advance to the press.

Advertising agency   An organization that prepares and designs advertisements for clients, and buys advertising space.

Agony column   A regular feature giving advice on personal problems to the mainly young; hence agony aunt.

Alts   Alterations made to copy or set matter.

Angle   A particular approach to a story.

Angling   Writing or editing a story from a particular angle, i.e. to bring out a particular aspect of its news content.

Art   Pertaining usually to design and layout of pages, the use of pictures and typography in newspaper display.

Art desk   Where page layouts are drawn in detail and the pictures edited.

Art editor   The person responsible for the art desk and for design of the newspaper.

Artwork   Prepared material for use in newspaper display.

Ascender   The part of a letter that rises above its x-height, as in h, k, l and f.

Author's marks   Corrections or amendments by the writer on an edited story.

Back bench   The control centre for a newspaper's production, where sit the night editor and other production executives.

Backgrounder   A feature giving background to the news.

Back numbers   Previous issues of a newspaper.

Bad break   Ugly or unacceptable hyphenation of a word made to justify line of type. See *Justify.*

Banner   A headline that crosses the top of a page – also *streamer.*

Bastard measure   Any typesetting of non-standard width.

Beard   The space between a letter and the edge of the base upon which it is designed.

Beat   An exclusive story or one that puts a newspaper's coverage ahead of another's.

Big quotes   Quotation marks larger than the typesize they enclose, i.e. used for display effect.

Big read   A long feature covering many columns – usually an instalment of a series.

Bill   A newspaper poster advertising the contents of the paper at selected sites.

Black   Used to describe certain boldface types.

Blanket   Newspaper page proof, i.e. print-out of page.

Bleach-out   A picture overdeveloped to intensify the blacks and remove the tones – useful in producing a motif to use as a display label on a story.

Blobs   Solid black discs used in front of type for display effect, or for tabulating lists.

Blow-up   Enlargement of a picture or type.

Blurb   A piece of self-advertisement composed of type, and sometimes illustrations, used to draw a reader's attention to the contents of other pages or issues to come.

Bodoni   A commonly used serif type, noted for clean lines and fine serifs.

Body   The space taken up by the strokes of a letter – the density of a letter.

Body matter   The reading text of a newspaper.

Body type   The type used for reading text.

Bold   Name given to type of a thicker than average body.

Border   A print rule or strip in the computer used to create panels for stories, or for display effects in layout.

BOT Type reversed as black on tone background.

Box A story enclosed by rules on all four sides – also *panel*.

Break 1 Convenient place to break the text with a quote or crosshead; 2 the moment of happening of news.

Breaker Any device such as a quote or crosshead which breaks up the text in the page.

Break-out A secondary story run on a page with a main story, usually on a feature page.

Brevier Old name for 8pt type.

Brief A short news story, usually one paragraph.

Bring up An editing instruction meaning use certain material earlier in a story.

Broadsheet Full size newspaper page approximately 22 in by 15 in, as opposed to tabloid, half size.

Bromide Emulsioned stiff paper on which type is printed, still used in cut-and-paste; any photographically printed material.

Bucket Rules on either side and below tying in printed matter to a picture.

Bureau The office of a news agency; in the US any newspaper office separate from the main one.

Buster Headline whose number of characters exceed the required measure.

By-line The writer's name at the beginning, or near the top, of a story.

c & lc Capital letters and lower case of type.

Caption Line(s) of type identifying or describing a picture.

Caps Capital letters of type.

Caslon A traditional-style seriffed typeface used for headlines.

Cast off To edit to a fixed length; the edited length of a story as estimated.

Catchline Syllable taken from a story and used on each folio, or section, along with folio number, to identify it in the typesetting system.

Centre spread Material extending across the two centre-facing pages in a newspaper. *Spread*: any material occupying two opposite pages.

Centred Type placed equidistant from each side of the column or columns.

Century Much used modern seriffed type with bold strokes.

Change pages Pages that are to be given new or revised material on an edition, or on which advertising material is being replaced.

Characters The letters, figures, symbols, etc. in a type range, hence *character count*, the number of characters that can be accommodated in a given line of type.

Circulation The number of copies of a newspaper sold, i.e. in circulation; hence *circulation manager*, the executive in charge of distributing copies and promoting circulation, also *circulation rep* (representative).

City editor Editor of financial page; in US the editor in charge of newsgathering in main office.

Clean up Editing instruction to improve tone of copy.

Cliché A well-worn, over-used phrase.

Cliffhanger A story that still awaits its climax or sequel.

Close quotes Punctuation marks closing quoted material.

Close up To reduce space between words or lines.

Col Short for column.

Column Standard vertical divisions of a newspaper page; hence column measure.

Column rule Fine rule marking out the columns.

Columnar space Vertical space separating one column of matter from another.

Command A keyboarded instruction to a computer.

Compo Composite artwork made up of type and half-tone.

Condensed type Type narrower than the standard founts; hence *extra condensed* and *medium condensed*.

Contents bill Bill or poster advertising a story or item in a newspaper.

Copy All material submitted for use in a newspaper.

Copy-taker Telephone typists who take down reporters' copy on a keyboard.

Copy-taster Person who sorts and classifies incoming copy in a newspaper.

Copyright Ownership of written or printed material.

Corr Short for correspondent.

Correction Published item putting right errors in a story.

Count   The number of characters in a line of type.

Coverage   The attendance at, and writing up, of news events; also the total number of stories covered.

Credit   Usually the photographer's or artist's name printed with an illustration; hence *credit line*.

Crop   To select the image of a picture required for printing.

Crosshead   Line or lines of type to break the text, placed between paragraphs.

Cross-reference   Line of type referring to matter elsewhere in the paper.

CRT   Cathode-ray tubes, used as a light source to create the type image in a photosetter (used now only in paste-up).

Cursive   Any flowing design of type based on handwriting.

Cursor   Electronic light 'pen' on VDU screen, used to manipulate text during writing and editing.

Cut   To reduce a story by deleting facts or words.

Cut-off   A story separated from the text above and below by type rules making it self-contained from the rest of the column; hence *cut-off rule*.

Cut-out   Half-tone picture in which the background has been cut away to leave the image in outline.

Cuttings   Catalogued material from newspapers cut out and stored in a cuttings library for future reference, (nowadays electronically) in US clippings.

Cuttings jobs   A story based on cuttings.

Cypher   A character in a type range which represents something else, i.e., ampersand (&) and £ and $ signs.

Database   The material to which a computer gives access.

Dateline   Place and date of a story given usually at the start.

Dead   Matter discarded and not to be used again.

Deadline   Latest time a story can be filed, accepted or set.

Deck   One unit of a headline.

Define   To specify on a computer screen the material a command is intended to cover.

Delayed drop   An intro which reserved the point of a story till later.

DA-notice   An official instruction to editors that a story is subject to the Official Secrets Act and therefore should not be used.

Descender   The part of a letter that projects below the x-line.

Diary   1 The newsroom list of jobs for the day or week; 2 A gossip column in a newspaper.

Didot point   Unit of type measurement slightly larger than the British–American point and used in Europe, except Britain and Belgium. Equal to 0.01483 of an inch.

Direct input   The inputting of material into a computer by writers for the purpose of screen editing.

Directory   A list of stories of a given classification held in a computer and available to those with access.

Disaster caps   Large heavy, sanserif type, used on a major (usually disaster) page one story.

Disclaimer   A printed item explaining that a story printed previously has nothing to do with persons or an organization with the same or similar name as used in the story.

Display ads   Advertisements in which large type or illustration predominate.

District reporter   Reporter working from a base away from the main office.

Double   The same story printed twice in the paper.

Double-column   Across two columns.

Dress   Redress or revision of a story; also *rejig*.

Drop letter   An outsize initial capital letter on the intro of a story; also *drop figure*.

Drop quotes   Outsize quotes used to mark off important quoted sections in a story.

Dummy   Blank copy of the paper (now on screen) showing the position and sizes of the advertisements and the space available for editorial use; also mock-up of editorial pages as preparation for a new format.

Earpieces   Advertisements on either side of the masthead, or centred titlepiece, of a newspaper's page one.

Edit   Prepare copy for the press.

Edition   An issue of the paper prepared for a specific area; hence *editionize*, to prepare such.

Editor   Chief editorial executive who is responsible for the editing and contents of a newspaper.

Editorial   The leading article or opinion of the paper.

Editorialize   To insert, or imbue with, the newspaper's own opinion.

Editor's conference   Main planning conference of a newspaper.

Egyptian   A type family which has heavy 'slab' serifs.

Ellipsis   Omission of letters or words in a sentence, represented by several dots.

Em   Unit of type measure based on the standard 12pt roman lower case letter 'm'; also called a *mutton* (in US a pica).

Embargo   Request not to publish before a nominated time.

En   Half an em, based on the standard roman lower case letter 'n'.

EPD   Electronic picture desk.

Exp   Expanded (of type).

Execute   Computer command meaning to put into effect.

Facsimile   Exact reproduction of an original, as in facsimile transmission of pages from one production centre to another by electronic means.

Family   All the type of any one type range.

Feature   Subjective articles used in newspapers, as opposed to objective news material; newspaper material containing advice, comment, opinion or assessment; sometimes any editorial content other than news.

File   A reporter's own computer input; to send or submit a story; a writer's or agency's day's output.

Files   Back issues.

Filler   A short news item of one or two paragraphs.

Filmset type   Photoset type, as used in a paste-up.

Fit-up   Artwork involving several elements joined together.

Flash   Urgent brief message on agency service – usually an important fact.

Flashback   A story or picture taken from a past issue.

Flush   Set to one side (as of type).

Fold   Point at which the paper is folded during printing; hence *folder*, a device attached to the press which does this.

Folio Page.

Follow-up A story that follows up information in a previous story in order to uncover new facts.

Format 1 The shape and regular features of a newspaper; its regular typographical appearance; 2 Any pre-set instruction programmed into a computer.

Font All the characters in a given size of any type.

Forme The completed newspaper page or pair of pages when ready to be made into a printing plate.

Frame The adjustable easel at which paste-up pages are made up from photoset and photographic elements.

Freelance Self-employed person, i.e. journalist.

Free sheets Newspapers that rely solely on advertising income and are given free to readers.

Front office Usually the advertising and editorial part of a newspaper office to which the public is admitted.

Full out Typeset to the full measure of a column.

Gatekeeper Sociologist's name for a copy-taster.

Gatherers Journalists who gather and write material for a newspaper – a sociologists' term.

Ghost writer One who writes under another's name; one who writes on behalf of someone else.

Good pages Pages that do not have to be changed for later editions.

Gothic Family of sanserif type with a great variety of available widths – medium condensed, extra condensed, square, etc.

Graphics Any drawn illustrative material used in page design.

Grot Abbreviation for Grotesque, a family of sans headline type.

Gutter The margin between two printed pages.

Hair space The thinnest space used between letters in typesetting systems.

Half lead (pronounced *leed*) The second most important story on a page.

Half-tone The reproduction process, consisting of dots of varying density, by which the tones of a photograph are reproduced on a page.

Handout Pre-printed material containing information supplied for the use of the press.

Hanging indent   Style of typesetting in which the first line of each paragraph is set full out and the remaining lines indented on the left.

Hard copy   Typewritten or handwritten copy, as opposed to copy centred into a computer.

Hard news   News based on solid fact.

Head, heading   Words for headline.

Header   The part of the computer screen in which commands and basic instructions are entered, and in which the computer communicates with the user.

Heavies   Name sometimes given to the quality or serious national press as opposed to the popular press; newspapers that specialize in serious news.

H & J   Computer term for 'hyphenated and justified', meaning that the material has been prepared on the screen in the length and sequence of equal lines in which it will be typeset.

Hold   To keep copy for use later.

Hood   Lines of type above a picture or story and attached by rules top and side.

Hook   A term used in some computer systems for a queue or desk to which stories can be sent after testing to await possible use.

Horizontal make-up   Page design in which stories and headlines cross the page in several legs as opposed to being run up and down.

Hot metal   The printing system in which type is cast from molten metal into 'slugs' for assembly into pages.

House style   Nominates spellings and usages used to produce consistency in a newspaper or printing house.

Imprint   Name and address of the printer and publisher, usually found at the bottom of the back page of a newspaper.

Indent   Material set narrower than the column measures, leaving white space either at the front or at both sides.

Insert   Any copy inserted into a story already written or in type.

Intro   The introduction or beginning of a story.

Investigative journalism   A form of reporting in which a news situation is examined in depth by a team of reporters under a project leader, i.e. as an investigation of all aspects.

Issue   All copies of a day's paper and its editions.

Italic   Type characters that slope from right to left.

Jack line   A short line left at the top of a column (usually avoided in page make-up). Also a *widow*.

Journalese   Newspaper-generated slang; shoddy, cliché-ridden language.

Justify   To space out a line of type to fit a nominated width.

Keyboard   The panel of keys on a computer or workstation by which copy is entered.

Kicker   A story in special type and setting that stands out from the main part of the page.

Kill   To erase or throw away a story so that it cannot be used.

Label   A headline without a verb.

Layout   The plan of a page.

Lead (pronounced *leed*)   The main story on a page; the page lead.

Lead (pronounced *led*)   The space between lines of type material derived from the hot metal system which used strips of metal, or leads, of set point width.

Leader   Editorial opinion, or leading article.

Leg   Any portion of text arranged in several columns on the page.

Legal kill   A legal instruction not to use.

Legman   A reporter who assists with gathering the facts but does not write the story; hence leg work.

Letterpress   A method of printing from a raised or relief surface, as with metal or polymer stereo plates on rotary presses.

Letter-spacing   Space the width of an average letter in a given type.

Lift   To use, and keep in a page, matter that has appeared in a previous edition.

Light box   A device consisting of a ground glass screen illuminated from below through which prints pictures can be viewed face downwards so that they can be cropped and scaled on the back.

Light face   Type of a lighter weight or character than standard.

Lineage   Computation of lines used as a basis of payment to writers; sometimes used for payment of non-staff newspaper contributors.

Line block   An engraved plate in the hot metal printing system, which reduced the lines of a drawing in continuous black, as opposed to a half-tone block which rendered tones by dots of varying density.

Line drawing   Drawing made up of black strokes, as with a cartoon or comic strip.

Literals   Typographical errors.

Local corr   A district correspondent.

Logo   Name, title, recognition word, as of a regular column or section of newspaper.

Long primer   Old name for 10pt type; also l.p.

Lower case   Small, as opposed to capital, letters of an alphabet.

Machine minder   Operator in charge of a press.

Make-up   The act of making up a page.

Masking   Excluding part of a photograph by paper overlay to indicate area to be printed.

Masthead   The name or title of a newspaper at the top of page one.

Measure   Width of any setting.

Medium   A weight of type between light and bold, or heavy.

Memory   The part of a computer that retains information fed into it; where written and edited stories are stored.

Merchandizing   Information about price and place of purchase in consumer journalism features.

MF   Abbreviation for more to follow.

MFL   More to follow later.

Milled rule   A Simplex rule or border with a serrated edge as on the edge of a coin.

Montage   A number of pictures mounted together.

Mood picture (or shot)   A picture in which atmosphere is more important than content.

Mop-up   A story that puts together different aspects of an event.

Morgue   Old name for newspaper picture and cuttings library.

Motif   Drawing or picture used to symbolize a subject, or to identify a feature or story.

MS   Manuscript of any text before printing.

Mug shot   Picture showing only a person's head.

Must   An item that must be used, and containing *must* in its instructions.

Mutton   Old name for an em.

Nationals   Newspapers on sale all over the country.

New lead   A version of a story based on later information.

News agency   An organization that collects, edits and distributes news to subscribing newspapers.

News desk   The newsroom, where the collection of news is organized, and where reporters are based (in US, city desk).

Nibs   News in brief.

Night editor   The senior production executive of a daily paper.

Nonpl   Norpareil, the old name for 6pt type.

Nose   The intro or start to a story; hence to *re-nose*.

NS   Newspaper Society, an association for provincial newspaper proprietors in Britain.

Nuggets   Small items of news; separate sections of a story.

NUJ   National Union of Journalists (in Britain).

Nut   Old name for an en; hence *nutted*, type indented one nut, or nut each side.

Obit   Obituary item.

Offset   Printing by transferring the page image from smooth plastic printing plate to a roller which then sets it off on to paper.

Open quotes   Punctuation marks denoting the start of a quoted section.

Overline   A line of smaller type over a main headline; also a *strapline*.

Overmatter   Left-over printed material not used in the edition.

PA   Press Association, home national news agency in Britain.

Page facsimile transmission   Method by which completed pages are digitized and reduced to an electronic signal for transmission by wire or satellite to another printing centre for simultaneous production.

Pagination   The numbering of pages; the number of pages to work towards.

Panel   Story enclosed in rules or borders; see *Box*.

Paste-up   The method of making up pages from photoset material by attaching them to a page card, as in cut-and-paste.

Photoset   The name given to photocomposed type; hence *phototypesetter*.

Pica   12pt type; unit of measurement based on multiples of 12 points (pica = one em).

Picture desk   Where collecting and checking of pictures is organized; hence *picture editor*.

Platen   Surface which holds the paper in a printing press and presses it against an inked surface.

Point   Unit of type measurement. The British-American point is 0.01383 in, or about one seventy-second of an inch. See also *Didot point*. The size of type is measured by depth in points.

Populars   Mass circulation newspapers of popular appeal.

Print   Total number of newspapers printed of one issue; also a picture or bromide printed from a photographic negative.

Print order   The number of copies of an issue ordered to be printed.

Print-out   A copy of material in a computer printed out for reference or filing.

Printing plate   The plate, metal or polymer, from which the page is printed.

Projection   The display and headline treatment given to a story in the page.

Promotion   Any form of planned publicity that has a specific aim.

Publishing room   Where the newspapers are counted, wrapped and prepared for distribution.

Puff   An item in a newspaper which publicizes something or somebody.

Pull-out   Separate section of a newspaper that can be pulled out, often with separate pagination.

Pundit   A regular newspaper columnist who dispenses opinion.

Qualities   Serious, as opposed to popular, newspapers.

Queue   A particular collection or directory of stories held in a computer – features queue, newsroom queue, etc.

Quire   Unit of freshly printed, ordered newspapers, usually twenty-six copies.

Quotes   Raised punctuation marks to indicate quoted speech.

Qwerty   Standard keyboard layout based on the first five characters of the top bank of letter keys.

Ragged (left or right)   Copy set justified on one side only, sometimes used in captions.

Range   The number and variety of characters available in a particular type.

Rate card   List of newspaper advertising charges based on specific sizes and placings.

Reader participation   Editorial material or items which involve contributions by readers, such as readers' letters, competitions and articles based on invited opinions.

Readership   The total number of people who read a newspaper – not the number of copies in circulation. The estimated number of readers per copy of magazines and newspapers can vary considerably.

Redress   See *Rejig*.

Reel   Spindle holding a roll of newsprint; sometimes, a roll of newsprint; hence *reel room*, where rolls of newsprint are stacked for use.

Register   The outline of printed matter as it appears on the paper; important in colour printing where the main colours are printed separately on to the picture image.

Rejig   The revision of a story in the light of later information, or a change of position in the paper, often between editions.

Release   The date or time that handout material becomes available for use.

Re-nose   To put a new intro on to a story, using different material or a different angle.

Re-plate   To replace a printing plate to allow a later version of a page on to the press.

Reporter   Person who gathers and writes up news.

Retainer   Periodic payment made to retain someone's services, as with local correspondents; see *Stringers*.

Retouching   Improving the quality of a photograph, now usually done electronically.

Reuters   British based international news agency.

Revamp   General change given to a story or page in the light of a reconsidered approach.

Reverse   Type printed white on a black or tone background.

Reverse indent   See *Hanging indent*.

Revise   To check and correct, or improve, edited material.

Rewrite   To turn a story into new words rather than to edit on copy.

ROP   Run of press. For instance colour is and printed during run of press rather than as a separate or additional process.

Rota picture   A news picture obtained under the rota system, in which limited coverage of an event is allowed on a shared basis.

Rotary press   Traditional press in which newspapers were printed by the letterpress method from curved metal or polymer relief plates.

Rough   Outline sketch of page layout.

Rule   A printed border of varying width.

Run   Length of time taken to print an issue of a newspaper.

Running story   A story that develops and continues over a long period.

Run on   To carry on printing without changing plates for an edition.

Rush   Second most urgent classification of news agency material after *flash*; hence *rushfull*, a full version based on rushes.

Saddle   A metal mount used for attaching polymer plates to a rotary press to achieve correct printing height.

Sale or return   Newspapers sold subject to a fixed payment for unsold copies carried.

Sans   Sanserif, types without tails, or serifs, at the end of the letter strokes.

Satellite printing   Printing at subsidiary production centres by the use of page facsimile transmission.

Scaling   Calculating the depth of a picture to be used.

Scalpel   Used to lift, cut up and place material in paste-up pages.

Schedule   List of reporting or feature jobs to be covered for use in an issue of a newspaper.

Scheme   To plan and draw a page; also a *page layout*.

Scoop   Exclusive story.

Screamer   Exclamation mark.

Screen   The density of dots in half-tone reproduction of photographs.

Screen   Where stories held in the computer are projected for reading or editing; hence *screen subbing*, subbing by electronic means by use of a cursor.

Scroll (up or down)   To display material on to a computer screen so that it can be read in sequence.

Seal   Standard words, often in colour, at the top of a page indicating the edition; also a logo.

Section   A separately folded part of a newspaper; hence sectional newspapers.

Send   A command to transfer material in a computer to another queue or desk, or to the page.

Separation   The separate elements of a colour picture by which the colour is transferred to the page.

Sequence   The order in which a story is presented (in subbing).

Series   Range of typesizes, or types.

Serif   Type characterized by strokes that have little tails, or serifs.

Service column   An advice, or consumer, column.

Set and hold   Put into type for use later.

Set flush   To set full to the margin.

Set forme   The last forme (of page or pair of pages) to go to press.

Set solid   To set without line spacing.

Setting format   Setting of a nominated size, width and spacing that is programmed into the computer for cases of frequent use.

Shorts   Short items of edited matter, usually of one, two or three paragraphs.

Sidebar   Story placed alongside a main story to which it relates.

Side-head   A headline or cross-head set flush left, or indented left.

Sign-off   The name of the writer at the end of a story.

Situationer   A story giving background to a situation.

Sizing   See *Scaling*.

Slab-serif   Type with heavy square-ended serifs.

Slip   To change a page between editions; hence *slip edition.*

Snap   Piece of information in advance of full details in news agency story.

Spike   Home for unwanted stories. Computers have an electronic *spike* to which stories can be sent.

Spill   To run down and fill space (of type).

Splash   The main page one story.

Split screen   The use of a terminal to display two stories at once.

Spot colour   Non-processed colour applied to the page during run of press.

Spread   A main story that crosses two adjoining pages.

Squares   Black or open, a species of type ornament used to mark off sections of text.

Stand-first   An explanation in special type set above the intro of a story, i.e. it stands first.

Stand-up drop   An initial letter in large type that stands above the line of the text at the start of a story.

Star   Type ornament; hence *star-line*, a line of stars.

Star-burst   Headline or slogan enclosed in star shaped outline used in blurbs and advertising.

Start-up   When the presses begin to print.

Stock bills   Newspaper display bills on fixed subject such as 'today's TV', 'latest scores', etc.

Stone   Bench where pages used to be made up under hot metal system; hence *stone sub*, the journalist who supervised this work in cut-and-paste make-up.

Stop press   Late news printed from a separate cylinder on to the page while on the press, or afterwards.

Strap-line   Headline in small type that goes above the main headline; also overline.

Streamer   Headline that crosses the top of the page, also a *banner* headline.

Stringer   A local correspondent.

Subeditor   Person who checks and edits material for a newspaper to fit set space, and writes the headline.

Subhead   Secondary headline.

Subst head   Headline in place of another.

Syndication   The means by which a newspaper's material is offered for a fee for use in other publications or countries.

Tabloid   Half size (newspaper).

Tag-line   An explanatory line or acknowledgement under the bottom line of a headline.

Tear-out   A picture printed with a simulated torn edge, usually a flashback of a printed picture, or a part of a document; also *rag-out*.

Telephoto lens   Camera lens that magnifies an image telescopically.

Textsize   A broadsheet, or full-size newspaper page.

Tie-in   A story that is connected with one alongside.

Tie-on   A story that is connected with the story above.

Tip-off   Information from an inside source.

Top   A top of the page story; mostly any story that merits a good headline and more than three paragraphs long.

Trim   To cut a story a little.

Turn head   A head covering a story that has been continued from another page.

Typebook   Catalogue of types held.

Typechart   A tabulated list giving character counts for given types.

Underscore   To carry a line or rule under type.

Update   To work in later information.

Visualize   To plan and work out how a page or display will look.

Web-offset   A system of printing in which the inked page image is transferred from a smooth printing plate on to a rubber roller and then offset on to paper, as opposed to being printed directly on to paper by relief impression, as in letter-press.

Weight   The thickness of a type.

Widow   A short line left at the top of a column of reading type; also *jack-line*.

Wing in   To set a headline within the top rule of a panel or box, leaving a piece of rule showing on either side.

Wire   A means of transmitting copy by electronic signal which requires a receiver or decoder; hence *wire room*, where such copy is transmitted or received.

Word processor   Electronic system by which text can be keyboarded into a computer, stored, edited, amended and finally printed (i.e. processed) when required.

Work station   Any computer connected to a system or network.

WOB   White on black type.

WOT   White on tone type.

WYSIWYG   What you see is what you get (acronym).

X-height   The mean height of letters in a type range, exclusive of ascenders or descenders.

INDEX

Abbreviations:
  in headlines, 131–2
  in text, 122
Aberdeen Press & Journal, 59
Accuracy:
  in features, 205–6
  in headlines, 129, 217
  in text, 70–3
Add matter, 170
Adobe PhotoShop, 9, 62
Advertising, 26–8, 31
Advice columns, 191–2
Agence France Presse, 14
Agony columns, 189, 192
Alternative words, 151–8
American words, 120
Angling stories, 166–7
Antelope, HMS, 50
Apple-Mac, 2–4, 7–8, 24
Ascenders, 39
Associated Press, 14

Back bench, 24
Background, 86
Bastard measure, 42, 65
Bembo (type), 39–40
Biafran War, 49
Bills, 174–5
Bit-mapping (of type), 38
Bleach-out, 64
Blobs, 43
Blurbs, 8, 66, 191, 212
Bodoni (type), 37, 39
Body type, 41

Breakers, 42–3
By-lines, 46, 195

Canary Wharf, 4
Capa, Robert, 56
Capital letters, 120–2
Captions:
  do's and don'ts, 172
  general, 52–3, 73
  typography, 173–4
  writing, 171–4
Cartier-Bresson, Henri, 56
Caslon (type), 37
Casting off, 75–7
Century (type), 37, 39, 194, 200
Check sources, 73–5
Cheltenham (type), 37
Chief subeditor, 16–17, 24, 29–30, 38
Children:
  intrusion, 219
  in sex cases, 219
Circumlocutions, 108–10
Clichés, 110–12
Code of Practice (PCC), 217–22
Column rules, 47
Column widths, 41–2
Columnists, 196
Command desk system, 6
Competitions, 206
Compos, 30, 64
Computer graphics, 8–9, 68, 194
Computerized setting, 28, 40
Condensed type, 39
Confessions, 205
Confidential sources, 221

Contempt of court, 162–4
Contents bills, 174–5
Control desk, 24
Copyright, 52
Copy sources:
    features, 190–1
    news, 13–15
Copy-tasting, 12, 17, 20–1, 24–5
Coren, Alan, 207
Creative writing, 206–8
Criminal Justice Acts, 161
Criminals (friends and relatives of), 220
Cropping (of pictures), 58–62, 66
Crossheads, 42–3, 195
Crossword puzzles, 189–90, 205
Cumberland News, 19, 21
Cut-and-paste, 4, 10
Cut-outs, 64–5
Cutting text, 75–81
Cuttings library, 73–4
Cyphers, 122

Daily Mail, 38, 44, 67, 200, 202, 214–15
Daily Telegraph, 4, 18, 38, 207, 215
DA-notices, 164
Decentralized printing, 4
Defamation Act 1952, 165
Delayed drop stories, 81–2
Descenders, 39
Design (of pages):
    asymmetrical patterns, 31
    focal points, 31–5
    general, 26–47
    in features pages, 189–204
    layouts, 32
    order, 35
    pictures in, 63
    principles, 30
    purposes, 36
    scheming pages, 30
    type character, 35–6
Disclaimers, 73
Discrimination, 220
Drop figures, 46
Drop letters, 42, 44, 195
Dummy (newspaper), 26

Editionizing, 169–71
Editorial manning, 28–30
Editorial production, 1, 8–11, 12–25

Editor's conference, 26
Electronic newsroom, 15–16
Electronic picture desk (EPD), 51, 55
Electronic tools, 108–9
English (spotting faults in):
    apostrophe, 104–5
    bracket, 102–3
    colon, 102
    dash, 102–3
    ellipsis, 103–4
    exclamation mark, 104–5
    full stop, 101
    guide to, 87–106
    hyphen, 105–6
    nouns, 95–6
    paragraphs, 96–100
    participles, 89–90
    prepositions, 96
    pronouns, 90–1
    punctuation, 100–6
    qualifiers, 94
    question mark, 105
    quotation mark, 105
    semi-colon, 101
    sentence, 87–9, 96–9
    split infinitives, 93
    tenses, 92
    verbs, 92–3
Evans, Harold, 56
Evening Mail, Birmingham, 22, 192, 196–9, 214
Evening papers, 12
Evening Post, Bristol, 22, 79
Evening Post, Nottingham, 7, 210
Evening Standard, London, 59, 65
Exclamation marks, 104–5
Exclusives, 13, 52
Expanded type, 79
Express, The, 66, 82, 215

Falklands War (picture), 49
Faults in English (see English: spotting faults)
Features:
    accuracy, need for, 205–6
    chief subeditor, 38
    copy flow, 190
    copy sources, 190–1
    design, 189–204
    editing, 205–16
    ghost writing, 208–9

handling text, 195, 205–9
headline writing, 213–16
language, 206–9
logos, 196
page design, 194–5
page furniture, 196
page planning, 191–3
pictures, use of, 194, 198–9, 202–4, 212–13
planning, 189–204
production, 193–4
projection, 205–13
reader participation, 209–11
readers' letters, 191–3, 209–11
style, 206–8
the law, 211
topicality, 193
typography, 194
Fillers, 24, 35
Financial Times, 18, 20–1, 23, 31, 35
Focal points, 31, 35
Follow-ups, 20
Fonts, 36–41
Foreign words, 108, 120
Formatted setting, 47
Fowler's Modern English Usage, 93, 99
Freelances, 4, 16
Fry, Stephen, 200, 202, 204
Futura (type), 37, 194

Garamond (type), 194
Garst and Bernstein, 151
Geography, 85–6, 134
Ghost writing, 208–9
Gill sans (type), 37
Glossary, 223–41
Gothic (type), 37, 39, 194
Gowers, Sir Ernest: *The Complete Plain Words*, 91
Graphics, 67–8
Grotesque, or Grot (type), 37
Guardian The, 18, 47, 67, 200–1, 214, 216

Half lead, 35
Handling text, 69–86
Handouts, 15
Harassment, 218
Headline typography:

arrangement, 142–3
character count, 144–7
shape, 140–2
spacing, 146–8
type style, 143
Headlines (writing):
abbreviations, 131–2
accuracy, 129
adjectives, 127–8
alternative words, 151–8
content, 132–4
creative moment, 148–50
direct approach, 134–5
features, 213–16
function, 125
geography, 134
nouns, 127–8
numbers, 132
oblique approach, 135–6
omission of words, 127
personal touch, 133
punctuation, 129
special words, 127
split headlines, 137–8
subject, 126
symbols, 128
taste, 132–3
thoughts, 137
time, 133–4
tinted or reversed, 46
turn heads, 138
verb, 126
words, 126–8
writing, 125–58
Helvetica (type), 38, 194
HMS Antelope, 50
Hospitals (intrusion), 219
House style:
abbreviations, 122
American words, 120
capital letters, 120–2
cyphers, 122
editor's phobias, 122
foreign names, 120
guide to, 119–23
names, 121
numbers, 121
spellings, 119–20
trade names, 123
typographical style, 123
Hull Daily Mail, 210
Hyphens, 105–6

Independent, The, 6, 215
Indicators (type, for use in lists), 45
Inserts, 171
Internet, 8
Intro writing, 78–81
Intrusion, 218, 219
Investigative journalism, 14
Italic type, 39

Jesperson, Otto: *Growth and Structure of the English Language*, 91
Journalese, 91

Law and the subeditor, 159–66
Lawson, Nigella, 207
Layouts, 30–2
Lead story, 35
Legal traps:
    absolute privilege, 164–5
    contempt of court, 162–4
    libel, 161–2
    Official Secrets Act, 164
    qualified privilege, 165–6
Libel, 161–2
Linotype machine, 3
Listening devices, 219
Liverpool Echo, 45, 203–4, 214–15
Liverpool Post, 9
Local correspondents, 14, 16
Logos, 23, 130, 195–6

McCullin, Don, 56
Measuring news, 18, 20–1
Microsoft Windows, 2, 7–8
Mirror Group Newspapers, 4
Mirror, The, 18, 38
Misrepresentation, 20
Mistaken identity, 72
Misused words, 116–19
Modern English Usage (Burchfield edition), 93
Modern Newspaper Practice, 191
Modular make–up, 9
Montage, 64
Morning papers, 13
Mouse controls, 4, 10, 48, 62
Multi-skilling, 49

News:
    agencies, 14–15
    copy flow, 16
    coverage, 19–20

    creating, 13–17
    editing, 15–17
    measurement, 18, 20–1
    origination, 12–13
    patterns, 21–3
    presentation, 19, 22–3
    reporting, 13–17
    tasting, 17
News agencies, 14–15
News Centre, Portsmouth, 11
News editor, 15–16
News of the World, 2, 48, 60, 73, 215
Newspaper:
    balance, 27–8
    content, 27–8
    design, 26–47
    dummy, 26
    focal points, 31–5
    format, 26–7
    layouts, 30
    logos, 27, 30
Newsroom, 12, 15–17
Nibs, 35
Numbers, 121, 132

Office lawyer, 159–61
Official Secrets Act, 164
Opportunity to reply, 218

PA News, 9–10
Page:
    building, 62
    design, 26–47
    editors, 6, 8, 29, 50
    furniture, 196
    layouts, 2, 4, 30, 32
    make-up, 1–5, 10
    pairing, 30
    planning, 63, 191–3
    sizes, 42
Pagination, 26
Pairing (of pages), 30
Paparazzi, 53
Paragraphs, 96–100
Payment for stories, 221
Photo-compositors, 2
Photographers:
    briefing, 55–6
    freelance, 51, 53
    paparazzi, 53
    rota jobs, 51, 54

staff, 51–2
telephoto cameras, 55
Photo-set type, 2
Pictures:
agencies, 51, 54
assessment, 61
black and white, 51
bleach–outs, 64
captions, 52–3, 73, 171–4
choice, 63
choosing, 56–7
collected, 54
colour, 51
copyright, 52
cropping, 58–62, 66
cut-outs, 64–5
display, 58–9
editing, 51–2, 55–67
electronic picture desk (EPD), 51, 55
files, 73
glamour, 54
handout, 54
libraries, 51, 55
montage, 64
news pictures, 51
photo-briefing, 55–6
pixel-moving, 50
qualities required, 56–7
retouching, 50, 62
role, 48–51
rota, 51, 54
scanning, 49–50
sizing, 61–2
sources, 51–5
telephoto, 55
transmission, 52
usage, 63–5
use in features, 194, 198–9, 201–4,
212–13
wrong identities, 72–3
Plate maker, 4, 30
Points system, 41
Press Complaints Commission:
Code of Practice, 217–22
general, 50, 211
Print rules, 43
Privacy, 218
Privilege:
absolute,164–5
qualified, 165–6
Public interest, the, 222
Punctuation:

in headlines, 129–31
in text, 100–6

QPS, 7–8
Quark revolution, 1–11
QuarkXpress, 2–4, 7–8, 24
Quotes:
as breakers, 43–4
marks, 105
paraphrasing, 72
speech, 72
using, 83–5

Ragged setting, 45
Reader participation, 191, 209, 211
Readers' letters, 191–3, 209–11
Reference books, 74–5
Reporters:
freelance, 14
local correspondents, 14
staff, 13–14
Retouching, 50, 62
Reuters, 14, 50
Revising text, 169–71
Rewrites:
angling, 166–7
bad copy, 168
multiple copy sources, 167–8
Rockwell (type), 38
Rota jobs, 51, 54
Running stories:
general, 12, 77
handling the text, 176–88

Sans type, 36, 38
Screen make-up, 4
Sentences:
general, 87–9
object, 87–8
subject, 87–8
Serif type, 34, 36–8
Sex Offenders Acts, 161
Side heads (shoulders), 42, 45
Sign-offs, 46, 195
Sizing (pictures), 61–2
Slab serif type, 38
Sociology and press, 1
Spacing (in headlines), 146–8
Splash (page one lead), 41
Split infinitives, 93
Sports production, 71
Stand-firsts, 195, 213

Stringers, 14
Strunk and White: *Elements of Style*, 91
Subeditors:
    and technology, 1, 4, 6, 8–11
    and the law, 159–66
    multi-skilling, 49
    required skills, 69–70
    staffing, 69
    table layout, 6, 16, 69
Sun, The, 18, 32, 38, 192, 215
Sunday Times, The, 27, 31, 34, 37
Symbol graphics, 67–8

Taste, 132–3
Technical words, 107–8
Tenses, 92
Text editing:
    accuracy, 70–3, 129, 205–6, 217
    angling, 166–7
    background, 86
    bad copy, 168
    casting off, 75–7
    check sources, 73–5
    cutting text, 75–8
    delayed drop, 81–2
    editionizing, 169–71
    features, 195, 205–9
    general, 69–86
    geography, 85–6
    intro, 78–81
    legal traps, 160–6
    misreadings, 72
    mistaken identity, 72
    multiple copy sources, 167–8
    order and shape, 78
    quoted speech, 72
    rejigs, 166–9
    revising, 169–71
    rewrites, 166–9
    running stories, 12, 27, 176–88
    story sequence, 82–3
    subs and the law, 159–66
    time, 86
    using quotes, 83–5
Time, 86, 133–4
Times Roman lower case, 23, 37, 39
Times, The, 18, 37, 38, 207, 209, 215
Titling Gothic (type), 39
Trade names, 123
Trooping the Colour, 56
Turn heads, 138
TV programme setting, 46, 196, 205

Type:
    bastard measure, 42
    body setting, 41
    character, 35–6
    computerized setting, 38, 40
    fonts, 36–41
    formatted setting, 47
    general, 1–11
    in captions, 173–4
    in features pages, 194
    ragged setting, 45
    setting width, 41–2
    sizes, 41
TV programme setting, 46, 196, 205
    using, 39–41
    variants, 39–41
    x-height, 39
Typography, 22–47, 36–42, 123, 140–8, 194

Unisys Hermes, 2, 5, 8–9
United Press International (UPI), 14
Univers (type), 37, 200

Variant types, 39–41
Victims of sex assault, 220
Vogue words, 112–16

Web-offset:
    presses, 3, 11
    printing, 11
Western Mail, 33, 44, 59, 67, 84
White space, 47
Word use:
    alternatives, 151–8
    American, 120
    circumlocutions, 108, 110
    clichés, 110–12
    foreign, 108, 120
    house style, 119–23
    journalese, 123–4
    misused, 116–19
    names, 121
    numbers, 121
    synonyms, 110
    technical, 107–8
    vogue words, 112–16
    word traps, 107–24
Working graphics, 67–8
Writing headlines, 125–58

x–height (of type), 39